This new reading of Baudelaire's *Le Spleen de Paris* is a response to Baudelaire's own challenge to read his text as one in which 'everything...is head and tail, alternately and reciprocally'. Margery Evans proposes that *Le Spleen de Paris* serves to question the conventions of prose forms such as the novel and the moral fable, problematising such conventions as the unitary narrator, the extended plot and the artifice of beginnings and endings, and making use of intertextual parody and ironic inversion.

Baudelaire's text probes the relationship between individuality and conformity to pre-existing codes, both in literature and in the world, explicitly re-writing a traditional philosophical topos which contrasts mankind's reclusive and sociable impulses. The giant metropolis provides a symbol of that drama.

Dr Evans explores the interconnections between the prose poems which make up *Le Spleen de Paris* and their intertextual relations with other, mostly prose, works, and shows how this anomalous, hybrid work raises far-reaching questions of general relevance to narratology.

Cambridge Studies in French 38

BAUDELAIRE AND INTERTEXTUALITY

Cambridge Studies in French

GENERAL EDITOR
Malcolm Bowie

Recent titles in this series include

26 JOHN FORRESTER
The Seductions of Psychoanalysis: Freud, Lacan and Derrida

27 JEROME SCHWARTZ
Irony and Ideology in Rabelais: Structures of Subversion

28 DAVID BAGULEY
Naturalist Fiction: The Entropic Vision

29 LESLIE HILL
Beckett's Fiction: In Different Words

30 F. W. LEAKEY
Baudelaire: Collected Essays, 1953–1988

31 SARAH KAY
Subjectivity in Troubadour Poetry

32 GILLIAN JONDORF
French Renaissance Tragedy: The Dramatic Word

33 LAWRENCE D. KRITZMAN
The Rhetoric of Sexuality and the Literature of the French Renaissance

34 JERRY C. NASH
The Love Aesthetics of Maurice Scève

35 PETER FRANCE
Politeness and its Discontents: Problems in French Classical Culture

36 MITCHELL GREENBERG
Subjectivity and Subjugation in Seventeenth-Century Drama and Prose: The Family Romance of French Classicism

37 TOM CONLEY
The Graphic Unconscious: The Letter of Early Modern French Writing

A complete list of books in the series is given at the end of the volume.

BAUDELAIRE AND INTERTEXTUALITY

Poetry at the crossroads

MARGERY A. EVANS

Lecturer, Department of French Studies, University of Warwick

CAMBRIDGE UNIVERSITY PRESS

Published by the Press Syndicate of the University of Cambridge
The Pitt Building, Trumpington Street, Cambridge CB2 1RP
40 West 20th Street, New York, NY 10011-4211, USA
10 Stamford Road, Oakleigh, Victoria 3166, Australia

© Cambridge University Press 1993

First published 1993

Printed in Great Britain at the University Press, Cambridge

A catalogue record for this book is available from the British Library

Library of Congress cataloguing in publication data

Evans, Margery A.
Baudelaire and intertextuality: poetry at the crossroads –
Margery A. Evans.
p. cm. – (Cambridge studies in French); 38
Includes bibliographical references and index.
ISBN 0 521 36508 2 hardback
1. Baudelaire, Charles, 1821–1867. Spleen de Paris. 2. Prose
poems. French – History and criticism. 3. Baudelaire, Charles,
1821–1867 – Prose. 4. Paris (France) in literature.
5. Intertextuality. I. Title. II. Series.
PQ2191.S63E9 1992
841'.8 – dc20   92-3404 CIP

ISBN 0 521 36508 2 hardback

For Michael, Helen and Laura

Contents

List of illustrations	*page* x
Preface	xi
Acknowledgements	xiv
Introduction	1
1 The city	12
2 Exchange codes	21
3 Poetry and desire	41
4 Unsententious moralities	59
5 Poetry and madness	75
6 Poetic cookery	95
7 The poet as savage: rewriting cliché	110
8 Musicality	121
9 Straight lines and arabesques	139
Conclusion	150
Notes	161
Select bibliography	182
Index of names	193
Index of prose poems	195

Illustrations

(*between pages 94 and 95*)

From Goya's *Los Caprichos*, engravings presented to the Colgratia Nacional, Madrid, October 1803.

1 *Capricho 43*: 'The sleep of reason produces monsters'
2 *Capricho 37*: 'Might not the pupil know more?'
3 *Capricho 38*: 'Bravo!'
4 *Capricho 40*: 'Of what ill will he die?'
5 *Capricho 41*: 'Neither more nor less'
6 *Capricho 42*: 'Thou who canst not'
7 *Capricho 63*: 'Look how solemn they are!'

Preface

Le Spleen de Paris has enjoyed increasing popularity both inside and outside France over a number of years now, to the extent that it has come to rival, even to eclipse, the success of *Les Fleurs du mal*. But it is a text which has always presented its audience with a major problem of reading strategy. This does not apply just to the French, who Claude Pichois engagingly suggests are handicapped by their Cartesian love of definitions and classifications.[1]

The problem arises partly from the difficulty of finding a reference point by which to situate a work which is so resolutely *hors série*. In his dedication Baudelaire cites Aloysius Bertrand's *Gaspard de la nuit* as a source of inspiration, but, traditionally, critics have not found this statement very fruitful and have shied away from a comparison which they suspect is couched in perplexing layers of irony. In any case, it is argued, Baudelaire states plainly that he has done something singularly different from Bertrand. This is clearly true, although some studies of Bertrand's use of parody and cliché suggest that he may have afforded Baudelaire some important examples of the *poème-lecture*.[2]

Baudelaire's comments on prose poetry in his *1859 Salon* imply that he saw the genre as being in some respects closer to the novel than to verse poetry ('la fantaisie est d'autant plus dangereuse qu'elle est plus facile et plus ouverte; dangereuse comme la poésie en prose, comme le roman').[3] *Le Spleen de Paris* invites comparison with other specifically Parisian prose works such as Diderot's equally *excentric*, non-conformist *Neveu de Rameau*, with Hugo's *Notre-Dame de Paris* or with Balzac's vast, interconnected Parisian novels. Also, the invocation of Sterne as a possible muse in 'Les Bons Chiens' provokes comparisons with *Tristram Shandy*, another rhapsodic or *fantaisiste* production. In this book I shall look at aspects of the intertext of the prose poems and these and other prose works alluded to in *Le Spleen de Paris*.

Despite Baudelaire's own admiration for 'la gravité, la beauté et le côté infini' of the novelist's art, and despite Michel Butor's talk of the 'roman inconnu' inherent in *Le Spleen de Paris*, the collection of prose poems is generically distinct from the novel and indeed from almost all the many earlier prose texts to which it refers.[4] Since it has always been difficult to find analogous prose works, one line of approach to the *Petits Poèmes en prose* has been to explore their degree of divergence from the norms of traditional lyric poetry. Here Barbara Johnson's lively study of the prose poems as a *remise en question* of Baudelaire's verse poetry offers a useful means of access.[5] However, I hope to show how *Le Spleen de Paris*, a self-consciously 'monstrous' or hybrid work, also sets itself up for comparison with the novel and with classic texts by the great moralists, calling into question the codes governing those genres, just as it calls into question the conventions of lyric poetry.

Whether one situates the prose poems in terms of their difference from traditional lyric poetry or of their relationship with a certain prose tradition, one is first inevitably drawn into deciding which basic reading approach to adopt towards the *Petits Poèmes en prose* as a collection. Do we read them as discrete entities, loosely grouped together within the 'album' of *Le Spleen de Paris*, or do they invite reading as an inter-related whole? The two ways of reading which Roland Barthes describes in his approach to La Rochefoucauld,[6] and which are on offer with most collections of maxims and reflections, are also available in this instance: one can read the short units (maxims, reflections, or here prose poems) individually *in isolation* or one can read them all together. The difference between *Le Spleen de Paris* and many of the edifying texts to which it alludes, either directly or indirectly, is that with the prose poems the reader is presented with 'une œuvre ouverte' and with the collections of maxims, moral tales or portraits, in most cases 'le discours cassé reste un discours enfermé' (Barthes).[7]

Baudelaire describes *Le Spleen de Paris* in the Dedication to Arsène Houssaye as a 'tortueuse fantaisie' and reinforces this suggestion of a sinuous, or convoluted, continuum when he goes on to describe the collection as a snake. It is true that he writes that each of the fragments which make up this serpentine structure *can* exist separately, but this is not to say that we are encouraged to read the poems as autonomous pieces; indeed the insistence that 'tout y est à la fois tête et queue' seems to imply the reverse. Is it possible that Baudelaire's emphasis on the *singularité* of the collection ('singulièrement différent' from *Gaspard de la nuit*, more 'singulier' than *Les Fleurs de mal*) signals not only their exceptional status but also the potential oneness concealed behind an apparent plurality? How does the collection reveal itself as one in which 'tout est à la fois tête et queue'? How can we interpret the poet's comparisons of his work with music and with great cities ('le croisement de leurs innombrables rapports')?[8] These are some of the questions which must form the starting point for our study of *Le Spleen de Paris* as a collection.

Acknowledgements

I should like to thank the university of Warwick for financing the later stages of my research for this book.

I am grateful to friends and colleagues at Warwick for their part in creating a climate of interest and commitment which helped to give this project meaning. Special thanks are owing to Christopher Thompson, Leslie Hill and Mark Treharne for helpful discussions over a number of years. I would also like to thank my Ph.D. supervisor, David Kelley, whose rigorous criticism was of immense value when I was writing the original thesis from which this book evolved. Finally, and not least, the encouragement and advice of Malcolm Bowie helped me through the last stages of the project.

The occasion of this publication allows me the opportunity to thank my parents, not just for their enthusiastic interest in this project, but for a lifetime of encouragement and example.

It is equally difficult to acknowledge adequately the great debt which I owe to my husband, Michael, whose patience and support sustained me through every stage. His comments and suggestions on points of theory helped to clarify much of my early thinking on *Le Spleen de Paris*, and his influence on my approach to literary criticism as a whole has been very great. The writing of this book was a part of his life as well as mine.

The preparation of the final version of the script for the press was made easier for me by the word-processing expertise and professionalism of Anne Lakey. Lastly, I want to express my gratitude to my friend and childminder, Ros Johnson, whose excellent and cheerful care of my younger daughter, Laura, was enormously important and greatly valued.

Introduction

A KALEIDOSCOPIC STRUCTURE

J'ai cherché des titres. Les 66. Quoique cependant cet ouvrage tenant de la vis et du kaleidoscope ... put [sic] bien être poussé jusqu'au cabalistique 666 et même 6666 ...

These remarks about the *Petits Poèmes en prose*, taken from the *Canevas de la dédicace* found amongst Baudelaire's papers after his death, provide a tantalisingly suggestive but enigmatic indication of the poet's conception of the collection of prose poems. The allusion to a cabalistic multiple of 6 clearly signals to us that meaning is being proffered but at the same time withheld, and we are immediately encouraged to cast ourselves in the role of *déchiffreurs/euses*, striving to resolve an enigma. In what way do the screw and the kaleidoscope resemble each other, and how do they afford a model for a collection of prose poetry? It is not difficult to see that both incorporate principles of linearity and circularity. The screw suggests also a capacity for penetration, and this seems consistent with the thematising of acts of psychological, sexual or artistic penetration in a number of the poems. The kaleidoscope image is equally suggestive and can be read as a metaphor for the 'spin-off', the patterns of association, linking an individual poem to others in the collection and beyond to the numerous other works by moralists, novelists and poets alluded to in *Le Spleen de Paris*.

Let us look at the different levels on which the comparison with the kaleidoscope might operate. One of these is the controlled randomness of the method of composition, a method which has even been described as 'desultory'. Certainly, the unfinished nature of the collection and the apparently haphazard order of composition have always caused problems for those critics who have sought to establish the poet's intention. Although the 1869 text, published posthumously by the poet's friends Asselineau and Banville, presents the poems in an order indicated by Baudelaire in late 1865 or early 1866, it seems that the collection might have contained additional poems and the structure might therefore have been modified had not sickness and death prematurely curtailed the project.[1] However, had Baudelaire lived longer there is nothing to suggest that the collection would have been given a more rigid structure or that the poet had conceived of such a structure at the time he embarked on writing the first poems.

It is true that no work of art is entirely preconceived and does not evolve in the course of its composition, and so the method of composition of the collection of prose poems cannot be placed in antithesis to that of *Les Fleurs du mal*. As a number of critics have emphasised, the collection of verse poetry was itself profoundly modified by rearrangements and additions in the years 1857 to 1861.[2] However, even if the difference can only be one of degree, *Le Spleen de Paris* does appear to have evolved more freely along its own self-determined paths, and with less deference to an architectural plan, than was the wont of contemporary nineteenth-century *prose* works (and particularly the novel with its fixed beginning and ending and its submission to the dictates of plot).

In his 1865 ordering Baudelaire seems to have deliberately alternated contrasting types of poems, and the resulting distribution is probably far less arbitrary, but nevertheless this has the effect of breaking down any impression of a progressive structure and of increasing the reader's sense of the work's heterogeneity. It is true that the 'Liste de Projets' found with Baudelaire's notes does contain a number of 'classements' ('Choses parisiennes', 'Onéirocritie' and 'Symboles et moralités'), but these seem to have served more as private reminders of the relative proportion of different categories of poems within the collection than as a planned linear structuring principle.

Introduction

Even if they might ultimately have served as the basis of some system of organising the poems, the fact that not all the planned poems come under headings suggests that this would always have been a *retrospective* patterning and not a rigid architecture. In a note included with the second list ('SPLEEN DE PARIS à faire') Baudelaire refers not only to 'Choses parisiennes', 'Rêves' and 'Symboles et Moralités', but also to 'Autres classes à trouver', as though these categories would emerge from the accumulating body of the text rather than dictate its development from the outset.

A kaleidoscope involves the compositional principle of *bricolage*, the *a posteriori* association of elements. Patterns emerge, rather than being preordained from the start (although materials are selected with a view to favouring these patterns).[3] If this is the governing principle, clearly it does not matter that the *Petits Poèmes en prose* may be an incomplete collection; indeed incompleteness scarcely matters in an open-ended work. Baudelaire would have been familiar with Hugo's assertion that the edifice of literature is 'toujours inachevé'. It is also the case, of course, that the twentieth-century reader of *Le Spleen de Paris*, familiar with Valéry's remark that 'un ouvrage n'est jamais achevé... mais abandonné', is unlikely to find incompleteness a barrier to either appreciation or analysis.[4]

But would not Baudelaire, like Edgar Allan Poe, have rejected the very notion of taxing the reader's memory with the effort of appreciating the extensive collection of prose poems as one long whole? Would it not then amount to the sort of long poem which Poe had so firmly condemned in *The Poetic Principle*? Do not the condescending remarks in the dedication about 'commodité' and the 'volonté rétif' of the reader indicate that we are being asked to read the poems as separate pieces, and are not required to draw connections between them? It is easier to answer these questions if we first consider Baudelaire's comments on epic poetry in his *Notes nouvelles sur Edgar Poe*.

Baudelaire's observations in the *Notes nouvelles* are particularly revealing of his views on the unity of effect to be produced by a work of art, and specifically poetry. When he discusses Poe's theories about long poems he distinguishes very clearly between the artistic conception, or prior intention, and the effect on the reader, the impression produced by the finished work. This is where he differs from Poe. The following passage is interesting as much for its divergence from Poe's *Poetic Principle* as for the similarities to it.

> Voilà évidemment le poème épique condamné. Car un ouvrage de cette dimension ne peut être considéré comme poétique qu'en tant qu'on sacrifie la condition vitale de toute œuvre d'art, l'Unité; – je ne veux pas parler de l'unité dans la conception, mais de l'unité dans l'impression, de la *totalité* de l'effet, comme je l'ai déjà dit quand j'ai eu à comparer le roman avec la nouvelle. Le poème épique nous apparaît donc, esthétiquement parlant, comme un paradox. Il est possible que les anciens âges aient produit des séries de poèmes lyriques, reliées postérieurement par les compilateurs en poèmes épiques; mais toute *intention épique* résulte évidemment d'un sens imparfait de l'art. Le temps de ces anomalies artistiques est passé, et il est même fort douteux qu'un long poème ait jamais pu être vraiment populaire dans toute la force du terme. (*Œuvres complètes* II, 332)

The epic poem is here seen as an 'artistic anomaly' which is inappropriate in modern nineteenth-century France. The aristocratic implication of a certain dislike for the capacities of the crowd is something which Baudelaire would have found in Poe. But the doubt as to whether the long poem could be *populaire* also tallies with other statements by the poet at this period, and with the condescending remarks about the 'volonté rétif' of the reader in the dedication to Houssaye. It is interesting that he links the problem of writing epic poetry to the problem of achieving totality of effect in the novel, as opposed to the *nouvelle*. Significantly, Baudelaire is much more reserved than Poe in his critique of the epic (if it even amounts to a critique), and he omits quoting Poe's outright dismissal of the idea that a long poem might have any advantages at all. Baudelaire refers to the epic as a paradox, but he prefers to stress the aesthetic error of 'epic intention' rather than linger over the problem of the possible unity of effect. Nor does he make any negative reference to Milton's *Paradise Lost*, as Poe had done. Instead, he alludes exclusively to the epic poets of antiquity, and here his description of the *retrospective organisation* of their work clearly invites comparison with his own compositional method in writing *Le Spleen de Paris*.

As early as 1846 Baudelaire had written of the challenge of creating a new artistic tradition which might rival the achievement of the Ancient World, and had paid tribute to Balzac's achievement in rendering 'le coté épique de la vie moderne'.[5] However, we know that Baudelaire's attraction to the power and vitality of the epic was accompanied by an equally intense attraction to poetic concentration and verbal economy. His comments in 1861 on Hugo's *Légende des siècles* make plain his interest in a truly modern epic which succeeds because its component parts are kept brief. The passage reveals his preoccupation with the problem of reconciling the impact of epic dimensions with the intensity of the short poem:

> Victor Hugo a créé le seul poème épique qui put être créé par un homme de son temps pour des lecteurs de son temps. D'abord les poèmes qui constituent l'ouvrage sont généralement courts, et même la brièveté de quelques-uns n'est pas moins extraordinaire que leur énergie. Ceci est déjà une considération importante, qui témoigne d'une connaissance absolue de tout le possible de la poésie moderne. (*Oc* II, 140)

Certainly, given Baudelaire's interest in Hugo's achievement, it does not come as a surprise that *Le Spleen de Paris* is covertly presented as rivalling the epic. 'Cela vaut mieux qu'une intrigue de 6000 pages', is the assertion we find in the notes for the dedication, pursuing the idea of infinite multiplication which is attached to the cabalistic number 6. The urban poet figure of 'Les Bons Chiens' specifically compares and contrasts himself with the pastoral minstrels of traditional epic poets:

> Les bergers de Virgile et de Théocrite attendaient, pour prix de leurs chants alternés, un bon fromage, une flûte du meilleur faiseur ou une chèvre aux mamelles gonflées. Le poète qui a chanté les pauvres chiens a reçu pour récompense un beau gilet... (*Oc* I, 362)

The alternative title, *Petits Poèmes en prose*, closely echoes Hugo's sub-title for *La Légende* (*Petites Epopées*). Did Baudelaire see *Le Spleen de Paris* as in some ways an analogous project?[6] Like the *Légende*, the collection of prose poems resembles the epic in its capacity to evoke an experience common to myriads of individuals (the poet is 'une âme collective'[7]). It differs from the epic of the Ancients in that it does not concern itself with the teleology of a particular racial destiny. Neither does it share the formal simplicity of the traditional epic.

The distinction which Baudelaire makes in the *Notes nouvelles* between the *retrospective* totality of effect of a work of art and what he calls 'l'unité dans la conception' or 'l'intention épique' is, of course, particularly relevant to *Le Spleen de Paris*. The prose poems do not each fall into place within a vast preconceived architecture, but this does not mean that ultimately they may not generate their own play of patterns and interconnections (although the poet's comments in the dedication imply that these may not be appreciated by the majority of readers). A poem which on a first reading may stand alone as an individual 'tronçon' will be remembered as the reader progresses through the text, and their understanding of it will be modified in the light of what they are now decoding. Michael Riffaterre gives a useful analysis of such stages in the reading of poetry in his *Semiotics of Poetry*:

The second stage is that of *retroactive reading*. This is the time for a second interpretation, for the truly *hermeneutic* reading...As the reader works forward from start to finish, he is reviewing, revising, comparing backwards. He is in effect performing a structural decoding: as he moves through the text he comes to recognize, by dint of comparisons or simply because he is now able to put them together, that successive and differing statements, first noticed as mere ungrammaticalities, are in fact equivalent, for they now appear as variants of the same structural matrix...The maximal effect of retroactive reading, the climax of its function as generator of significance, naturally comes at the end...poeticalness is thus a function coextensive with the text...This is why, whereas units of meaning may be words or phrases, *the unit of significance is the text*. To discover the significance at last, the reader must surmount the mimesis hurdle: in fact this hurdle is essential to the reader's change of mind. The reader's acceptance of the mimesis sets up the grammar as the background from which the ungrammaticalities will thrust themselves forward as stumbling blocks, to be understood eventually on a second level. I cannot emphasize strongly enough that the obstacle that threatens meaning when seen in isolation at first reading is also the guideline to semiosis, the key to significance in the higher system, where the reader perceives it as part of a complex network.[8]

Riffaterre's theory is based on the unit of the individual poem, but it also works well when we apply it to the prose poems, taking the collection as a whole as the ultimate unit of significance. His analysis does not fully take account of the mobility of the reading opportunity afforded by *Le Spleen de Paris*. But it conveys well the idea of the reading of poetry as a movement from the initial perception of what he terms 'ungrammaticalities', or elements which resist immediate understanding, to their ultimate integration within new semiotic networks. Joseph Frank was already feeling his way towards a similar formulation twenty years earlier in his chapter 'Spatial Form in Modern Literature' in *Criticism: The Foundation of Modern Literary Judgement*:

> Since the primary reference of any word group is to something inside the poem itself, language in modern poetry is really reflexive... instead of the instinctive and immediate reference of words and word groups to the objects and events they symbolise, and the construction of meaning from the sequence of these references, modern poetry asks its readers to suspend the process of individual references temporarily until the entire pattern of internal references can be apprehended as a unity.[9]

Certainly Baudelaire's own description of the collection as a kaleidoscope already suggests the complexity of the reading process which it solicits. Like a kaleidoscope the *Petits Poèmes* offer a structure which is both single and multiple. The collection is described in the dedication as being a unit. Even if an element is removed, the organic whole is preserved: 'Enlevez une vertèbre et les deux morceaux de cette tortueuse fantaisie se rejoindront sans peine.' Moreover, we know from Baudelaire's correspondence that he thought of the prose poems as functioning together, and that his sense of the unity of the work was such that he referred to the whole collection in the singular as 'LA LUEUR ET LA FUMEE: POEME, EN PROSE'. At the time he mentioned this title (in a letter to Arsène Houssaye, around 20 December 1861) he was proposing that the 'poème, en prose' should comprise forty or fifty pieces, of which he claimed to have written twelve. Three years later, although he had abandoned the idea of calling the collection a 'poème, en prose' and had adopted the plural 'poèmes en prose', he still saw the collection as one unit whose composition necessitated a continuous chain of thought:

> Le Spleen de Paris, ce maudit livre sur lequel je comptais tant, est resté suspendu à la moitié. Ah! qu'il me tarde d'être chez moi! Il y a décidément un grand danger à laisser longtemps un travail interrompu, et à faire plusieurs à la fois. Le fil de la pensée se perd souvent, et on ne peut plus retrouver l'atmosphère spirituelle où on s'était d'abord placé. (Letter to Madame Aupick, 3 November 1864)

However, it is also true that Le Spleen de Paris resembles a kaleidoscope in that it gains its effects from a sequence of fragments which appears at first sight to be completely random. Critics have often remarked on the heterogeneous nature of the collection, and on the whole have accepted the poet's suggestions in the dedication as indicating that the prose poems need not be read in a fixed sequence and that their ordering is not so important as, for example, the disposition of the poems in Les Fleurs du mal. The arrangement of the verse collection has often been held to correspond, broadly speaking, to the logical progression of a deductive argument, although in recent years critics have argued that too rigid an adherence to such a view can impede one's reading of Les Fleurs du mal.[10]

Few have argued that any progressive structure may be traced in the prose poems.[11] Certainly, Baudelaire's comparison of the work to a kaleidoscope suggests that it does not, even tenuously, take its shape from a thesis. The randomness of sequence is drawn attention to in the first sentence of the dedication:

> Mon cher ami, je vous envoie un petit ouvrage dont on ne pourrait pas dire, sans injustice, qu'il n'a ni queue ni tête, puisque tout au contraire y est à la fois tête et queue, alternativement et réciproquement. (Oc I, 275)

The affirmation here gains strength from its formulation in terms of a double negative: 'on ne pourrait pas dire, sans injustice, qu'il n'a ni queue ni tête'. By withholding its meaning, keeping it at several removes from the obvious, the sentence makes the reader hesitate, fixes their attention. And the conclusion, whose syntax might at first sight appear reassuring (since the negatives are abandoned in favour of a positive statement of fact), proves to be deceptive since it teases one's powers of logic with the apparently absurd claim that head and tail, beginning and ending, may be the same thing. The contrast with *Les Fleurs du mal*, where the recognition of a beginning and an ending was considered by the poet to be of such importance, is striking.

The unstable structure of the collection, and the absence of any continuous *narrative* thread linking the different poems, encourages the reading of a given element to benefit from an effect of inter-reflection or collaboration with other elements in the whole. The metaphor of the kaleidoscope suggests the possibility of unity without the rigidity of a fixed order. It reconciles two often ambivalent Romantic aesthetic ideals: the ideal of incompleteness (because it is constantly becoming) and that of coherence (all its parts are interconnected and contribute to the whole). At the same time, it implies a radically modern view of the reader's role and of the degree of control exercised by the poet over his product. For however many additions Baudelaire might have been able to make to the collection, his description of the work as a kaleidoscope suggests an awareness that it would always remain in some sense incomplete. Because of its mobile structure it is a work which is conspicuously 'en devenir', and which actively encourages the reader to participate in its creation by perceiving patterns and associations within the text, in the same way that Baudelaire describes the poet in his article on Hugo as actively discerning the correspondences in nature. Baudelaire, then, before Mallarmé, already forcefully implies that it is ultimately the audience which produces the book.

The collection of prose poems does not solely offer a play of internal correspondences; at the same time it draws attention to a further level of correspondences linking it intertextually to other works by different authors. The reader is actively encouraged to read not only across an individual poem to others in the collection, but also across the whole collection to other works. Born of an ideal derived from observing '(les) villes énormes' and the 'croisement de leurs innombrables rapports', *Le Spleen de Paris* is presented in the dedication as a kind of infinite crossroads. It can be viewed as the point of convergence not only of a number of internal cross-reflections but also of a cultural heritage: an 'écho redit par mille labyrinthes'. Chateaubriand, Balzac, Nerval, Rabelais, Rousseau, La Fontaine, Vauvenargues, Defoe, La Bruyère, Pascal, Aloysius Bertrand, Diderot, Horace, Régnier, Sterne, Sainte-Beuve, Cervantes, Virgil, Lucan and Theocritus are all directly or indirectly invoked in the text, sometimes with detailed reference to specific passages in individual works. This reworking of literary *topoi* is consistent with Baudelaire's fascination with the advantage of the *lieu commun* (itself, of course, a similar metaphor to the *carrefour*). 'Sois toujours poète, même en prose', the poet exhorts himself in his private diary, '(g)rand style (rien de plus beau que le lieu commun). In his *1859 Salon* he remarks: 'existe-t-il (...) quelque chose de plus charmant, de plus fertile et d'une nature plus positivement *excitante* que le lieu commun?'[12]

The descent into prose was to be a descent into the *carrefour* and the *lieu commun*, a metaphor which is taken up again and expanded in the poem 'Perte d'auréole'. This move is appropriate to the urban subject matter and it is in keeping with the climate of the period in which Hugo writes his celebration of William Shakespeare '(pris) en flagrant délit de fréquentation populaire, allant et venant dans les carrefours, "trivial", disant à tous le mot de tous, parlant la langue publique'.[13] It is a move which implies an awareness of the collective discourse and a recognition of the magical concentration and suggestiveness of cliché and hence of language in general, which, at the same time that it may take the form of a single articulation, also bears clustering around it the myriad associations of past utterances.

We can see, then, that at the dawn of our era *Le Spleen de Paris* is self-consciously offered to the reader as a mobile or open structure which invites each interpreter to discover interconnections within the whole, and to pursue the multiple intratextual and intertextual avenues in the labyrinth of the text. The collection of prose poems can be seen as anticipating Mallarmé's utopic *Livre*, whose pages were not to have followed one another according to a predetermined order but which would have allowed its readers to make their own grouping within a system of possible permutations. Baudelaire, before Mallarmé, can be seen as the real forerunner of the modern *œuvre en mouvement*. Baudelaire too, before Mallarmé, would have recognised the importance of Richard Wagner's belief that poetry had in the nineteenth century reached a critical juncture in its development when it might evolve either towards science or towards music. His conception of *Le Spleen de Paris* as a structure which would be 'musicale sans rythme et sans rime' signals a move in the direction which Mallarmé was to accentuate and prolong with his concept of poetry as a music of *signification* and his ideal of a book which derives its mobility and spaciousness from the power of letters themselves, through a play of correspondences.[14]

CHAPTER I

The city

THE CROSSROADS METAPHOR

C'est surtout de la fréquentation des villes énormes, c'est du croisement de leurs innombrables rapports que naît cet idéal obsédant.
(Dedication to Arsène Houssaye)

Je chante les chiens calamiteux...ceux qui errent, solitaires, dans les ravines sinueuses des immenses villes.
('Les Bons Chiens')

C'était l'explosion du nouvel an: chaos de boue et de neige, traversé de mille carosses, étincelant de joujoux et de bonbons, grouillant de cupidités et de désespoirs, délire officiel d'une grande ville fait pour troubler le cerveau du solitaire le plus fort.
('Un Plaisant')

The dominant image of Baudelaire's Paris is one of a cluster of intersecting trajectories, a fantastic, palimpsest arabesque of criss-crossing paths. It recalls similar *mises en abyme* in works by Baudelaire's contemporaries and by earlier prose writers such as Laurence Sterne. Perhaps above all one is reminded of the 'dédale inextricable de ruelles, de carrefours et de culs de sacs' evoked by Hugo in *Notre-Dame de Paris* (1831), a work which has itself been seen as furthering an aesthetics of digression as a 'roman poème' anticipating the modern 'polycentric' novel.[1] Hugo declared in his 1829 Preface to 'Les Orientales' that he was aiming to create 'une œuvre assimilable à une ville du Moyen Age'. But it is his prose work *Notre-Dame de Paris* which offers the most striking exploration of analogies between the monument or city and the palimpsest architecture of text itself.

Progression through the city text is associated in *Notre-Dame de Paris*, as in *Le Spleen de Paris*, with the pursuit of fantasy, which is linked with meandering and amorous pursuit. Hugo's 'mauvais poète', Pierre Gringoire, notices that 'rien n'est propice à la rêverie comme de suivre une jolie femme sans savoir où elle va'. And in a description which on one level closely mirrors the reader's activity of following the text (and which offers parallels with Baudelaire's description of the behaviour of his 'bons chiens') Hugo continues:

> Il y a dans cette abdication volontaire de son libre arbitre, dans cette fantaisie qui se soumet à une autre fantaisie, laquelle ne s'en doute pas, un mélange d'indépendence fantasque et d'obéissance aveugle...je ne sais quoi d'intermédiaire entre l'esclavage et la liberté.[2]

But it is beyond the wit of Gringoire to find his way alone through the maze of city streets described by Hugo in self-consciously *textual* terms ('un tricot inextricable de rues bizarrement brouillées').[3] And, just as the *ligne droite* of the novel's plot begins itself to become increasingly 'brouillée', so at the same moment Gringoire first loses the 'fil de ses idées' and then loses his way in a Hoffmanesque labyrinth of streets 'qui ressemble à un écheveau de fil brouillé par un chat'.[4] These are streets which, as Gringoire laments, 'ont bien peu de logique'. A little later his exasperated cry, 'Maudits soient les carrefours! C'est le diable qui les a faits à l'image de sa fourche',[5] casts some light on Baudelaire's own choice of the devil as patron of a work directly inspired by the 'innombrables rapports' characteristic of the modern city (and one which, again like *Notre-Dame de Paris*, associates itself with hermeticism and freemasonry).[6] Hugo's Paris is likened to a labyrinth and also to a beehive, the same self-consciously intertextual metaphor which is used later in *Notre-Dame*, after the manner of Montaigne, to evoke the totality of productions associated with the printed word ('C'est la fourmilière des intelligences. C'est la ruche où toutes les imaginations, ces abeilles dorées, arrivent avec leur miel').[7]

Like the cathedral itself which is seen to lie symbolically at its heart and like the Babel's tower of works emanating from the printing press ('cette *métropole* de le pensée universelle' (my italics)),[8] the city is perceived as the complex accretion of the centuries rather than the product of individual genius. The images of the cathedral, the city and the Babel's tower of literary productions here help to promote what Victor Brombert has seen as the characteristically Hugolien vision of 'une poésie ininterrompue (...) une textualité sans frontières', 'une vision du monde en tant que livre, et de la création en tant que texte'.[9] Later, in a musical comparison which offers striking analogies with Baudelaire's references to music in the Dedication to Arsène Houssaye and in the prose poem 'Les Veuves',[10] Hugo portrays Paris as 'une mer d'harmonie', 'une fournaise de musique', the source of a 'symphonie qui fait le bruit d'une tempête' and which incorporates passages which are 'tour à tour grave(s) et criard(s)'.[11] Here, as in the *Petits Poèmes en prose*, music provides a model of structural complexity and extremes of contrast analogous with the complexity of the modern city. Here too, writing about music appears to offer Hugo a way of writing about the structural complexity of the novel itself, without necessarily implying any analogy between the sound qualities of music and prose.

The *Petits Poèmes en prose* also encourage one to read metatextually certain descriptions of Paris by Balzac and to see them as reworkings of a self-reflexive metaphor common to a great number of 'urban' texts by different writers. Balzac's thematising of the labyrinthine interconnections in the capital city is too complex and extensive for me to do more than briefly allude to it here, and recall perhaps such a salient description as that of Rastignac's closing vision of Paris at the end of *Le Père Goriot*, when, viewed from the height of the Père-Lachaise cemetery, the city is characterised by its tortuousness and likened also to the familiar image of a 'ruche bourdonnante' whose frenzied activity here contrasts powerfully with the immobility of the microcosmic 'cité des morts' in which Rastignac is standing. Balzac too, like Hugo in *Notre-Dame de Paris* and Diderot before him in *Le Neveu de Rameau*, presents voyeurism and amorous pursuit in the heart of Paris as metaphors for the mind and its digressive movement, particularly the mind engaged in the process of creating and reading the text itself.

> Une bien belle chose est le métier d'espion, quand on le fait pour son compte et au profit d'une passion. N'est-ce pas se donner les plaisirs du voleur en restant honnête homme?... Mais c'est la chasse, la chasse dans Paris, la chasse avec tous ses accidents, moins les chiens, le fusil et la taïaut! Il n'est de comparable à ces scènes que celles de la vie des joueurs. Puis besoin est d'un cœur gros d'amour ou de vengeance pour s'embusquer dans Paris,... et pour jouir alors de tous les accidents de Paris et d'un quartier, en leur prêtant un intérêt de plus que celui dont ils abondent déjà. Alors ne faut-il pas avoir une âme multiple? N'est-ce pas vivre de mille passions, de mille sentiments ensemble?[12]

This description of 'spying' in Balzac's *Ferragus* can be read as a celebration of the imaginative receptiveness or 'âme multiple' demanded by literary creation and by the reading process. It can be compared with Baudelaire's celebration of poetic activity in 'Les Foules', the 'sainte prostitution de l'âme' which is associated, as in Balzac, with those laws of chance which are so vividly illustrated by the random encounters in big cities:

> Ce que les hommes nomment amour est bien petit, bien restreint et bien faible comparé à cette prostitution de l'âme qui se donne tout entière, poésie et charité, à l'imprévu qui se montre, à l'inconnu qui passe. ('Les Foules')

The images of Paris in the prose poems may also bring to mind a description in Edgar Allan Poe's *Tale of the Ragged Mountains* (1844), in which a labyrinth of sinuous paths leads the chief protagonist to his dream city of innumerable streets crossing each other in all directions. They also invite comparison with the *mise en abyme* of the frozen lake in Gautier's *Spirite* (1865), in which the winter skaters leave their intricate tracery of criss-crossing pathways as on a magic mirror.[13]

In a more jocular vein, Sterne's Tristram remarks on how, as his pen journeyed over the barren track of the white page, *by making the most of every chance encounter* and 'hailing all those who were coming through cross roads' 'I turned my *plain* into a *city*'.[14] More overtly than Balzac, or Hugo, Poe or Gautier, Sterne here uses the city as a metaphor for the text. The precedent is a particularly striking one, especially given the fact that *Tristram Shandy* is mentioned in 'Les Bons Chiens' when Sterne is evoked as a possible muse.

All these images in this diverse collection of texts have in common the fact that they may be interpreted as offering paradigms of the reader's sense of awe, and even perplexity, on confronting the complex fabric of a literary text. With the *mise en abyme* of the 'carrefour', the network of interconnections within the city, Baudelaire is crucially and characteristically reworking a common literary topos. In other words, his 'carrefour' is a *lieu commun* in two senses of the word. In the case of *Le Spleen de Paris*, with its conspicuously kaleidoscopic or open structure, the 'carrefour' can be seen as a variant on the image of the *réseau* and read, after Barthes, as a metaphor for Text (Text which, like language itself, was seen by Barthes as being 'structured but decentred and without closure').[15] A century before Barthes and Derrida Baudelaire's metatextual imagery in *Le Spleen de Paris* reflects his reading of Hugo and his interest in the cabalistic tradition which saw the world as a book and the creation as an external text, an enigmatic hermeneutic system.

It is tempting to read in Baudelaire's metaphor of the 'carrefour' an implicit recognition of what we would nowadays term intertextuality and of the seamless continuity of world and text, 'l'espace d'inscription' envisaged in modern philosophical and literary criticism.[16]

But as well as offering a network image, Baudelaire's 'carrefour' is above all specifically *urban*. We know that he considered titles such as *Le Promeneur solitaire* and *Le Rodeur parisien* as alternatives to *Le Spleen de Paris*, titles which relate more closely to the dominant image of a solitary individual wandering through the city labyrinth (an individual whose solitude, in one reading, might link him to the reader, engaged in the quintessentially solitary exercise of exploring/creating the written text). Quite apart from the *carrefour* image, what are the attractions of the city landscape? Why is it a peculiarly appropriate reflection of the poetic ideal behind the *Petits Poèmes en prose*, as is claimed in the dedication? Why, in 'Les Bons Chiens', does the poet reject the academic muse in favour of the city muse: 'la muse familière, la citadine, la vivante'? Why, in 'Laquelle est la vraie?', is the ideal muse, the beautiful and infinitely precious first Benedicta, replaced by a vulgar, bizarre and hysterical figure who cackles with laughter as she announces: 'C'est moi, la vraie Bénédicta! C'est moi, une fameuse canaille!'?

The answer to these questions lies partly in the mobility and vitality of the metropolis and partly, paradoxically, in those very qualities which make the city abhorrent to the *flâneur* poet. The first of these aspects is perhaps the easiest to understand. As in Diderot's *Neveu de Rameau*, a work with which the *Petits Poèmes* offer a number of intertextual links,[17] or *Tristram Shandy* with its emphasis on the 'chance encounter', *Le Spleen de Paris* exploits the image of the metropolis as a way of thematising its own apparent contingency, as well as the *folie* or *lunatisme* of capricious association which forms one important aspect of the poetic imagination. The mutability of Diderot's Nephew ('Rien ne dissemble plus de lui que lui-même') is paralleled by the *libertinage* of the Philosopher's imagination, the errant fancies which are themselves compared to the amorous meanderings of flirtatious young people in the heart of the city. In a similar manner, the frenetic movements and chance encounters of the city-dwellers in the *Petits Poèmes* (perhaps best expressed in 'Perte d'auréole') are matched by the caprice and 'lunacy' of the artist or poet as depicted in such poems as 'Le *Confiteor* de l'artiste', 'Le Mauvais Vitrier', 'Le Fou et la Vénus', 'Les Bienfaits de la lune' and 'Assommons les pauvres!', amongst others. Caprice here includes the capacity for sudden reversals and changes of idea or mood, but also the arabesque or lateral movement of fantasy or 'musical' association, which is compared in 'Le Thyrse' to the flowers which spiral and play around the rod of an emblematic thyrsus.

It is this *mobile* quality of the city which more than any other feature allows it to be compared to the unstable, kaleidoscopic structure of the collection of prose poems. It is also one of the features which provokes comparisons in the poems between the city and the sea. The irresistible tidal force of the crowds ('le flot mouvant') in 'Le Vieux Saltimbanque' is the source of one of the most powerful images of the modern condition to figure in *Le Spleen de Paris*. Baudelaire's poet, swept along and unable to resist the surge which pulls him away from the chance encounter which a similar, sea-like movement of the crowd had brought about a moment before, has left an immense legacy. Even in twentieth-century film one finds an echo in the image of Marcel Carné's Mime in *Les Enfants du Paradis* (in success terms a mirror reversal of Baudelaire's failed Saltimbank), who is swept along in a vast Parisian crowd all of whom are dressed in the same Pierrot costume, a human tide of look-alikes who, even whilst paying tribute to his talent, deny him his most basic autonomy as an individual.

Baudelaire's poet, gazing out over 'des vagues de toits' ('Les Fenêtres') or leaning on his balcony listening to the oceanic roar of diverse discordant cries from the city asylum ('Le Crépuscule du soir'), poses both as the observer of the city, or outsider, and as an *homme cité* in himself. We can compare him to Hugo's *homme océan*: a mind containing and expressing the flux and reflux, the extremes of contrast, the whole fantastic diversity of 'une vie moderne'.[18]

It is not only the mobility of the modern crowd which dominates the Paris of *Petits Poèmes en prose*. The very architecture is seen to be itself in a state of flux and ferment.[19] The activities stemming from Baron Haussmann's great political initiative to transform the metropolis are incidentally recorded in 'Les Yeux des pauvres' with the description of 'un café neuf qui formait le coin d'un boulevard neuf, encore tout plein de gravois', which contributes to the central image of the city as a place of continuous change.

It is here that we see how closely related are two of the aspects of the city which inspire the new poetic venture: its mobility and its distastefulness. The irony of the poet's reference to the 'boulevard neuf montrant déjà glorieusement ses splendeurs inachevées' is matched by his description of the café itself and its grotesque trivialisation of a cultural heritage to serve the ends of the new materialist consumerism. The irony here, so characteristic of the 'raillerie' which Baudelaire saw as a distinctive feature of the *Petits Poèmes en prose*, is in the same spirit that Hugo advocates in his *William Shakespeare*:

Résumer l'horreur par le rire, ce n'est pas la manière la moins terrible.[20]

This is why a number of poems suggest that the more horrible the poet's material, the greater is its power to inspire him. If the poet's new urban muse is bizarre, hysterical and repellent, as is suggested in 'Laquelle est la vraie?', she also resembles the 'inévitable et impitoyable Muse' of 'Le Galant Tireur' (a poem which can be read as an allegory of the poet's activity): that is, a creature whose hatefulness inspires him above all to 'tirer juste'.[21] And we know from the dedication to Houssaye that the poet is 'un esprit qui regarde comme le plus grand honneur d'accomplir *juste* ce qu'il a projeté de faire'. The title *Le Spleen de Paris* focusses even more acutely than alternatives such as *Le Promeneur solitaire* or *Le Rodeur parisien* on the source of the poet's spleen and of his *raillerie*, in other words on his most valuable source of inspiration.

As Philippe Hamon has convincingly demonstrated in a very rich article on 'Texte et architecture', buildings and cities crowd many poetic works, suggesting amongst other things poets' interest in *where* humanity lives, in the space which conditions men's and women's lives, a habitat which is also an *habitude* or *routine*: 'une façon de se faire manipuler par l'espace'.[22] As we shall see in the next chapter, Baudelaire's 'Spleen' for Paris can be seen as coextensive with the literary function of the prose poems to break with mental routine as well as with genre conventions. It is a spleen which will fuel the disruption of that conventional and unthinking, if sometimes comforting, subservience to habitual perceptions which infantilises humanity. Proust's more compassionate, or indulgent, exploration of the force of habit, and its power to put us to sleep like children, was to deal essentially with the same question. In a variant of the same conjuring with 'route' and 'routine', the world of habit, and more specifically habitual perception, is of course symbolically shattered in *A la Recherche*, when Marcel discovers that the two Combray walks or *routines*, which he had thought of as quite separate and distinct, are in fact connected.

CHAPTER 2

Exchange codes

J'estime de l'essence de la Poésie qu'elle soit selon les diverses natures des esprits, ou de valeur nulle ou d'importance infinie; ce qui l'assimile à Dieu même.
Valéry, *Questions de poésie*

...tout ce qui ne sera pas l'ardeur vers Plutus sera réputé un immense ridicule...Ces temps sont peut-être bien proches; qui saît même s'ils ne sont pas venus...Quant à moi qui sens quelquefois en moi le ridicule d'un prophète, je sais que je n'y trouverai jamais la charité d'un médecin.
Baudelaire, *Fusées* (*Oc* I, 667)

...chaos de boue et de neige...grouillant de cupidités et de désespoirs, délire officiel d'une grande ville fait pour troubler le cerveau du solitaire le plus fort.
Baudelaire, 'Un Plaisant'

The city offers Baudelaire, as we have seen, the image of a giant, mobile *carrefour* of interconnecting ways, a model of such structural complexity that it invites comparison with music and with textuality, suggesting the possibility of a harmony which might include the possibility of dissonance and extremes of contrast. At the same time, the phenomenon of an individual mind confronted by the city crowd provides a focus for the exploration of profound tensions between individuality and conformity to the group. It is the locus for a paradoxical reversal: the infinite fecundity of the individual, solitary imagination (its *multiplicity*) contrasts with the atrophying and simplifying force of the 'collective' mind with its anti-vital subservience to cliché (its *singleness*). Clearly it is no coincidence that this is a central theme of a work whose own structure constitutes, as we have seen, a play on the concepts of singleness and multiplicity.

Among the received codes which control and ordain the thinking of the group, the collective and unthinking madness which *Le Spleen de Paris* foregrounds above all others is the commercial exchange code ('l'ardeur vers Plutus'). Baudelaire's Paris is dominated by commercialism, and the prose poems foreground this quintessential feature of its modernity, comparing and contrasting commercial exchange with that other process of exchange in which the poet and his reader are engaged. Paris serves here, of course, as a symbol of the modern urban condition and the poet's depiction of the Paris phenomenon is no more restricted to one fixed metropolis than his remarks in *Pauvre Belgique!* are specific to the Belgian race. His thoughts on the materialist consumerism that so dominated the Paris of the mid-nineteenth century have in no way lost their immediacy for the modern reader. Indeed, one reason for the popularity of *Le Spleen de Paris* with a twentieth-century readership must undoubtedly be that the poems still surprise us with the cutting edge of their *raillerie*, startle us with sudden, discomforting insights into a reality which we recognise as our own. With stridency and passion, with irony and humour, Baudelaire invites his readers to espouse an alienated, marginal and exceptional vision of modern social processes, and to divest themselves of any comforting identification with mainstream, collective 'sanity', or accepted wisdom. Modern society's conventional distinctions are persuasively interrogated; categories such as normality and madness, civilisation and savagery are revealed as arbitrary conveniences serving the group's own need for self-justification and self-definition. By problematising some of society's most cherished assumptions and categories of thought the poems powerfully implicate and involve their readership in a reappraisal of their own 'point de départ'. The logic of the poetry itself works to invalidate the criticism which dismisses it as the product of a 'sick', marginal, maladjusted, social and financial failure.

The very first poem in the collection foregrounds the

importance of gold, the symbol of supreme worth in contemporary nineteenth-century Paris.

L'ETRANGER
– Qui aimes-tu le mieux, homme énigmatique, dis? ton père, ta mère, ta soeur ou ton frère?
– Je n'ai ni père, ni mère, ni soeur, ni frère.
– Tes amis?
– Vous vous servez là d'une parole dont le sens m'est resté jusqu'à ce jour inconnu.
– Ta patrie?
– J'ignore sous quelle latitude elle est située.
– La beauté?
– Je l'aimerais volontiers, déesse et immortelle.
– L'or?
– Je le hais comme vous haissez Dieu.
– Eh! qu'aimes-tu donc, extraordinaire étranger?
– J'aime les nuages... les nuages qui passent... là-bas... là-bas... les merveilleux nuages!

The subject of this poem (the 'outsider') is in many ways a perfect example of the 'uncivilised' Romantic hero with an eccentric preference for solitude. He is asked a number of questions regarding his values in life, and when asked if gold is his greatest love he astonishes his interrogator by replying: 'Je le hais comme vous haissez Dieu.'

The comment earns him the epithet 'extraordinaire', and seems more than any of his other answers to confer on him the status of a 'sauvage'. It is this reply which presages the poem's climax, and which seems to prove conclusively that the subject's norms are not those of society (as represented by his interlocutor). The self exclusion of this outsider is not based, then, merely on vague emotionalism or self-absorption but on the rejection of a specific code of values. The immaterial marvels represented by the clouds ('les nuages... les nuages qui passent... les merveilleux nuages') may be of interest to the outsider but they are unlikely to impress his interrogator, who appears as the representative of a society which already respects material commodities above all else. The outsider is an 'homme singulier': 'singular' in his oddness or difference: *one* man outside the *multiple* collective consciousness of the group. The dialogue form is here the perfect vehicle for the expression of conflicting codes of value. The outsider figure has none of the complexity of, for example, the narrator of 'Les Tentations'. His voice expresses a difference from the norm and the 'portrait' functions more to interrogate society's mental habits than to evoke a 'rounded' individual persona. Paris is the capital or 'head' of a world where, as Baudelaire argues elsewhere, in his article on Gautier, 'les vrais poètes apparaissent comme des êtres fabuleux et étrangers' and of which he writes: 'on peut dire que dans tous les genres d'invention le grand homme ici est un monstre'.[1]

'L'Etranger', then, initiates a thematising of 'singularité', the exceptional and unconventional, a breaking away from the normative, in this work which is itself a 'monster' or hybrid breaking with all previous poetic norms. The poem takes on further resonance when it is read in relation to 'Les Tentations' with its description of Plutus, one of the devils who appear before the poet in a dream and who try to distract him from his true vocation. Here, as in 'L'Etranger', gold represents an alternative anti-poetic value system, but in this instance the tone is more jocular and the poet's stance is modest, self-critical and bantering. Gold constitutes a real temptation: one which the poet will reject with disgust, but not without retrospective qualms. The poet figure is not himself exempt from the code of values he describes and 'Les Tentations' ironically dispels any impression of moral one-upmanship which might be inferred from a reading of 'L'Etranger'. The skin of Plutus is golden, and the long metallic rattling sound which comes from his stomach suggests that he is sustained by the ingestion of precious metals. Humorously, but insistently, we are reminded that, like the 'little savages' of 'Le Gâteau', this devil consumes a strictly finite commodity and his greed is clearly shown to be at the expense of others' suffering. By amusingly acknowledging the poet's own greed, the poem is able disarmingly to confront this particularly bitter equation, so unpalatable in any consumer society.

Plutus has no eyes and therefore never could have been and

never will be capable of seeing. In contrast, the poor are memorable because of the fascination which their eyes exert over the poet–narrator. It is in the eyes of the poor that he reads the reflection of his own imaginings. Amongst the figures illustrated on Plutus's skin the poet discerns 'de petits gnomes difformes, maigres, dont les yeux réclamaient l'aumône mieux encore que leurs mains tremblantes'. To accept the material gifts of Plutus would mean also assuming his sightlessness and indifference. It would mean opting for egoism rather than the charity associated with the artistic process itself, a charity which in the context of the wider collection of poems takes the comical or grotesque form of a Sterne/Tristram extending to an ass 'son immortel macaron' ('Les Bons Chiens').[2]

The humour of 'Les Tentations' offers a relatively gentle form of persuasion, but in 'Les Yeux des pauvres', with its ambiguous reproach to an insensitive and unreceptive addressee, the reader is more aggressively implicated in the social canvas. Here the poet–narrator recalls his own sense of shame when, sitting in a brash new café, he felt himself to be part of a vulgar display of affluence which dazzled an impoverished family standing outside in the street. The 'gold' which the new café boasts on its walls may only be giltwood, but the counterfeit nevertheless seems to amaze the trio of observers:

Les yeux du père disaient 'Que c'est beau! que c'est beau! on dirait que tout l'or du pauvre monde est venu se porter sur ces murs.' (*Oc* I, 318)

Indeed, this fake gold is prized as the 'beauty' of contemporary Paris ('Que c'est beau! que c'est beau!'), and it seems to express the highest values of a *poor* or degraded reality ('tout l'or du pauvre monde').

The exploration of counterfeit values is continued in 'La Fausse Monnaie', where the hypocrisy of a materialistic society which still retains a vestigial respect for inherited mythical and religious beliefs is suggested in the description of a rich man who thinks to have accomplished both a charitable act and 'une bonne affaire' by giving a beggar a counterfeit coin:

Comme nous nous éloignions du bureau de tabac, mon ami fit un soigneux triage de sa monnaie; dans la poche gauche de son gilet il glissa de petites pièces d'or, dans la droite, de petites pièces d'argent; dans la poche gauche de sa culotte, une masse de gros sols, et enfin, dans la droite, une pièce d'argent de deux francs qu'il avait particulièrement examinée. (*Oc* I, 323)

The meticulous distribution of the change underlines the hierarchical nature of the commercial exchange system, whilst reflecting the pecuniary preoccupations of the modern city dweller and presaging the action which is to follow. The poet narrator misinterprets his friend's charitable gesture, and at first sees the gift of the counterfeit coin as a pretext for imaginative *speculation*. For him (if not for his friend) it might serve as a form of low-budget down-payment on fantasy:

une pareille conduite, de la part de mon ami, n'était excusable que par le désir de créer un évènement dans la vie de ce pauvre diable, peut-être même de connaître les conséquences diverses, funestes ou autres, que peut engendrer une pièce fausse dans la main d'un mendiant. Ne pouvait-elle pas se multiplier en pièces vraies? ne pouvait-elle pas aussi le conduire en prison?... Et ainsi ma fantaisie allait son train, prêtant des ailes à l'esprit de mon ami et tirant toutes les déductions possibles de toutes les hypothèses possibles. (*Oc* I, 324)

For the poet-figure, then, the act of 'charity' derives from perverse curiosity, the same sort of motivation which might lie behind the gesture of offering perfume to a dog ('Le Chien et le flacon') or a macaroon to an ass ('Les Bons Chiens'). Even the philanthropic beating of the beggar in 'Assommons les pauvres!' invites association with the same perverse desire to ape the powers of the Almighty.

But this 'artistic' or *gratuitous* form of investment offers the possibility of an almost infinite return. In 'La Fausse Monnaie', the multiplication of the poet-figure's own hypotheses and deductions far outstrips the finite rewards which the beggar might gain from commercial speculation. As Roland Barthes pointed out in his essay 'Pouvoir nous brûle', speculation is a sublimated alchemical form of capitalist profit.[3] Its fascination for Baudelaire is similar to its fascination for the Balzac of *Le*

Faiseur: both writers associate it with a form of absolute creation or alchemical power. In the *Petits Poèmes* the perverse *gamble* of art itself, even if it has satanic sponsorship (as suggested in 'Le Joueur généreux'), is presented as analogous but infinitely superior to commercial investment. Baudelaire's notes for a possible title in the draft dedication suggest the idea of a quasi-infinite multiplication as opposed to a distinct sum ('66...jusqu'au cabalistique 666 et même 6666'). Like his 'mentor' Sterne, Baudelaire seems to be recognising in 'La Fausse Monnaie' that the most interesting thing about money is its power to stimulate the imagination. (In Sterne's novel, Tristram tells us how the *finite* sum bequeathed by his Aunt Dinah has the effect of arousing his father's imagination to such a degree that 'a hundred-and-fifty odd projects took possession of his brain by turns' (*TS* IV, 328).)

However, in 'La Fausse Monnaie' the rich man's motivation is different from the poet's, and reveals how hypocrisy is bred of the union between commercialism and religious optimism (based on the quid pro quo of 'investment' in personal salvation rather than the gamble of imaginative speculation). The act of charity is motivated by the same thinking as the commercialism which Baudelaire defines in *Mon Coeur mis à nu* as 'le prêté-rendu...le prêt avec le sous-entendu: *Rends-moi plus que je ne te donne.*'[4] The rich man's illusion that he can 'emporter le paradis économiquement' is more misplaced than the drug addict's desire to 'acheter avec un peu de monnaie le bonheur et le génie' which the poet criticises in *Le Poème du hachisch*.[5] Both are unlike the paradise attained through art itself, which is compared in 'L'Invitation au voyage' to a reward bestowed on 'un homme laborieux et qui a bien mérité du monde entier': the reward for a superior kind of 'stake', one which ultimately has more in common with Aloysius Bertrand's 'jeton du fou' than with capitalist investment.[6] In 'Le Tir et le cimetière', the play on the expression 'tirage' suggests the printing and circulation of a work such as *Le Spleen de Paris* itself, and at the same time evokes a lottery draw for winning numbers. It develops and prolongs in a vein of dark humour Bertrand's image of the book itself as a counter, cast in the face of time, on the gambling table of destiny. By contrast, the rich man's counterfeit coin in 'La Fausse Monnaie' seems ultimately to symbolise the counterfeit values of commercialism itself. 'Le commerce' may be 'naturel', in that for Baudelaire it reflects man's infamous and fallen state, but the values which it promotes are unreal. The reality of modern commercial Paris is shown in the prose poems to be sham, and there is a sense in which the only 'real' gold (the only true value) presented in the *Spleen de Paris* exists in dream or in art. This whole network of poems illustrates well the poet's remark in the dedication for *Les Paradis Artificiels*: 'Le bon sens nous dit que les choses de la terre n'existent que bien peu, et que la vraie réalité n'est que dans les rêves.'[7]

However, the nature of the poetic 'treasure' may be one which takes account of the reality of the world in which it is to be read. In 'Laquelle est la vraie?' a conundrum as to the nature of illusion and reality centres on the description of a buried 'treasure': the poet's defunct love, Bénédicta, 'qui remplissait l'atmosphère d'idéal et dont les yeux répandaient le désir de la grandeur, de la gloire et de tout ce qui fait croire à l'immortalité'. Bénédicta's name means 'fine words' or 'true expression'. The muse of those who aspire to greatness and to glory, she is buried in a coffin of scented wood as incorruptible as the treasure chests of India (or, as Etienne Gilson has remarked, as a poetic text like *Les Fleurs du mal*).[8] It is whilst gazing on the spot where this 'treasure' lies buried that the poet is confronted with a second Bénédicta who curiously resembles the first, but whose raucous and common tones he finds shocking. In the version of 'Laquelle est la vraie?' published in *Le Boulevard* (14 June 1863), the 'inferior' or 'common' language of the second Bénédicta is emphasised by the poet's coyly pedantic comment: '*dans ce patois familier de la canaille que ma pudeur ne saurait reproduire*'.[9] Although this description of the poet's attitude towards the language of the second Bénédicta does not appear in the 1869 text, Bénédicta's words are in themselves sufficient to suggest the antithesis between 'fine expression' and vulgarity: 'C'est moi, la vraie Bénédicta! C'est moi, une fameuse canaille!' But the poet figure angrily rejects this second muse:

Mais moi, furieux, j'ai répondu: 'Non! non! non!' Et pour mieux accentuer mon refus, j'ai frappé si violemment la terre du pied que ma jambe s'est enfoncée jusqu'au genou dans la sépulture récente, et que, comme un loup pris au piège, je reste attaché, pour toujours peut-être, à la fosse de l'idéal. (*Oc* I, 342)

By rejecting this vulgar reincarnation of his first muse the poet finds himself in a tragi-comic position: he must remain forever trapped in the quicksand grave of his first love. The ideal of lyric poetry, associated in *Les Fleurs du mal* with a movement of 'Elévation', has here become a dead weight dragging the poet down. With the confusion of identity as to which is the 'real' Bénédicta the question is posed as to what really constitutes 'fine expression', what constitutes the *real* treasure. Must poetry always affect the noble tones of the traditional lyric or can it be constructed out of the most vulgar idioms, the language of the people? Language too is coextensive with social hierarchies, and with the divisions which separate the rich from 'la canaille'. The ridiculous posture of the poet-figure in 'Laquelle est la vraie?' suggests the dangers of clinging to a chimera of the past, and of rejecting the inspiration of 'la canaille', the vile or *dog-like* populace (from the Latin 'canis').

The common urban Bénédicta evoked in 'Laquelle est la vraie?' is clearly also identifiable with the muse of the poet of 'Perte d'auréole' who resigns himself to losing his halo in the mire of the city street and who abandons the trappings of poetic distinction (ambrosia and so on), commenting in the language of the street: '*à quelque chose malheur est bon.* Je puis maintenant me promener incognito, faire des actions basses, et me livrer à la crapule, comme les simples mortels' (my italics). The greatness of glory associated with the nobility of the first Bénédicta are renounced in favour of a hysterical democratic muse associated with madness and capriciousness.

The traditional artistic glory cult is presented here as just another manifestation of the exchange ethos, and when 'Perte d'auréole' is read in the context of other poems its ironic subversion of this cult takes on further significance. For if the rich man of 'La Fausse Monnaie' looks for redemption in exchange for charity, the poet-figure of 'A une heure du matin' is seeking glory (even if it is initially a private distinction) *in exchange for* social isolation and suffering. The poem's concluding prayer may appear lyrical and moving, but it nevertheless invokes the Deity for dubious purposes: 'Accordez-moi la grâce de produire quelques beaux vers qui me prouvent à moi-même...que je ne suis pas inférieur à ceux que je méprise!' Artistic glory, even if it is superior to the cheap renown associated with journalism in 'Les Tentations', is, nevertheless, only another form of 'brevet' in a complex system of social rewards. In 'Assommons les pauvres!' the poet-figure finally opts instead for the 'brevet de folie', recognising that this is in reality the only sort of 'distinction' which his society will accord him.

The defunct muse of 'Laquelle est la vraie?' is portrayed as a buried 'treasure', but the realm of art celebrated in 'L'Invitation au voyage' is compared to a revealed treasure. The 'pays de Cocagne' evoked in this poem is described as a treasure-house, and the ships which supply it with its riches ('ces énormes navires...tout chargés de richesses') are explicitly acknowledged as a metaphor for the poet's thoughts: 'ce sont encore mes pensées enrichies qui reviennent de l'infini vers toi'. The poet boasts:

Qu'ils cherchent, qu'ils cherchent encore, qu'ils reculent sans cesse les limites de leur bonheur, ces alchimistes de l'horticulture! Qu'ils proposent des prix de soixante et de cent mille florins pour qui résoudra leurs ambitieux problèmes! Moi, j'ai trouvé ma *tulipe noire* et mon *dahlia bleu*! (*Oc* I, 303)

The commercial comparison is once again foregrounded. But on this occasion the poet-figure boasts that his own alchemy has proved more successful than the magic of the horticulturalists who quest for the commercial mine of the black tulip or the blue dahlia. He has discovered his own priceless ideal which cannot be evaluated and sorted, like the rich man's change, into 'petites pièces d'or', 'gros sols', 'pièces d'argent' and so on.[10] But with the image of the blue dahlia the reader is again made aware of the complexity and ambivalence of Baudelaire's presentation of art's relationship to consumerism. He is describing a world

Exchange codes 31

where beauty is *not* exempt from the pressures of the marketplace but where it can be forced in a hot-house and sold to the highest bidder. This is a world where alchemy is truly at the service of the devil and where 'flowers' have become the battleground for commercial rivalry and greed. There are two ways of looking at this. On the one hand, commercial exchange is evoked as a system that is ultimately transcended and rejected in the privacy of the individual imagination, but on the other hand the social reality of commercialism is shown to be a force which vitally conditions the circumstances of the production and reception of the work of art.

Elsewhere in the *Petites Poèmes en prose* gold is sometimes associated with the riches of the imagination, rather than with a finished work of art. In 'Les Vocations' the opening description of the evening sky ('un ciel déjà verdâtre où des *nuages d'or* flottaient *comme des continents en voyage*' (my italics)) prepares the reader for the description of the first child, whose preoccupations echo those of the protagonists in 'L'Etranger', 'Le *Confiteor* de l'artiste', 'La Soupe et les nuages', 'Le Port' and 'Déjà!' But the gold which in 'L'Etranger' was contrasted with the clouds is here identified with them. The value symbol has, as it were, migrated from the material to the immaterial world and to the spiritual values which Baudelaire associates with God. In implied comparison with the values of commercial Paris, where vocation is often synonymous with the struggle for material success, this poem celebrates man's spiritual and aesthetic values, the riches of the imagination. The child cloud-gazer of 'Les Vocations' may be compared with the poet of 'Le *Confiteor* de l'artiste', his eyes fixed on the horizon between sea and sky:

Et l'enfant resta longtemps tourné du meme côté, fixant sur la ligne qui sépare la terre du ciel des yeux où brillait une inexprimable expression d'extase et de regret. (*Oc* I, 333)

The dividing-line between sky and sea, or sky and earth, can be interpreted as a paradigm of man's own divided nature. The poet of 'Le *Confiteor* de l'artiste' sees the 'petite voile frissonante à l'horizon' as a metaphor for his own 'irrémédiable existence'. Half angel, half beast, the humanity of *Le Spleen de Paris* is on the one hand hungry for the ambrosia of poetry and on the other hand subject to egoistic and carnal appetites, aspiring to the spiritual 'gold' of the imagination and yet forced to make money in order to survive, thirsting for a value which cannot be quantified yet continually returning to a petty commercialism, the counting of change ('La Fausse Monnaie') or of takings ('Les Vocations').

Another aspect of commercialism is the phenomenon of prostitution. Critics have traditionally linked Baudelaire's references to prostitution with his interest in city life: for example, Albert Thibaudet commented that prostitution was of interest to Baudelaire because it was a special characteristic of the city, unlike pure love which is traditionally associated with pastoral settings. However, in the prose poems prostitution is a symbol which extends beyond the confines of the metropolis, suggesting that the city is presented not as the antithesis of an ideal rural setting but rather as expressing in a concentrated form the inherent evils of a dangerously colonising and invasive code of values.

This is particularly evident in 'La Belle Dorothée', when it is revealed that the exotic and beautiful subject of the portrait is in fact a whore. The manner in which this revelation is made is so gradual that the fact is in danger of being ignored until the very end of the poem, when, like the startled dog in 'Le Chien et le flacon', the reader is pained at discovering something quite different from what was anticipated. At first, lulled by the delicately balanced prose, we read without suspicion the erotic description of Dorothée's posture and clothing. Even the reference to the illusion of blood-red rouge cast by the reflection of her sunshade probably does not at first arouse suspicion. It is not until the account of Dorothée's relationship with European naval officers that we begin to realise the commercial nature of the 'puissant motif' which forces her to go out in the heat of the afternoon sun ('obligée d'entasser piastre sur piastre pour racheter sa petite soeur'). Only then is it realised that this is not the world of the pure savage, but a parody (even if a nostalgic one) of that early Romantic chimera. It is a parody which exploits the time involved in the reading process in order to humiliate the gullible reader, who has perhaps at first enjoyed rediscovering the seductive cliché and escaping from the spleen of the overtly Parisian poems.

The selling of personal intimacy for money was, of course, a process also experienced by artists. And, as Walter Benjamin shows, the corruption possible in such a situation had been especially evident since the late 1830s when the growth of the 'feuilleton' had provided a vast new audience for belles-lettres. In Baudelaire's lifetime the high fees paid for these new 'feuilletons' had opened up new career possibilities for writers.[11] The analogy between poet and prostitute, naively expressed in Baudelaire's early verse poem 'Je n'ai pas pour maîtresse une lionne illustre', was to be transformed with the *Petits Poèmes en prose* into a more complex and indirect series of associations.

The play of analogy and inversion in 'Mademoiselle Bistouri', associating and contrasting the two night workers, poet and prostitute, centres most obviously on their shared fate as obsessional 'monsters'. But also, the similarity between them as victims of the commercial exchange ethos becomes particularly obvious when 'Mademoiselle Bistouri' is read in relation to the concluding paragraph of 'L'Horloge'. The addition of this paragraph in 1862 forms an important modification of the original 1857 text, serving ironically to expose the conventions behind the traditional madrigal and to situate the poem within a wider network of allusions to the theme of prostitution:

N'est-ce pas, madame, que voici un madrigal vraiment méritoire, et aussi emphatique que vous-même? En vérité, j'ai eu tant de plaisir à broder cette prétentieuse galanterie, que je vous demanderai rien en échange. (*Oc* I, 300)

This appended paragraph is an example of the way in which Baudelaire's later modifications often seem to have favoured inter-reflections within the widening collection, actively facilitating and signposting a further level of reading available to the reader. The non-exchange of 'L'Horloge', where the poet does not ask for the 'favour' which would 'repay' his gallant literary gesture, can be seen ironically to invert the non-exchange of

'Mademoiselle Bistouri', where the prostitute tells of how she refuses to take money from her favourite young intern:

Je lui ai dit: 'Viens me voir, viens me voir souvent. Et avec moi, ne te gêne pas; je n'ai pas besoin d'argent.' Mais tu comprends que je lui ai fait entendre ça par une foule de façons; je ne le lui ai pas dit tout crûment. (*Oc* I, 355)

The prostitute's pride in the delicate formation of her message, which she recounts in a language full of inelegant colloquialisms, adds ironic piquancy to the parallel with the gallant poet. In both instances the negative, the non-exchange, serves to draw attention to the habitual process of exchange, the convention which otherwise might pass almost unnoticed. Although the poet-figure in 'L'Horloge' ostensibly addresses his mistress, the reader too is implicated by the ambiguous use of the second person. In the normal course of events the public pays the poet like a prostitute for his services. The refusal of this payment becomes an exaggerated gesture of defiance and mock-aggressiveness towards the reader as well as towards the imaginary mistress.

In 'La Chambre double' the emphasis on everyday wrangling and commercial pressures serves as a reminder that the poet does not divorce himself from the environment in which he lives, does not present the artist as being outside the problem. The poet must transform himself into an effective 'marchand de nuages' if he is to survive in modern society; like the musicians of 'Les Vocations', at the end of the day he must count his takings; if he fails to entertain he must join the old showman, whose financial plight is emphasised in 'Le Vieux Saltimbanque' by the context in which he is depicted, the description of a bank holiday crowd driven by modern commercial frenzy ('les uns dépensaient, les autres gagnaient, les uns et les autres également joyeux').

THE '*BREVET D'HONNEUR*'[12]

Je ne vois que la condamnation à mort qui distingue un homme, pensa Mathilde: c'est la seule chose qui ne s'achète pas.

Stendhal, *Le Rouge et le noir*

The last poem in the collection, 'Les Bons Chiens', brings the motif of exchange full circle and is a poem which depends more on its context within the collection as a whole than perhaps any other of the pieces. Indeed, one could argue that it does not really succeed if it is taken as an isolated piece, a detached 'tronçon', as under these conditions its readability is excessively restricted. The artists mentioned in the poem's conclusion may not worship gold, but all are presented as being engaged in the process of exchanging the spiritual for the material:

Les bergers de Virgile et de Théocrite attendaient, pour prix de leurs chants alternés, un bon fromage, une flûte du meilleur faiseur ou une chèvre aux mamelles gonflées. Le poète qui a chanté les pauvres chiens a reçu pour récompense un beau gilet, d'une couleur, à la fois riche et fanée... (*Oc* I, 362)

Virgil's shepherds may have bartered their poems for a fine cheese, or a swollen-uddered goat, but not all the artists mentioned are so fortunate in the rewards bestowed on them. As for the poet–narrator, his traditional poet's mantle may have shrunk to the proportions of a mere waistcoat, but its colour at least is noble, though faded, and it symbolically places him in a tradition stretching from Virgil and Theocritus down to Aretino and beyond. However, the comparison between this gift received by the poet and those offered to Aretino introduces a graver note, although still in the same ironic vein:

Tel un magnifique italien, du bon temps, offrait au divin Arétin soit une dague enrichie de pierreries, soit un manteau de cour, en échange d'un précieux sonnet ou d'un curieux poème satirique. (*Oc* I, 363)

If one turns to Dujardin's short biography of Aretino which is included in the 1845 collection of selected works by Aretino (one of the very few translations available to Baudelaire and the one which he was most likely to have consulted), one discovers various levels of possible innuendo concentrated in the brief allusion to this sixteenth-century predecessor. The Dujardin biography refers to the riches and honours which the Italian poet was said to have extorted from men of power, and it also throws light on the role which daggers played in his career. It tells of how a satirical poem slandering a domestic in the employ of Aretino's enemy Jean-Mathieu Gilberti was used as a pretext for an assassination attempt on Aretino by one of Gilberti's men, who was the woman's lover. The man, Achille de la Volta, attacked Aretino with a dagger. Aretino protested to the pope but his complaints were ignored as the pope had already been forewarned by Gilberti. Part of the official reply to Aretino's complaints (composed by the poet Berni and cited by Dujardin) reads as follows:

> Ta langue, qui le fiel distille,
> Te fera trouver tôt or tard
> Un vengeur muni d'un poignard,
> Plus tranchant que celui d'Achille.
> Pauvre, mais insolent esprit
> Que la médisance nourrit
> Haï des hommes et de Dieu,
> Détesté par le diable même,
> Ta bouche, mère du blasphème,
> Te fait chasser de chaque lieu,
> Nous te verrons dans peu sur le haut d'une échelle,
> De valets de taverne et de crocs entouré,
> Danser au bout d'une ficelle,
> Au doux branle de leur *salve*,
> Or va, poursuis la triste chance;
> Mais sois assuré qu'un cordeau,
> Ou le bâton, ou le couteau
> Feront taire ta médisance.[13]

In the passage from 'Les Bons Chiens' which I have quoted, Aretino is described as having to choose between 'une dague enrichie de pierreries' or 'un manteau de cour'. The latter suggests the idea of royal protection, whilst the former may be read, in the light of biographical circumstance, as suggesting the glittering suicide instrument of Aretino's own satiric verse. Dujardin tells of how, if the satire worked in someone's favour, that man offered Aretino his protection, while if it operated against him (as in Strozzi's case for example), the man in question might take a summary revenge. The implied reference to the Aretino dagger incident draws attention, then, to the condition of the artist as someone marked out by fate, a martyr by vocation, engaged 'in a long and deliberate suicide' (Butor).

It reverberates within a network of similar references in other poems echoing indirectly the analogy between the poet-figure and Christ, suggested in 'L'Etranger' and in 'Les Tentations'. It invites comparison too with the ironic reference to the artist's halo in 'Perte d'auréole' and 'Une Mort héroique', and with the description of the symbolic poses of martyrdom enacted by the child model in 'La Corde'.

In 'Les Bons Chiens' the 'magnifique tyran du bon temps' who would repay Aretino for his poetry by proffering him a murder instrument ('une dague') would grant him the same paradoxical *favour* as the one which the prince in 'Une Mort héroique' accords to Fancioulle:

Depuis lors, plusieurs mimes... sont venus jouer devant la cour de — , mais aucun d'eux n'a pu rappeler les merveilleux talents de Fancioulle, ni s'élever jusqu'à la même *faveur*. (*Oc* I, 323)

Once again, modern society's habitual value systems are stood on their head. The artistic talents which charm an audience and which are here celebrated as 'merveilleux' are the same as are deemed worthless by the 'brave petit commerçant' of 'Le Don des fées'. In 'Une Mort héroique' the poet reveals how a genius like Fancioulle is 'favoured' with a martyrdom which takes the form of violent penetration, as though by a blade ('un coup de sifflet aigu... Le sifflet, rapide comme un glaive...'). If this were not enough, the mention of a 'tyran italien' provides further encouragement to the reader to make comparisons between the Aretino reference in 'Les Bons Chiens' and the earlier poem 'Une Mort héroique'. In this way, a detail which perplexes and resists integration on the level of an individual poem offers further levels of meaning once it is read in relation to the whole collection.

It is by a similar process that the description of the artist's martyrdom in 'Une Mort héroique' throws light on another poem, 'La Corde', which further contributes to the motif of exchange. The name Fancioulle indicates a child-like personality (Ross Chambers has noted its affinity with the Italian 'fanciullo'), and the child suicide of 'La Corde' is also like Fancioulle in that he is cast in the role of a martyr. The description of the various guises in which the child is painted anticipates the tragedy of the poem's conclusion:

Il a posé plus d'une fois pour moi, et je l'ai transformé tantôt en petit bohémien, tantôt en ange, tantôt en Amour mythologique. Je lui ai fait porter la Couronne d'Epines et les Clous de la Passion, et la Torche d'Eros. (*Oc* I, 329)

The reference to the 'violon du vagabond' encourages the reader to compare the child to another small 'incompris', the fourth boy in 'Les Vocations'; whilst the allusion to the 'Amour mythologique' recalls 'Les Tentations' with its description of another, inferior form of self-sacrifice associated with Eros. But it is the reference to the 'Clous de la Passion' which is echoed later in 'La Corde', when much emphasis is placed on the nail which attaches the suicide rope to the top of the painter's cupboard. The crown of thorns image also evokes the description in 'Une Mort héroïque' of Fancioulle, with his halo symbolising the association between art and martyrdom (a halo which will be recalled again, ironically, in 'Perte d'auréole').

Once he has been denied access to his customary intoxicants ('le sucre et les liqueurs'), the only other escape route open to the child is death. This suicide, which is prefigured by the various transformations he has undergone (into gypsy, angel and cupid), is itself a form of metempsychosis or spiritual exchange, here associated with the magical and forbidden escape of the drug addict, but at the same time offering implicit parallels with the artistic experience.[14] It contrasts with the crushing materialism of a society where a mother will not neglect the commercial potential of selling off her child's suicide rope to superstitious bidders.

We can see, then, that the motif of exchange opens up a dynamic confrontation between the commercial values of a mercantile metropolis and the spiritual values associated with art. In general, the provocativeness of Baudelaire's attack on bourgeois ideology is often underestimated. As Claude Pichois and Jean Ziegler have shown in their sympathetic new biography, Baudelaire's enthusiasm of 1848 for the radical economist and polemicist Pierre-Joseph Proudhon did not disappear with the political disenchantment of the post-revolutionary years.[15] Instead, in his 1851 article *Les Drames et les romans honnêtes* he asserted, not without some personal courage: 'Proudhon est un écrivain que l'Europe nous enviera toujours.' A marginal note to 'Assommons les pauvres!' ('Qu'en dis-tu, citoyen Proudhon?') reveals that Proudhon still represented a cornerstone of his mental life at the time of the composition of the prose poems, although the implication appears to be that his own socio-economic *moralité* is here an exercise in the ironic mode from which Proudhon, with his excessively direct formulations, might have profited. Certainly his letter to Narcisse Ancelle of February 1865 reveals that his underlying sympathy for Proudhon's economic theories remained unchanged:

> La lettre de Proudhon ne vous a pas assez frappé et vous le traitez de fou beaucoup trop légèrement. Je vous ai envoyé cette lettre pour vous prouvez que Proudhon, quoi qu'on ait dit, *n'avait jamais varié*. A la fin de sa vie, comme à ses débuts, les questions de production et de finance étaient celles qui l'obsédaient particulièrement. S'il etait question d'art, oui, vous auriez raison de dire de Proudhon: Il est fou. – Mais en matière d'économie, il me paraît singulièrement respectable.
>
> Je ne vois qu'une seule manière de mettre à néant les utopiés, les idées, les paradoxes et les prophéties de Proudhon sur la rente et sur la propriété, c'est de prouver péremptoirement (l'a-t-on fait? je ne suis pas érudit en ces choses) *que le peuple s'enrichissent en s'endettant*. Vous êtes plus financier que moi; vous devez savoir si cette thèse a été soutenue.[16]

Too much a philosopher and a poet to be at ease with politics, and ever aware of the dangers of pontificating, Baudelaire was uncomfortable at perceiving in himself 'le ridicule d'un prophète'.[17] However, through their complex interplay of strident and contrasting voices, the *Petits Poèmes en Prose* nevertheless offer a powerful *mise en question* of a society continuously threatened by its unthinking adherence to a reductive and subtly brutalising code of values. It is true, undoubtedly, that this vision of Parisian society was rooted in the personal trials and vicissitudes of a man who experienced at first hand the humiliation of financial dependence on the whims of his ageing bourgeois mother and the legal financial control of a judiciary counsel imposed on him by his family. A notion of the poet's financial imprudence or incapacity may have helped to sustain his family in the conviction that their actions were justified, but the reassuring, anaesthetising cliché of the poet as inadequate misfit, somehow deserving of social and financial failure, is difficult to accept in the twentieth century as an alibi for the injustice of the system that dictated Baudelaire's fate. It can only be with a profound sense of retrospective irony that we now assess a situation in which one of the great individuals of literary history, a man whose work has given pleasure to millions and who helped to shape the course of European culture in his own generation and generations to come, should have experienced such humiliation.

In a particularly telling presentation of Baudelaire's financial situation in the years from 1844 to 1864, Claude Pichois and Jean Ziegler note that the twenty prose poems that were bought by Arsène Houssaye for *La Presse* went for fifteen centimes a line. Professor Pichois estimates that in total the publication of the poems might have earned the poet a merè 800 francs in all.[18] This, then, was the mathematics of the inverse ratio of cultural value and financial reward, this was the bizarre yet logically appropriate result of the dominant commercial exchange code which *Le Spleen de Paris* both thematised and concretely illustrated by its own history as a product in the market-place of literary transaction.

CHAPTER 3

Poetry and desire

– Malheureux peut-être l'homme, mais heureux l'artiste que le désir déchire!
(*Oc* I, 340)

Plus l'homme cultive les arts, moins il bande. Il se fait un divorce de plus en plus sensible entre l'esprit et la brute... Foutre, c'est aspirer à entrer dans un autre, et l'artiste ne sort jamais de lui-même.
(*Oc* I, 702)

N'est-ce pas, madame que voici un madrigal vraiment méritoire... En vérité, j'ai eu tant de plaisir à border cette prétentieuse galanterie, que je ne vous demanderai rien en échange.
(*Oc* I, 300)

SWORDS, DAGGERS, LANCETS AND BULLETS

One of the commonplaces of our western literary heritage has been the perception of literature and sexuality as offering rival forms of communication. Literature has often presented itself as a substitute for sexual fulfilment or as something offered in exchange for sexual favours, and references in literature to sexuality have sometimes been used to signal the processes of substitution inherent in artistic creation. This may, for example, be central to the plot, as in the *Thousand and One Nights*, where the telling of stories by Shahrazad serves both as a *substitute* for the fulfilment of the Sultan's perverse and excessive sadistic lust and as a cure for it. Narrative itself becomes the *medication* which will enable the Sultan to return to a socially acceptable erotic state, marrying Shahrazad, the story-teller, who thereby saves his other subjects, the population of the city, from his transgressive excesses. Or again, Italo Calvino's *If on a Winter's Night a Traveller* features an author-figure obsessed with sexual fantasies about his ideal female reader and offers a happy ending in the comic mode where *two* readers, one male and one female, enjoy marital harmony engrossed in parallel readings of his book in a vast double bed. In other instances, the theme of substitution may emerge more indirectly, as in, say, *La Chartreuse de Parme*, where in the Farnesi prison Clélia communicates passionately with Fabrice in an outburst of feigned operatic recitative on the piano, with Fabrice responding by tracing charcoal letters on the palms of his hands. At this point in the story Fabrice's whole endeavour is to obtain the further, more significant favour of pen and paper communication with the object of his desire. As Gérard Genette has observed when discussing this passage in the context of his reading of Stendhalien love as a system and an exchange of signs, the link between the exchange of writing and the erotic commerce (a link based on substitution) is plainly evident.

In recent years, critics influenced by the work of Jacques Lacan and his interpretation of Freud's concept of Eros have drawn particular attention to self-reflexive narratives such as Balzac's *Peau de chagrin*, which lay bare the nature of narration itself as 'a form of human desire...a force including sexual desire but larger and more polymorphous...desire in its plastic and totalizing function'.[1] Narration is seen as a manifestation of a force as basic as Freud's Eros, which 'seeks to combine organic substances into ever greater unities'.[2] Male narratives in particular are seen as characterised by a dynamic of eroticism, whether they take the form of love stories, picaresque adventures, or, less obviously, Bildungsroman novels of ambition where social success is co-relative with sexual success and where the movement of ambition is itself, in any case, seen as inherently 'totalising' and 'self-aggrandising'.[3]

Even if we leave aside the question of plot, it is clearly the case that, traditionally, the narrator or poet-figure has often been cast in the role of a seducer. There is the obvious generic example of love poetry. But also, in a more comic vein, self-conscious allusions in poetry and the novel to the addressee have often made humorously salacious play of the quasi-sexual intimacy of the tryst between reader and author-figure. Sterne's *Tristram Shandy* offers some particularly conspicuous examples of this variety of facetious innuendo. At one point Tristram rounds on 'Madam Reader' for her 'quest for adventures' and lack of interest in the digressions en route.[4] On another level, the whole farcical, warm-hearted saga of Uncle Toby's obsession with fortification develops into a marvellously witty meta-fictional *jeu de force* in which the displacement of Toby's sexual and other passions comes to symbolise the process of displacement and substitution inherent in the creative process itself, the rule of metaphor and indirection.[5]

In *Le Spleen de Paris* Baudelaire is doing something very similar, rewriting familiar metaphors, in particular echoing Sterne, Diderot and Balzac in his usage of the arabesque as a figure of capricious mobility and freedom associated with the imagination and with sexual desire. In *Tristram Shandy* the arabesque traced by Corporal Trim's cane as he brandishes it in the air both represents the freedom of the bachelor life and, like other arabesques in Sterne's novel, gestures towards the free untrammelled digressive movement of Tristram's narrative, that is, as Peter Brooks has written, 'the fantastic designs drawn by narrative desire'.[6] In other words it offers a variant of the parallelism of capricious sexual pursuit and spontaneous imaginative vagary which figures so prominently in the following lines from the opening of Diderot's *Neveu de Rameau*:

J'abandonne mon esprit à tout son libertinage. Je le laisse maître de suivre la première idée sage ou folle qui se présente, comme on voit dans l'allée de Foy nos jeunes dissolus marcher sur les pas d'une cortisane... quitter celle-ci pour une autre, les attaquant toutes et ne s'attachant à aucune. Mes pensées, ce sont mes catins.[7]

The peregrinations of Baudelaire's gallant dogs ('Les Bons Chiens') as they snake through labyrinthine city ways, coming and going, responding to the needs and passions of the moment ('*la première venue*'), pursue and prolong the same analogy.

Another way of putting this is to say that in the *Petits Poèmes en prose*, as in *Tristram Shandy*, *Le Neveu de Rameau* and *La Peau de chagrin*, the references to sexuality contribute to a self-reflexive exploration of the creative process itself, and the relationship of the author to his material and to the reader. As we shall see, this is also illustrated by the fact that the 'tutelage' traditionally implicit in all author/reader relationships is drawn attention to in *Le Spleen de Paris* and problematised by a series of bantering references which transpose into the sexual arena the proselytising of the disciple by the moral authority. In this respect, as in others, *Le Spleen de Paris* offers a striking display of poetry provocatively abandoning earlier codes of seemliness and courtly preciosity and delighting in the most indelicate of metaphors. Recurrent images of violent penetration by daggers, blades, surgical instruments or 'piercing eyes' underscore, often with humorous and self-parodying insistence, the comparison between poetry and eroticism as forms of transgression.

We saw earlier that in 'Les Bons Chiens' the Italian tyrant's gift of a dagger invites comparison with the metaphorical 'stabbing' of Fancioulle in 'Une Mort héroïque'. These passages reverberate in the context of a number of poems in the collection all of which make reference to forms of violent penetration. The movements of penetration work in at least four ways: nature enters the artist; the artist attempts to enter nature (although the success of this enterprise is open to doubt); the work of art (and by association the artist) is entered by the reader or audience, and vice versa.

'Que les fins de journées d'automne sont pénétrantes! Ah! pénétrantes jusqu'à la douleur', exclaims the poet in 'Le Confiteor de l'artiste'. And, as if this repetition of the adjective were not enough to draw attention to the unspoken metaphor, it is immediately followed by comparison between the intensity of two opposing extremes of concentration and expansion:

Car il est de certaines sensations délicieuses dont le vague n'exclut pas l'intensité; et il n'est pas de point plus acérée que celle de l'Infini. (*Oc* I, 278)

The image of the whetted blade of the Infinite prepares the

reader for the poem's conclusion: the implied sword-thrust of the duel, the victory of nature as she penetrates the artist.

'Le *Confiteor* de l'artiste' brings to mind a passage from the *Dédicace* of *Les Paradis artificiels* which describes how the natural world (exemplified by women) penetrates the spiritual world of the poetic imagination:

> *comme le monde naturel pénètre dans le spirituel*, lui sert de pâture, et concourt ainsi à opérer cet amalgame indéfinissable que nous nommons notre individualité, la femme est l'être qui projette la plus grand ombre et la plus grande lumière dans nos rêves. *La femme est fatalement suggestive*; elle vit d'une autre vie que la sienne propre; *elle vit spirituellement dans les imaginations qu'elle hante et qu'elle féconde*. (my italics; *Oc* I, 399)

The same inverted metaphor of the normal sexual order, whereby the female (Nature) makes it possible for the male poet to conceive, is also pursued in 'Mademoiselle Bistouri' and 'Le Désir de peindre'. In both these poems the female models represent the role of Nature in relation to the artist (Nature here signifying the whole of reality, that is, human nature and the modern urban context just as much as the vegetable world). Both poems, in their different ways, echo the paradigm relationship of 'Le *Confiteor* de l'artiste'. The analogy with a fatal love affair, implicit in the description of Nature as an 'enchanteresse sans pitié, rivale toujours victorieuse' ('Le *Confiteor* de l'artiste'), is developed in more detail in 'Le Désir de peindre', and at the conclusion of the poem the portraitist expresses a death-wish which recalls the last lines of 'Le *Confiteor* de l'artiste', although here the artist collaborates willingly in his martyrdom:

> Il y a des femmes qui inspirent l'envie de vaincre et de jouir d'elles; mais celle-ci donne le désir de mourir lentement sous son regard. (*Oc* I, 340)

Here as in a number of other prose poems, eyes replace the metal blade as agents of penetration. As the opening aphorism implies with its balanced antithesis, the penetration of the artist by his subject is an exact inversion of the sexual act:

Malheureux peut-être l'homme, mais heureux l'artiste que le désir déchire! (*Oc* I, 340)

Again, in 'Les Tentations' in a passage which parodies Balzac, an allusion is made to the penetrating magic of mature women:

ce charme...de très belles femmes sur le retour, qui cependant ne vieillissent plus, et dont la beauté garde *le magie pénétrante* des ruines. (my italics; *Oc* I, 309)

It is this 'magie pénétrante' that seems to be recalled by the poet of 'Les Bons Chiens' when in the poem's conclusion he observes that every time he dons his painter's waistcoat he is forced to recall 'la beauté des femmes très mûres'. The beauty of these women is analogous to the beauty of Nature, the 'enchanteresse' of 'Le *Confiteor* de l'artiste'. This enchantress too is not young: Nature is described as being at her most 'penetrating' on 'les fins de journées d'automne'. This means that the allusion in 'Les Bons Chiens' to the beauty of mature women, by recalling other images of penetration associated with the poetic process, effectively encourages one to situate the Aretino dagger reference which follows shortly afterwards in the context of a whole network of references in other poems. This is important because in this way the allusion acquires a density of significance which it does not carry if the poem is read in isolation.

Some further examples will, perhaps, help to make the point more vividly. A particularly blatant and humorous use of penetration symbolism occurs in 'Les Tentations, ou Eros, Plutus et la gloire', a poem which, amongst other things, ironically weighs in the balance the rival attractions of eroticism and poetry. Providing an interesting exemplification of Lacanian theory, the poem seems to confirm the suggestion that poetry, eroticism and ambition coexist on a profound level in the individual consciousness as different and rival manifestations of a deep, totalising impulse towards appropriation and self-aggrandisement. In 'Les Tentations', Eros, the first devil to tempt the sleeping poet, has various gleaming knives and surgical instruments dangling from his belt, and it is this 'mystérieuse coutellerie', along with other sinister symbolic accoutrements, which leads the poet-figure to reject him.

It is clear that in these poems, as in other writings discussed by Leo Bersani (*Baudelaire and Freud*), 'psychic penetrability is fantasised as sexual penetrability', and it is true that Baudelaire seems here to be acknowledging an aspect of artistic receptiveness which 'may change him into a woman'.[8] This is one aspect of the use of sexual metaphors in the prose poems. But we shall see that on other occasions they operate quite differently and there is less emphasis on the artist being penetrated by his subject and more on his role as a would-be agent of penetration, with the addressee and, ambiguously, the implied reader being chastised on one occasion for her 'imperméabilité féminine' ('Les Yeux des pauvres').[9]

PENETRATING EYES: PARADIGMS AND PARODIES OF 'READING'

One of the most striking uses of this imagery occurs in 'Mademoiselle Bistouri', a poem which explores at length the nature of the poet's relationship to his subject or model. Offering a certain parodic resemblance to many a Balzacian 'femme d'un certain âge', the subject of the portrait here is not young, although she considers herself to be still attractive ('Après tout, je suis assez belle femme, quoique pas trop jeune').[10] From the moment when the prostitute first accosts the poet–narrator she insists that he is a doctor, or, more precisely, the former assistant of a surgeon, a man whose *incisive* qualities she greatly admires:

Je me souviens que c'était vous qui l'assistiez dans les opérations graves. En voilà un homme qui aime couper, tailler et rogner! C'était vous qui lui tendiez les instruments, les fils et les éponges. (*Oc* I, 353–4)

Bistouri's insistence on the poet's medical status is, for him, an 'inintelligible refrain', and when she asks him if he is a surgeon he exclaims: 'Non! non! à moins que ce ne soit pour te couper la tête!' But the poet's indignation only serves to emphasise the comparison between the activity of the portraitist or moralist and that of the surgeon.

From the beginning the narrator-figure has confessed his desire to 'penetrate' the mystery of Mademoiselle Bistouri's character:

> J'aime passionnément le mystère, parce que j'ai toujours l'espoir de la débrouiller. Je me laissai donc entraîner par cette compagne, ou plutôt par cette énigme inespérée. (*Oc* I, 353)

As the poem progresses, the parallel between the poet and the prostitute becomes increasingly clear. The subject of the poetic 'portrait' herself requests a portrait of the poet, to add to her collection of pictures of doctors and surgeons. The narrator figure brushes aside her request, which he scarcely seems to notice, so intent is he on completing *his* analysis of *her*, the poetic portrait which will contribute to his own 'collection':

> 'Quand nous nous reverrons, tu me donneras ton portrait, n'est-ce pas, chéri?'
> – 'Mais' lui dis-je, suivant à mon tour, moi aussi, mon idée fixe, – 'pourquoi me crois-tu médicin?' (*Oc* I, 354)

The mutual concern with portraiture draws attention to the poet's own 'idée fixe': his activity too may be perceived as a sign of monstrousness. Trying to 'fix' and penetrate the Other with a portrait is another form of lunacy.

The prostitute may be a monster (as the poet suggests by the remark 'la vie fourmille de monstres innocents'), but so too are some of the surgeons she admires, and they are perhaps less innocent:

> Tiens! voilà Z., celui qui disait à son cours, en parlant de X.: 'Ce monstre qui porte sur son visage la noirceur de son âme!' Tout cela parce que l'autre n'était pas de son avis dans le même affaire!... Tiens, voila K., celui qui dénonçait au gouvernement les insurgés qu'il soignait à son hôpital. C'était le temps des émeutes. Comment est-ce possible qu'un si bel homme ait si peu de cœur? (*Oc* I, 354)

Appearances are deceptive: the 'bel homme' may be a heartless monster who denounces wounded revolutionaries to the government. Bistouri's simple observation demonstrates the fallacy of trusting to external appearance, and belies the facile judgements of those, like the surgeon she recalls, who talk of monsters whose faces convey the evil of their souls. Her comments have the effect of casting doubt on a common misconception which has important consequences for the portraitist: that is, the belief that a person's inner character, or 'soul', is clearly visible, and has therefore only to be 'copied' in a straightforward manner by the painter. This was the accepted bourgeois belief held up to ridicule in the ironic conclusion to Laclos's *Liaisons dangereuses* and vehemently attacked by Baudelaire in his *1859 Salon*.[11] It is a belief which is implicit, of course, in much of Balzac's narrative method. In 'Mademoiselle Bistouri' the prostitute's comments prepare the way for the poem's conclusion, where the roles of patient and surgeon, model and portraitist are inverted, and the ironic significance of the prostitute's name becomes clear. The poet's taste for the macabre will perhaps prove to be the source of his own salvation, and it is possible that he will heal himself in the process of trying to penetrate the character of Mademoiselle Bistouri ('comme la guérison au bout d'une lame'). It is she who may prove to be the instrument of his cure: the lancet which will radically cure his soul. The surgical blade initially intended for the penetration of 'Nature', the artist's model, is turned against the artist/surgeon himself, and the poet's initial movement to dissect the external world ('débrouiller le mystère') becomes a means of self-penetration. The portrait will be an amalgam of both artist and subject.

The poem can be seen, then, to explore the same paradox as that evoked at the conclusion of 'Les Fenêtres':

Peut-être me direz-vous: 'Es-tu sûr que cette légende soit la vraie?' Qu'importe ce que peut être la réalité placée hors de moi, si elle m'a aidé à vivre, à sentir que je suis et ce que je suis? (*Oc* I, 339)

The poet who goes to bed 'fier d'avoir vécu et souffert dans d'autres que lui-même' may not perhaps have penetrated external reality at all. This prolongs the suggestion already hinted at in 'Le *Confiteor* de l'artiste' where a doubt is expressed as to whether the penetrating blade which pierces the poet is wielded by Nature or by the poet himself ('Toutefois, ces pensées, qu'elles sortent de moi ou s'élancent des choses, deviennent bientôt trop intenses').

The parodic analogy between narrator, observer and surgeon, which finds its fullest expression in 'Mademoiselle Bistouri', is also implicit in 'Une Mort héroique', where the narrator vaunts his acumen in probing and dissecting the curious and sick character of the Prince:

De la part d'un homme aussi naturellement et volontairement excentrique, tout était possible, même la vertu... Mais pour *ceux, qui, comme moi, avaient pu pénétrer plus avant dans les profondeurs de cette âme curieuse et malade*, il était infiniment plus probable que le Prince voulait juger de la valeur des talents scéniques d'un homme condamné à mort. (my italics; *Oc* I, 320)

Despite his claim that the Prince's character may be penetrated by 'un œil clairvoyant' (*Oc* I, 322) and his earlier boasting as to his own powers of penetration, the narrator is reduced to concluding his analysis with a series of 'suppositions non exactement justifiées, mais non absolument injustifiables'. The intimations of solipsism in 'Mademoiselle Bistouri', 'Les Fenêtres', 'Le *Confiteor* de l'artiste' and 'Les Yeux des pauvres' are humorously confirmed here.

BALZAC: AN UNSPOKEN COMPARISON

Far from probing the depths of another person's soul with macho Balzacian acuity, in the *Petits Poèmes en prose* Baudelaire's references to eyes invariably suggest that communication with the Other is problematic, if not impossible. Several poems dramatise the phenomenon of eye-to-eye scrutiny ('L'Horloge', 'Les Yeux des pauvres', 'Le Fou et la Vénus' and 'Portraits de maîtresses') as well as the phenomenon of the self-scrutinising eye focussed on a mirror ('Le Miroir'), and the importance of the eye is in any case foregrounded because of the prominence of a number of 'flâneur' protagonists. The stooge narrators of 'Les Veuves' and 'Une Mort héroique' may boast of their acute vision, their piercing observation, but they have as their counterparts the disabused and cynical protagonists of such poems as 'Les Yeux des pauvres' and 'Les Fenêtres', who find themselves obliged to recognise the limitations of their own powers to perceive exterior reality or to communicate and to interpret feelings.

The relationships between lovers only serve to confirm this awareness. A woman's eyes may inspire the poet of 'Le Désir de peindre' with the thought of complete self-abandonment, 'le désir de mourir lentement sous son regard', but, like the renunciation of identity described in 'L'Horloge', such an experience is one of Lethean forgetfulness, 'une heure immobile', but not a process of communication, or not, at least, between the artist and his model. When, in 'L'Horloge', the poet gazes into the eyes of his 'feline' mistress the experience is analogous with the drug-induced evasion of 'La Chambre double', where time disappears and where impressions are unanalysed. In 'La Chambre double' the use of an unexpected colloquialism attracts the reader's attention to the mirror-like quality of the eyes which the poet associates with the opium dream. The protagonist is fascinated by his Idol's 'subtiles et terribles *mirettes*' and drawn towards them.[12] The word 'mirettes', conspicuous because of its colloquial register, echoes and prolongs the intimations of *dédoublement* already announced in the poem's title. The eyes are described as 'devouring' and the addict is cast in the passive role of the one devoured (in contrast with the poet figure of 'Un Hémisphère dans une chevelure'):

Voilà bien ces yeux dont la flamme traverse le crépuscule, ces subtiles et terribles *mirettes* que je reconnais à leur effrayante malice! Elles attirent, elles subjuguent, elles dévorent le regard de l'imprudent qui les contemple. Je les ai souvent étudiées, ces étoiles noires qui commandent la curiosité et l'admiration. (*Oc* I, 280)

Gazing into his Idol's eyes the observer enjoys for a short while the beatitude of an existence from which 'le temps a disparu'.

As well as evoking a state of amnesia, 'L'Horloge', like 'Portraits de maîtresses' and 'Un Hémisphère dans une chevelure', places emphasis on the lack of communication between the lovers. Barbara Johnson's remark about narcissism in 'Un Hémisphère dans une chevelure' could apply here too: the poem pointedly reveals the essentially narcissistic character of the poet's pleasure.[13] Indeed in 'L'Horloge' the exclusion of the woman from the experience she has occasioned is even more striking, since this time the poet is not describing himself gazing at some part of her body that she herself cannot see and which does not involve her personality (such as her hair), but is describing the form of eye-to-eye contemplation conventionally believed to involve dialogue or spiritual exchange.

Clearly, the powers of perception of the narrator-figures in 'Les Veuves', 'Les Fenêtres' and 'Le Joujou du pauvre' are cast in doubt although they are not involved in any erotic attachment. Also, the impotence of figures such as 'le vieux saltimbanque' and the beggar of 'Assommons les pauvres!' is conveyed by the description of eyes in which all the vital energy of the individual seems concentrated, weapons which are rendered totally ineffective by the indifference of the crowd. Because of this the reader is encouraged to situate the descriptions of 'seeing' in poems such as 'L'Horloge' and 'Le Désir de peindre' within a wider context. In other words, more than just relating to the specific relationship of lovers these poems draw attention to the wider problem of communication and to the functioning of the text itself. The eye is the organ relating the reader to the poetry. The description of the erotic relationship is not presented in isolation. But as an example of a situation where expectations of communication are conventionally strongest, it has the effect of dramatising the problem of human solitude and the difficulty of achieving true communication. The problem of communication between the sexes is subsumed within a more far-reaching ontological discourse.

Take 'Les Yeux des pauvres', for example: here, the beautiful green eyes of the poet's mistress give him the illusion that he can 'plunge' into her soul. But, like the capricious sea which the poet of 'Déjà!' finds 'si monstrueusement séduisante', the seductiveness of her gaze is like that of a mirror which returns his own thoughts ('Je tournais mes regards vers les vôtres, cher amour, pour y lire ma pensée').[14] Her hatefulness lies in the fact of her reminding him of the 'impermeability' of the medium which he had thought transparent. The woman's unexpectedly spiteful resentment of the presence of the poverty-stricken onlookers leaves the poet with an awareness of the incommunicable nature of thought, 'même entre gens qui s'aiment'. At the same time, the *reader* is left with an ironic awareness that the poet's interpretation of 'les yeux des pauvres' may have been as unfounded as his analysis of his mistress. In this way the poem draws attention to the fragility of its links with the real world, and casts doubt on its own power to communicate with the reader, who is aggressively stigmatised along with the poet's insensitive companion:

> Ah! vous voulez savoir pourquoi je vous hais aujourd'hui. Il vous sera sans doute moins facile de le comprendre qu'à moi de vous l'expliquer; car vous êtes, je crois, le plus bel exemple d'imperméabilité féminine qui se puisse rencontrer. (*Oc* I, 317)

The lover's eyes, commonly the focus for all the aspirations for communication which go along with sexual attraction, merely return the onlooker to his own inevitable subjectivity. The woman's eyes appear 'bizarrement doux' when, in 'Les Yeux des pauvres', they reflect back to the poet his own charitable emotions. They appear unbearably oppressive when, in the case of the 'perfect' mistress in 'Portraits de maîtresses', they remind the lover of his own guilty conscience:

> L'histoire de mon amour ressemble à un interminable voyage sur une surface pure et polie comme un miroir, vertigineusement monotone, qui aurait réfléchi tous mes sentiments et mes gestes avec l'exactitude ironique de ma propre conscience... Un soir, dans un bois... au bord d'une mare... après un mélancolique promenade où ses yeux, à elle, réfléchissait la douceur du ciel, et où mon cœur, à moi, était crispé comme l'enfer... (*Oc* I, 348–9)

In both poems the eyes are opaque, mirror-like and fundamentally impenetrable.

The mirror to mirror gaze of Baudelaire's protagonists in such poems as 'Les Yeux des pauvres' and 'Portraits de maîtresses' exemplifies the inaccessibility of the Other and points disturbingly to an absence at the heart of social relationships. In the endless self-conscious fictioning or 'figuring' of its models, *Le Spleen de Paris* suggests that the subject's relationship to the world and to the Other is always one of a *reading*. Seen like this, portraiture becomes a means of self-penetration: the arena of a duel between opposing realities, that of the observer and the observed. Either the observer's own fictions dominate and annihilate that Otherness in the very moment of figuring it on paper, in the very act of production ('Les Fenêtres'), or the poet is himself depicted as the victim of his model, transfixed by a mirror return of his own initial transgressive movement of penetration (figured as a blade, scalpel or penetrating gaze in 'Le *Confiteor* de l'artiste', 'Mademoiselle Bistouri', 'Le Desir de peindre').

It is this wider context which informs 'Le Galant Tireur' and 'Le Tir et la cimetière', poems which are resonant with the multiple associations of 'le tirage' and 'le tir': that is, with shooting ranges, with the explosive uncorking of bottles, with lottery draws for fate's winning numbers, and with *the act of printing* itself, and *the product of the printing press*. In 'Le Galant Tireur' the act of figuring, the production of the poem itself as the object of 'le tirage', is in its turn figured as an act of assassinating the model in a simulacrum of fatal penetration:

Comme la voiture traversait le bois, il la fit arrêter dans le voisinage d'un tir, disant qu'il lui serait agréable de tirer quelques balles pour tuer le Temps. Tuer ce monstre-là, n'est-ce pas l'occupation la plus ordinaire et la plus légitime de chacun? – Et il offrit galamment la main à sa chère, délicieuse et exécrable femme, à cette mystérieuse femme à laquelle il doit tant de plaisirs, tant de douleurs, et peut-être aussi une grande partie de son génie.

Plusieurs balles frappèrent loin du but proposé; l'une d'elles s'enfonça même dans la plafond; et comme la charmante créature riait follement, se moquant de la maladresse de son époux, celui-ci se tourna brusquement vers elle, et lui dit: 'Observez cette poupée, là-bas, à droite, qui porte le nez en l'air et qui a la mine si hautaine. Eh bien! cher ange, je me figure que c'est vous.' Et il ferma les yeux et il lâcha la détente. La poupée fut nettement décapitée.

Alors s'inclinant vers sa chère, sa délicieuse, son exécrable femme, son inévitable et impitoyable Muse, et lui baisant respectueusement la main, il ajouta: 'Ah! mon cher ange, combien je vous remercie de mon adresse!'

Baudelaire is here reformulating a *topos* that is prominent also in Nerval's *Sylvie*, which was published in the *Revue des Deux Mondes* in August 1853, four years earlier than 'Le Tir et le cimetière' and a decade before the probable composition of 'Le Galant Tireur'. With 'Le Galant Tireur' and 'Le Tir et le cimetière' *Le Spleen de Paris* brings together a network of enigmatic images of human mortality (the power of Time), of fate's lottery, of bottles, and invitations to 'tirer juste'. In this it closely resembles a passage in *Sylvie* in which the narrator recalls a scene from the past in which he had a vision of his 'muse' Adrienne. He is uncertain whether the scene was real or whether it was a dream:

Nous nous étions arrêtés quelques instants dans la maison du garde, où, ce qui m'a frappé beaucoup, il y avait un cygne éployé sur la porte, puis, au dedans, de hautes armoires en noyer sculpté, une grande horloge dans sa gaine, et des trophées d'arcs de flèches d'honneur au-dessus d'une carte de tir rouge et verte. Un nain bizarre, coiffé d'un bonnet chinois, tenant d'une main une bouteille et de l'autre une bague, semblait inviter les tireurs à viser juste. Ce nain, je le crois bien, était en tôle découpée. Mais l'apparition d'Adrienne est-elle aussi vraie que ces détails...[15]

The Baudelaire prose poem, like the *Sylvie* passage, focusses on art's relationship to reality and to time, or, in the case of 'Le Galant Tireur', on the act of 'tirage' as a means of killing time. The narrator's pursuit of Adrienne in the Nerval text is presented as a transgression of chronology, as we are forcefully reminded at the conclusion by the insistence on the disjuncture between the narrator's continuing obsession with Adrienne and the reality of her earlier death, unknown to him at the time. 'Laquelle est la vraie?', published in 1863, a poem which deals with the poet's obsessional attachment to an ideal but defunct muse, explores the same ground.

In 'Le Galant Tireur' to figure the model, to read the muse, is also to kill her. Implicitly, there seems to be an acknowledgement that any figurative rendering of the poet's vulgar urban muse (i.e. the reality of contemporary Paris) is an act of assassination. This idea is, of course, already implied by the 'duel' between nature and artist in 'Le *Confiteor* de l'artiste'.

Nothing, it would seem, could be further from, say, the Balzacian novel's refusal to acknowledge the problematic nature of its own activity of figuring (comparisons with Balzac are repeatedly solicited in *Le Spleen de Paris*). Indeed, the combined and complex effect of the prose poems is flagrantly to undermine the contemporary Balzacian thesis that the artist may take the scientist's methodology as a model for the penetration and analysis of external reality. Accumulatively, the *Petits Poèmes en prose* expose this myth of penetration as the unconscious expression of a particular sexual identity. 'Les Yeux des pauvres', for example, has the effect of refuting the Balzacian premise of the expressiveness of the human face and subverts Balzac's presupposition of cause and effect relation between outer forms and inner life. In the prose poems, eyes offers themselves not as texts to be read by the discerning (male) observer, as in Balzac's novels, but as mirrors which return the onlooker's own gaze, imprisoning him in the universe of his own thoughts: his 'readings' are his own creations. In Balzac's *Illusions perdues*, in a passage which directly addresses the problem of artistic 'penetration', the narrator declares that 'les poètes aiment plutôt à recevoir en eux des impressions que d'entrer chez les autres y étudier le mécanisme des sentiments', and poets are specifically presented by Balzac as effeminate.[16] Baudelaire's 'Mademoiselle Bistouri', 'Les Fenêtres' and 'Les Yeux des pauvres' can be viewed as a direct riposte to Balzac, affirming as they do that penetration of the Other is in any case liable to failure and that the observer's findings are impossible to substantiate. Given the solipsistic bias of so many of the *Petits Poèmes en prose*, it is perhaps not surprising to find that when he is casting around for a muse the poet of 'Les Bons Chiens' rejects the 'Balzacian' muse Buffon in favour of Laurence Sterne. This would seem to imply a formal rejection of the Balzacian presentation of the artist as a detached and 'superior' quasi-scientific analyst of the exterior world, and instead an acknowledgment of the problematic nature of the relationship between artist and model.

This means, amongst other things, that in *Le Spleen de Paris* the presentation of 'woman' never pretends to be a scientific, objective analysis of a reality foreign to the male poet-figure. The descriptions of women are, quite self-consciously, a series of fictions which may help to give the poet a sense of his own existence ('à sentir que je suis et ce que je suis') but which in no way purport to be an objective rendering of a common, shared reality. The myth of intellectual neutrality, so central to the Balzacian narrative project, is explicitly rejected. This is important as it helps to dispel any uneasiness which might be provoked by a superficial reading of the text's aggressive dichotomising of 'masculine' and 'feminine' signifiers.

When Balzac refers in *La Muse du département* to a means of penetrating 'les coins obscurs du cœur' by applying to private life 'l'avide scalpel du Dix-Neuvième',[17] he is proposing a pseudo-scientific theory of the artist's relationship to reality with which Baudelaire cannot identify, and which, as we have seen, is vigorously parodied in 'Mademoiselle Bistouri', as it is also in the following passage from 'Les Veuves':

C'est surtout vers ces lieux 'les jardins publics' que le poète et le philosophe aiment diriger leurs avides conjectures. Il y a là une pâture certaine... *Un oeil experimenté ne s'y trompe jamais*. Dans ces traits rigides ou abattus, dans ces yeux caves et ternes, ou brillants des derniers éclairs de la lutte, dans ces démarches si lentes ou si saccadées, *il déchiffre tout de suite les innombrables légendes* de l'amour trompé, du dévouement méconnu, des efforts non récompensés, de la faim et du froid, humblement, silencieusement supportés. (my italics; *Oc* I, 292)

Reading this in the context of other, more solipsistic, poems we have already looked at, one is conscious of the ironic exaggeration evident in the pompous certainty of the narrator–observer, and notably in the lightning rapidity of his 'reading' of the Parisian reality before his eyes. The emphasis on the narrator-figure's penetration of his subjects is quite different here from the celebration of the poet's own independent and exclusive 'rêverie' in the counterpart verse poem, 'Les Petites Vieilles'.

In summary, then, we can say that the parodying of Balzacian 'penetration theory' provides a means of presenting a much more 'modern' awareness of the individual's relationship to the world through language. The sense of incompleteness which is painful and tragic on a personal level, and which is co-relative with the erotic or desiring impulse described by Freud, appears in *Le Spleen de Paris* as analogous with the driving force behind artistic creation. The sense of solitude and the desire to reach outside the self is celebrated as a catalyst for the imagination, triggering the process which can conjure a teeming 'city' from the empty air ('Les Foules'). The poetic experience itself is presented as intoxicating, but the powers of the artist to objectively penetrate external reality, or even to communicate directly with his audience, are cast in doubt. Through the unremitting parody of the Balzacian 'penetration metaphor', Baudelaire effectively dismantles one of realism's most cherished conventions and pushes literature decisively *away* from 'science' (as understood in the 1860s) and towards a more 'musical' conceptualisation.

Finally, if we look at the question from a Lacanian perspective, we can say that the *Petits Poèmes en prose* do explicitly dramatise the subject's severance from the 'real', and they do call attention to the inaccessibility of final meaning. However, in their representation of the poetic process itself they characterise this awareness both in terms of loss ('l'artiste crie de frayeur avant d'être vaincu'), and also, more positively, in terms of ecstatic stimulus to the imagination ('heureux l'artiste que le désir déchire').

CHAPTER 4

Unsententious moralities

All narrative is sententious insofar as it lays down a certain law...
     G. Bennington, *Sententiousness and the Novel*[1]

Le récit est une figure de discours qui emprunte sa forme au mythe et au conte et...a comme eux pour fonction de distribuer les 'données' en une succession toujours édifiante, d'en tirer une 'morale'; de la sorte le récit accomplit toujours le désir; et d'abord, par sa forme même, le désir que la temporalité soit sensée et l'histoire signifiable.
     Dérivé à partir de Marx et Freud[2]

...je ne suspends pas la volonté rétive (du lecteur) au fil interminable d'une intrigue superflue.
     Baudelaire, *Dédicace à Arsène Houssaye*

PARODYING THE ARGUMENT OF THE STICK

If the masculine poet–narrator is no longer cast in the mould of sententious observer, 'l'homme supérieur', and is failing to promote himself convincingly like the Balzacian narrator as the detached analyst of one common, shared historical reality, then his role as moral authority is immediately jeopardised. With the commonsense view of reality and its attendant assumption of intellectual neutrality radically problematised, any new form of *moralité* which may be delineated necessarily operates within a network of inescapable ironies. What we find with the *Petits Poèmes en prose* is that, whilst exposing the arbitrary and relative character of human codes and laws, at the same time the poems appear to invite a reader response which depends for its effect on the existence of such codes. However, this time the codes are not entirely *unwritten* but are generated by the text itself, the whole collection of poems, through the complex play of intratextual association which enables individual poems to be read in the light of others in the collection. Thus it is that despite the parody of Balzacian sententiousness that we saw earlier one nevertheless finds Baudelaire in the *Listes de projets* proposing a whole series of poems under the category of SYMBOLES ET MORALITES[3] and repeatedly invoking in the prose poems such writers as Régnier, Vauvenargues, Pascal, Rousseau, Horace and La Fontaine and offering such elegantly polished exercises in the *poème–maxime* as 'Le Miroir', and 'Le Chien et le flacon'. One of the central paradoxes of the work lies in the way that the relativising and problematising of moral codes and attempts to 'lay down the law' coexist with an atmosphere of extraordinary indignation and spleen provoked by many different aspects of modern city experience.

How could the modern artist sit in judgement over the morality of his fellows? Or to put it another way, how could the writer of a modern 'moralité' avoid the trap of 'attacking sententiousness sententiously', an eighteenth-century problem conspicuous in the work of Voltaire, Vauvenargues and Chamfort?[4]

Vauvenargues is specifically invoked by Baudelaire in the opening lines of 'Les Veuves', where the reference to the Vauvenargues text 'Sur les misères cachées' from the *Réflexions sur divers sujets* further develops the intertextual resonances on the *multitude/solitude* topos already introduced by the preceding poems 'A une heure du matin' and 'Les Foules'. Vauvenargues, writing of 'ces solitaires', 'jeunes gens que l'erreur de la gloire entretient à l'écart de ses chimères', states with nuanced sympathy, but nevertheless sententiously: 'le plaisir et la société n'ont plus de charmes pour ceux que l'illusion de la gloire asservit...je plains ces misères cachées'. There is an obvious tension between the sympathy expressed in the Vauvenargues text and the judgemental self-distancing by the philosopher–narrator. This tension does not exist in the same way in *Le Spleen de Paris*. The prose poems, by alternately and simultaneously espousing and ironically distancing themselves from the persona of, say, the solitary glory-seeker ('A une heure du matin', 'Les Foules', 'Le Vieux Saltimbanque', 'La Solitude', 'Assommons les pauvres!'), effectively expose the limitations inherent in the unitary narrator persona of much traditional edifying discourse. The philosophical dialogue with its generally wooden and inflexible tradition of the 'winner' and the 'loser' of the argument did not, of course, really overcome these limitations. It was not until Diderot that the philosophical dialogue was to push towards a more ambivalent status, resisting classification either as poetry or philosophy, moving away from the tradition of using the magisterial 'winner' of the argument as the mouthpiece of impersonal, rational truth.[5]

Certainly, the *mise en question* of the underlying codes of the traditional *moralité* is central to the achievement of *Le Spleen de Paris*, perhaps more central than its interrogation of the conventions governing lyric poetry. Implicitly and explicitly, the prose poems set themselves up for comparison with texts by writers such as Vauvenargues, Pascal, Régnier and Rousseau, and at the same time, as I hope to show in Chapter 4, they acknowledge their debt to Diderot's *Neveu de Rameau*, a work which represented a glorious precedent in the art of taking sentientiousness to task, unsententiously.

The only appropriate mode for the 'moralité' in so profoundly self-reflexive a work as *Le Spleen de Paris* had to be a humorous, indirect and self-deprecating one. Moreover, the rewriting of the *moralité*, the ironic rejection of sententious moralising which is parodied in simulacrum in such poems as 'La Femme sauvage et la petite-maîtresse' and 'Assommons les pauvres!', itself goes hand in hand with the rejection of linearity and unicity on the formal level of the collection as a whole. By multiplying the voices in the different poems, allowing one poem to stand in contrast to another, or by introducing an exaggeratedly strident narrator whose utterances seem to preclude unthinking complicity by the reader, *Le Spleen de Paris* manoeuvres the reader into a more active role of reflexion and comparison. Given this plurivocality, it is impossible for the reader's relationship with the text to remain one of simple 'tutelage'.

It is in this sense that the mobility of the collection of prose poems militates against what has been seen by some critics as the inherent sententiousness of all narrative succession: the tyranny of the beginning and the ending which one finds in the case of the novel. Certainly many novels of the period and of the late eighteenth century seem to illustrate the tensions which the choice of an ending implied. *Les Liaisons dangereuses*, *La Nouvelle Héloïse*, and *Le Rouge et le noir* are amongst the more prominent examples of novels exemplifying some resistance or tension between the necessity of choosing an ending and the reluctance to 'lay down the law' or opt sententiously, and reductively, for any single moral message. The importance of the absence of this law of succession imposed by a continuous narrative thread cannot be over-emphasised. The fact that Baudelaire chose to foreground this absence in the dedication to Houssaye is of the utmost significance.

THE NEW *MORALITE* AND THE NEW MAN

The *mise en question* of sententiousness seems to be at work in a number of poems. A series of ironic allusions to 'cudgel moralism' or punitive didacticism suggested by repeated references to sticks and cudgels underscores the comparison between art, violence and sexuality which is implicit in the thematising of penetration symbolism which we have already looked at.

'La Femme sauvage et la petite-maîtresse' provides a good example. In this poem the masculine poet-figure points out to the addressee, his own 'victim' lover, that the wild woman who is the subject of his exemplar is confined in a cage like an animal and 'controlled' by her husband, who shouts at her and beats her with a stick. The enclosure draws attention to the text's own ambiguous status as *either* a crude exercise in the 'moralité' genre *or* an ironic parody of just that type of unsubtle didactic literature. Is the *mise en abyme* spectacle 'make-believe' or 'genuine'? 'Faites bien attention', the poet urges, 'voyez avec quelle voracité (non simulée peut-être?) elle déchire les lapins vivants et des volailles piaillantes.' A little later comes the revelation that what had been thought to be a fiction is in fact a reality (the stick has been wielded in earnest):

Grand Dieu! le bâton n'est pas un bâton de comédie, avez-vous entendez résonner la chair, malgré le poil postiche? (*Oc* I, 290)

This contributes to highlighting the ambiguity of the poet–narrator's own utterances. Are his words joking or serious, playfully exaggerated or to be taken literally? Is *he* using a 'bâton de comédie' or a 'real' stick?

Tant poète que je sois, je ne suis pas assez dupe que vous voudriez le croire, et si vous me fatiguez trop souvent de vos précieuses pleurnicheries, je vous traiterai en *femme sauvage*, ou je vous jetterai par la fenêtre comme une bouteille vide. (*Oc* I, 290)

If the window is interpreted as a symbol of the artistic medium (a reading encouraged by the presence in the collection of 'Le Mauvais Vitrier'), then it appears that the threat has already been carried out. The poet's aggression is channelled through his art: the addressee is ill-advised to despise the inert 'soliveau' poet, for it is in this role, by means of these same artistic powers, that he can batter and torment her like the 'femme sauvage' of the carnival. The poem, presented in its entirety in quotation marks, offers itself exaggeratedly as an instrument of assault, as crude an essay in dominance as the one perpetrated by the husband of the wild woman. The aggression seems to be only at one degree removed from the real reader, for whom the necessary association with the vaporous mistress is as much an abuse and an affront as, for the mistress, the implied comparison with the wild woman. Moral didacticism seems here to be equated with masculinity and sexual dominance in an elementary power struggle. But at the same time the whole exercise invites reading as a simulacrum, a self-consciously ritualistic and exaggerated display of a punitive move which the whole context of other poems in the collection conspires to negate and reject.

By 'having it both ways' the poem effectively interrogates underlying codes of masculinity and sententious didacticism whilst still situating itself as essentially masculine discourse. It could be seen as a way of exorcising Balzac's accusation, which I cited earlier, that poets were 'feminine'. Certainly Baudelaire associates the 'laying down of the law', either by quasi-medical 'diagnosis' or punitive didacticism, with *masculinity*. By ironically undermining such discourse the prose poems call into question contemporary nineteenth-century assumptions about both *genre* and *gender* identity.

The metaphoric association of 'cudgel' and moral argument is a literary cliché, as we are reminded in 'La Femme sauvage' when the link between the 'bâton' and the didactic stance of the poem ('je veux essayer de vous guérir') is highlighted by the poet-figure's self-comparison with a small joist or length of wood. The intertextual resonances here are multiple. On the one hand, the poem directly invites comparison with La Fontaine's moral fable 'Les Grenouilles qui demandent un roi' by making allusion to the 'soliveau' king of the frogs who is replaced by a murderous crane when the frogs complain to God about the inadequacies of their first monarch. In other words, like the cudgel which is wielded in the carnival stunt, the 'soliveau' poet is characterised as simple and inert, but capable of sudden transformation into an instrument of fatal violence against the addressee and, by extension, Baudelaire's Parisian readership. But, additionally, the *soliveau/poutre* which hails down on the Parisian populace like a species of retribution has more extensive intertextual resonances which link it to texts by Hugo, Diderot and Rabelais amongst others.

Baudelaire's allusion to the 'soliveau' poet calls to mind the passage in Hugo's *Notre-Dame de Paris*, where Quasimodo casts down a giant beam from the height of Notre-Dame cathedral on to the 'frog' populace of Paris, an incident which in turn recalls the exploits of Gargantua and conspicuously draws attention to the fact that it is a reworking of a literary *topos*.[6] The Hugo passage contains a number of features which encourage one to compare it with the 'cudgel' *réseau* in *Le Spleen de Paris*. Notably, it draws attention to the verb 'assommer' ('Pierre l'Assommeur est assommé'[7]), whose two meanings – 'to batter to death or knock senseless' and, colloquially, 'to bore to death or to bore stiff' – are exploited by Baudelaire in 'Assommons les pauvres!'

The phallic connotations of the beam and the reflexive or intertextual nature of Hugo's passage are clearly hinted at in the following comic dialogue between members of the crowd jostling in the streets below the cathedral:

– C'est la lune qui nous jette cette bûche, dit Andry le Rouge.
– Avec cela, reprit François Chanteprune, qu'on dit la lune amie de la Vierge![8]

Paradoxically, the virgin text keeps company with the queen of reflexivity, the *moon*, which shines with a 'borrowed light' and is commonly used to symbolise intertextuality, that is the *non-virginity* of the text.[9]

A similar *raillerie* and indirection characterise *Le Spleen de Paris*, and an awareness of the intertextual context, the links with Hugo, Diderot and Rabelais, together with a knowledge of the immediate context of other poems in the collection, furthers the reader's sense of the complexity of the irony unfolding in such exaggeratedly strident essays in cudgel moralism as 'La Femme sauvage et la petite-maîtresse' and 'Assommons les pauvres!'

Equally, the references in 'La Femme sauvage' to the 'cudgel' and to the 'soliveau' (and their association with a power struggle between masculine poet and feminine addressee) can be read in relation to similar imagery in 'Le Thyrse':

physiquement ce n'est qu'un bâton, un pur bâton, perche à houblon, tuteur de vigne, sec, dur et droit. Autour de ce bâton, dans des méandres capricieux, se jouent et folâtrent des tiges et des fleurs, celles-ci sinueuses et fuyardes, celles-là penchées comme des cloches ou des coupes renversées. Et une gloire étonnante jaillit de cette complexité de lignes et de couleurs, tendres ou éclatantes. Ne dirait-on pas que la ligne courbe et la spirale font leur cour à la ligne droite et dansent autour dans une muette adoration? (*Oc* I, 335–6)

The 'bâton' of 'Le Thyrse' resembles the 'soliveau' and the 'bâton' of 'La Femme sauvage' in that it is 'dur et droit' and it is also 'tuteur' ('prop' or 'stake' but also 'guardian'). The wild and capricious vine, on the other hand, offers parallels with the 'femme sauvage' who lunges restlessly around her fairground cage, circling her husband and his cudgel at a chain's length away. In both poems it is the feminine element which is associated with nature,[10] the 'masculine' cudgel which is associated with 'culture'. The immobile supporting rod of the thyrsus serves as a means of symbolically 'domesticating' the capricious exuberance of the plant in the same way that the husband's stick is used to tame the wild woman.

But in contrast with 'La Femme sauvage et la petite-maîtresse', 'Le Thyrse' provides an image of the complementarity of feminine and masculine elements, nature and culture, fantasy (or digressiveness) and rigour. In the first poem the sexes are at war, 'nature' must be violently constrained by 'culture', and fantasy and rigour are at odds: the dreamy mistress, 'les yeux tournés vaporeusement vers le ciel', provokes the poet to a paroxysm of cruel 'realism'. Though it is true that here 'nature' (the wild woman) is a fake, 'culture' (the husband) a travesty. The wistfulness of the 'petite-maîtresse' is not an equivalent of the 'rêverie' depicted in, say, 'L'Etranger' or 'Les Vocations', but is merely a pose ('toutes ces affectations apprises dans les livres'), whilst the aggressiveness of the poet-figure is so exaggerated that it appears like a mask. In 'Le Thyrse', on the other hand, feminine and masculine elements are harmoniously fused. In its complementary fusion of the masculine and the feminine, the straight line and the arabesque, the image of the thyrsus recalls Sterne's model of narrative progression in *Tristram Shandy* and Diderot's analogous model of song in *Le Neveu de Rameau*.[11] Caprice and rigour, movement and stasis, complexity and simplicity, 'fantaisie' and 'volonté' are held in a perfect equilibrium:

Le bâton, c'est votre volonté, droite, ferme et inébranlable; les fleurs, c'est la promenade de votre fantaisie autour de votre volonté; c'est l'élément féminin exécutant autour du mâle ses prestigieuses pirouettes. Ligne droite et ligne arabesque, intention et expression, roideur de la volonté, sinuosité du verbe, unité du but, variété des moyens, amalgame tout-puissant et indivisible du génie, quel analyste aura le détestable courage de vous diviser et de vous séparer? (*Oc* I, 336)

On one level 'Le Thyrse' suggests an ideal reconciliation of masculine and feminine elements, a discourse which resolves the tension between masculine rigour and feminine rhapsody. But on another level it recalls the power struggle of 'La Femme sauvage' and ultimately makes the same association between the artist figure, the 'bâton', and a certain kind of dominance. The thyrsus is a sacred emblem which, as well as inspiring adoration, also provokes fear. The nymph who wields it is able to strike terror into the hearts of her companions, and her dominance is compared to that of Liszt, whose genius also inspires his audience with a sense of fear:

> Jamais nymphe exaspérée par l'invincible Bacchus ne secoua son thyrse sur les têtes de ses compagnes affolées avec autant d'énergie et de caprice que vous agitez votre génie sur les cœurs de vos frères. (*Oc* I, 336)

The artist's emblem, then, is associated with a dominance which verges on violence. In this respect the sacred rod is like other sticks and cudgels in the prose poems which are associated with gestures of dominance on the part of the poet-figure.

The imagery which presents itself in a serious, even tragic light in one poem can create an effect of bathos in another, and 'Assommons les pauvres!' provides the occasion for a grotesque parody of the power symbols we have been looking at. Here, in contrast with the shocking presentation of the poet and the sadistic husband in 'La Femme sauvage', the poet-narrator is cast as a perverse and ludicrous moralist whose didactic theory is translated into a farcical attack on an old beggar.

ASSOMMONS LES PAUVRES!

Pendant quinze jours je m'étais confiné dans ma chambre, et je m'étais entouré des livres à la mode dans ce temps-là (il y a seize ou dix-sept ans); je veux parler des livres où il est traité de l'art de rendre les peuples heureux, sages et riches, en vingt-quatre heures. J'avais donc digéré, – avalé, veux-je dire, – toutes les élucubrations de tous ces entrepreneurs de bonheur public, – de ceux qui conseillent à tous les pauvres de se faire esclaves, et de ceux qui leur persuadent qu'ils sont tous des rois détrônés. – On ne état d'esprit avoisinant le vertige ou la stupidité.

Il m'avait semblé seulement que je sentais, confiné au fond de mon intellect, le germe obscur d'une idée supérieure à toutes les formules de bonne femme dont j'avais récemment parcouru le dictionnaire. Mais ce n'était que l'idée d'une idée, quelque chose d'infiniment vague.

Et je sortis avec une grande soif. Car le goût passionné des mauvaises lectures engendre un besoin proportionnel du grand air et des rafraîchissants. Comme j'allais entrer dans un cabaret, un mendiant me tendit son chapeau, avec un de ces regards inoubliables qui culbuteraient les trônes, si l'esprit remuait la matière, et si l'œil d'un magnétiseur faisait mûrir les raisins.

En même temps, j'entendis une voix qui chuchotait à mon oreille, une voix que je reconnus bien; c'était celle d'un bon Ange, ou d'un bon Démon, qui m'accompagne partout. Puisque Socrate avait son bon Démon, pourquoi n'aurais-je pas mon bon Ange, et pourquoi n'aurais-je pas l'honneur, comme Socrate, d'obtenir mon brevet de folie, signé du subtil Lélut et du bien-avisé Baillarger?

Il existe cette différence entre le Démon de Socrate et le mien, que celui de Socrate ne se manifestait à lui que pour défendre, avertir, empêcher, et que le mien daigne conseiller, suggérer, persuader. Ce pauvre Socrate n'avait qu'un Démon prohibiteur; le mien est un grand affirmateur, le mien est un Démon d'action, un Démon de combat.

Or, sa voix me chuchotait ceci: 'Celui-là seul est l'égal d'un autre, qui le prouve, et celui-là seul est digne de la liberté, qui sait la conquérir'.

Immédiatement, je sautai sur mon mendiant. D'un seul coup de poing, je lui bouchai un œil, qui devint, en une seconde, gros come une balle. Je cassai un de mes ongles à lui briser deux dents, et comme je ne me sentais pas assez fort, étant né délicat et m'étant peu exercé à la boxe, pour assommer rapidement ce vieillard, je le saisis d'une main par le collet de son habit, de l'autre, je l'empoignai à la gorge, et je me mis à lui secouer vigoureusement la tête contre un mur. Je dois avouer que j'avais préalablement inspecté les environs d'un coup d'œil, et que j'avais vérifié que dans cette banlieue déserte je me trouvais, pour un assez long temps, hors de la portée de tout agent de police.

The two meanings of the verb 'assommer' are humorously exploited in this exemplary cudgelling incident, which is more exaggeratedly and farcically *boring* in its 'heavy-handed' didacticism than even the turgid moralising tracts evoked for implied comparison by the poet–narrator. For the poet–moralist, on this occasion, uses not just a mere stick but 'une grosse branche d'arbre' in order to drive home his lesson:

je me saisis d'une grosse branche d'arbre qui traînait à terre, et je le battis avec l'énergie obstinée des cuisiniers qui veulent attendrir un beefteack. (*Oc* I, 359)

In other words, this poem provides a burlesque representation of the *Argumentum Baculinum* or 'argument of the stick' which is mentioned by Laurence Sterne, the mentor Baudelaire invokes in 'Les Bons Chiens'. In Sterne's novel, Tristram seems to favour instead the 'Argumentum Fistulatorium', the argument of a player on the shepherd's pipe, that is, the 'musical' argument of metaphor or indirection (typified in *Tristram Shandy* by Uncle Toby's practice of whistling half a dozen bars of *Lillabulero* as a means of venting his passion).[12]

In the exaggeratedly chauvinistic 'Portraits de maîtresses', the sexual associations of the 'bâton' are humorously exploited in a parody of 'edifying' male narratives. As we have already seen, the description of the third woman in this poem recalls the alimentary references in 'La Femme sauvage'. The third raconteur tells of how his mistress, a 'monstre polyphage', left him for another man who was able to supply her with all the food she wanted. The figure of speech describing the manner in which the new lover managed to satisfy his voracious companion humorously confirms the association between the two poems.

Je la nourrissais bien; et cependant elle m'a quitté – Pour un fournisseur aux vivres, sans doute? – Quelque chose d'approchant, une espèce d'employé dans l'intendance qui, *par quelque tour de bâton à lui connu*, fournit peut-être à cette pauvre enfant la ration de plusieurs soldats. C'est du moins ce que j'ai supposé. (my italics; *Oc* I, 347)

Here the associations of the word 'bâton' with a clandestine act mean that it has the effect of drawing attention once again to the 'secret' character of the text itself. A number of possible meanings cluster around the word: didactic message, cudgel, phallus, magician's wand or pen?

If the figure of speech 'tour de bâton' is taken literally, it suggests an image of the enigmatic employee of the mysterious Supplies Office brandishing a 'bâton' wand which will enable him (like the 'escamoteur éblouissant comme un dieu' glimpsed in 'Le Vieux Saltimbanque') to conjure up for his mistress the rations of several soldiers. Presumably, the cudgel-wielding husband of 'La Femme sauvage' engages in a similar feat of mystification, or hoax, for the same ends: in order to supply himself and his own 'monstre polyphage' with food. As we have seen, implicit in the comparison between this sadistic husband and the poet–narrator lies the suggestion that the 'soliveau' poet brandishes his own magical pen in order to achieve the same result: the addressee and, by extension, the reader are cast in role of 'engloutisseuse'.

'Portraits de maîtresses' is a poem whose title itself echoes the formulation of the traditional philosophical genre of the 'Portrait', but the conversational and anecdotal discourse of the poem suggests an exaggerated ironic caricature of male philosophical discourse. The anecdotes exchanged by the four men about mistresses are presented as an example of male discourse which is nevertheless not wholly masculine since there is the suggestion that even the mentioning of women or a feminine element is not 'philosophical'. A conversation about women introduces a feminine *non-philosophical* element, like listening to dance music:

L'un d'eux jeta la causerie sur *le sujet des femmes. Il eût été plus philosophique de n'en parler du tout*; mais il y a des gens d'esprit qui, après boire, ne méprise pas les conversations banales. *On écoute alors celui qui parle, comme on écouterait de la musique de danse*. (my italics; *Oc* I, 345)

The comparison between masculine philosophical discourse and conversation about subservient women or mistresses foregrounds the notion of a discourse which is compared to dance music. This is, then, a conversation which presents itself as *musical*, a musical prose poem. Comparisons with 'Le Thyrse', the model of a musical ideal which combines the masculine and the feminine, the rigour of the rod and the dancing freedom of the vine, are furthered by the poem's conclusion. Here, the apotheosis of masculine behaviour and discourse, the positive assassination of the perfect mistress, is presented as a transgressive excess of male *rectitude* the moral import or message of which stuns even its male audience, and also recalls the didactic edifying and threatening gesture of the male narrator in 'Le Galant Tireur':

Les trois autres compagnons regardèrent celui-ci avec un regard vague et légèrement hébété, comme feignant de ne pas comprendre et comme avouant implicitement qu'ils ne se sentaient pas, quant à eux, capables *d'une action aussi rigoureuse, quoique suffisamment expliquée d'ailleurs*.

Ensuite on fit apporter de nouvelles bouteilles, pour tuer le Temps qui a la vie si dure, et accélérer la vie qui coule si lentement. (my italics; *Oc* I, 349)[13]

THE CLOWN DOCTOR

At the same time that the didactic 'Argument of the stick' is held up to ridicule by a strategy of exaggeration, 'Les Veuves', 'Mademoiselle Bistouri' and 'Une Mort héroique' can be read as offering equally tongue-in-cheek renderings of the 'doctor' moralist convention. As we have seen, the title 'Assommons les pauvres!' can be seen as an incitement to 'cudgel' moralism ('Let's knock out the poor!') or as an ironic parody of turgid and indigestible moralising tracts ('Let's bore them stiff!') and, additionally, the absurdly strident narrator of this poem describes the application of his own moral theory on a poor beggar as an 'énergique médication'. Similarly, in 'La Femme sauvage et la petite-maîtresse', the narrator adopts the role of a fairground quack peddling cheap miracle cures. He announces to his mistress: 'Tenez, je veux essayez de vous guérir, nous en trouverons peut-être le moyen pour deux sols, au milieu d'une fête, et sans aller plus loin.' But before we reach the poem's conclusion his patronising stance is shown to be absurd because by his sadism he reveals himself to be as despicable as his companion. The reader, drawing the parallel with the carnival act, may conclude that, like the husband in the stunt, the moralising narrator is himself as loathsome as the 'femme sauvage'.

In a passage from 'Le Mauvais Vitrier' which directly compares the professions of moralist and doctor, the poet–narrator draws attention to their fallibility and casts himself in the opposite role of the potential patient. The passage, with its exaggeratedly ponderous address to the reader, seems to go out of its way to poke fun at the characteristic pronouncements of sententious Balzacian narrators:

Le moraliste et le médecin, qui prétendent tout savoir, ne peuvent pas expliquer d'où vient si subitement une si folle énergie à ces âmes voluptueuses... (Observez, je vous prie, que l'esprit de mystification qui, chez quelques personnes, n'est pas le résultat d'un travail ou d'une combinaison, mais d'une inspiration fortuite, participe beaucoup, ne fût-ce par l'ardeur du désir, de cette humeur, hystérique selon les médecins, satanique selon ceux qui pensent un peu mieux que les médecins, qui nous poussent vers une foule d'actions dangereuses ou inconvenantes.) (*Oc* I, 285–6)

How can the moralist and the doctor pretend to know all the answers to life's mysteries and to the enigma of the human heart? The narrator of 'Anywhere out of the World' forcefully implies that, far from enjoying the position of a detached and 'superior' observer, he is a victim of the same disease as his fellows. Once again, a medical metaphor conveys a moral condition: in a phrase which recalls Emerson,[14] the poet portrays himself as just another restless in-patient of a world from which he longs to escape:

Cette vie est un hôpital où chaque malade est possédé du désir de changer de lit. Celui-ci voudrait souffrir en face du poêle, celui-là croit qu'il guérirait à côté de la fenêtre. (*Oc* I, 356)

In a universe where *all* men are sick, including the doctors or moralists, such terms as 'malade' or 'fou' may only be employed ironically.

The medical metaphors in 'Mademoiselle Bistouri' and 'Anywhere out of the world' convey the same awareness as that expressed in the poet's *Notes Nouvelles sur Edgar Poe* that 'nous sommes tous nés marquis [*sic*] pour le mal'.[15] Baudelaire wrote in his notes on *Les Liaisons dangereuses* that 'le mal se connaissant était moins affreux et plus près de la guérison que le mal s'ignorant' and in 'Mademoiselle Bistouri' offers echoes of Laclos's satire of hypocritical moralising. For example, the pharisaical condemnation of X by doctor Z, instanced by Bistouri, strikingly parallels Madame de Volange's report of the judgement passed on Madame de Merteuil at the conclusion of Laclos's novel.[16]

If the modern poet was to be a moralist or 'doctor' then, like Bistouri's portraitist, he must be a 'médecin farceur', aware that his imaginative excursions into the exterior world and into the souls of his fellows were probably more revelatory of his own moral and psychological condition than of anything else. The most hopeless cases of sickness or 'savagery' would be those who might think to exempt themselves by pointing the finger at their fellows. Baudelaire would have been familiar with Poe's comment that 'in efforts to rise above our nature, we invariably fall below it. Your reformist demigods are merely devils turned inside out',[17] and the prose poems seem to echo the quizzical uncertainty expressed in the following passage from Poe's *Marginalia*:

'This is right', says Epicurus, 'precisely because the people are displeased with it.'
    'Il y a "à parier"', says Chamfort – one of the *Kankars of Mirabeau* – 'que toute idée publique – toute convention reçue – est une sottise; car elle a convenu au plus grand nombre.'
    'Si proficere cupis', says the great African bishop, 'primo id verum puta quod sana mens omnium hominum attestatur.'
    Now, 'Who shall decide where Doctors disagree?'
    To me, it appears that, in all ages, the *most* preposterous falsities have been received as truths by at least the *mens* omnium hominum. As for the *sana* mens – how are we ever to determine what this is?[18]

Once again reworking a familiar *topos*, 'Mademoiselle Bistouri' conveys well an awareness perhaps best exemplified by Diderot's *Neveu de Rameau*[19] and succinctly expressed for a post-Freudian audience by Shoshana Felman:

To talk about madness is always, in fact, to deny it. However one represents madness to oneself or others, to represent *madness* is always, consciously or unconsciously, to play out the scene of the denial of one's own madness.[20]

This may go a considerable way towards explaining the particular fascination of 'lunacy' for the Baudelaire of *Le Spleen de Paris*, who was already living under the fear of 'le vent de l'aile de l'imbécillité', as for the Sterne who wrote *Tristram Shandy* at a time when his wife was suffering from temporary insanity. But equally, a poem like 'Le Thyrse', with its 'defiguration' of the 'madness of rhetoric' (Johnson),[21] goes beyond simple biographical circumstances to reveal the centrality of madness to all works of literature, the intrinsic 'folie' of metaphoric association and, by extension, of language itself. The thematising of this madness in *Le Spleen de Paris* will be the subject of my next chapter.

CHAPTER 5

Poetry and madness

Madness...like literature itself, becomes a metaphor whose referent is a metaphor: *the figure of a figure*...What kind of madness interconnects madness with the language of fiction?

S. Felman, *Writing and Madness*[1]

Imagination abandoned by reason produces impossible monsters: united with her, she is the mother of the arts and the source of their wonders.

Goya, *Los caprichos*[2]

Toute figure, en fait comporte un processus de décodage en deux temps, dont le premier est la perception de l'anomalie...

J. Cohen, '*Théorie de la figure*'[3]

La raison s'aliène dans le mouvement même ou elle prend possession de la folie.

Foucault, *Histoire de la folie à l'âge classique*[4]

EXCEPTIONALITY AND CONFORMITY

A number of the *Petits Poèmes en prose* deal explicitly with the theme of madness, whilst others, less conspicuously, extend the network of associations in such a way as to link whimsy, caprice and mad unpredictability to a poetics of the exceptional and surprising. This seems to operate both with respect to metaphor and simple comparison within individual poems and also with respect to those migratory, lateral associations which link elements from one poem to others in the collection. On the most obvious level, as we have seen, the opening poem associates the poet-figure, or outsider, with a romantic archetype of uncivilised eccentricity, underscoring the difference that separates his perceptions from those around him. Similarly, the poet narrators of 'Le *Confiteor* de l'artiste' and 'Le Mauvais Vitrier' present themselves as overtly hysterical. In 'Le Crépuscule du soir' the mad 'friend', who rejects the gastronomic delights of a skilfully prepared restaurant chicken because of a private 'hieroglyphic' interpretation of its significance, is compared with the poet, here as in 'Les Bienfaits de la lune' characterised as another species of '*lunatique*', excited by the arrival of the night.

Echoing Pascal's perception of men as 'si nécessairement fou, que ce serait être fou par un autre tour de folie de n'être pas fou',[5] Baudelaire portrays humanity as occupants of a vast hospital in which each of the inmates deludes himself that he would be better off in another bed in a different position ('Anywhere out of the world'). Or again, reversing conventional distinctions, 'Un Plaisant' explores the nature of the 'délire officiel' of the metropolitan masses; the accepted, traditional insanity of a capital city's greedy New Year celebrations: 'chaos de boue et de neige...grouillant de cupidités et de désespoirs'. Similarly, the reclusive narrator of 'La Solitude' cites Pascal's thoughts on 'le divertissement' when writing of 'tous ces *affolés* [my italics] qui cherchent le bonheur dans le mouvement et dans une prostitution que je pourrais appeler *fraternitaire*, si je voulais parler le belle langue de mon siècle'. The diptych confrontation between two contrasting forms of madness is violently dramatised by the phenomenon of the *city*: the madness of the eccentric poet recluse, and that of the teeming majority who immerse themselves in 'le bruit et le remuement' (Pascal),[6] in the tumult and frenzy of the collective tide of the moment. The metropolis offers a perfect image of the vast and unself-conscious processes of that necessary madness which is conformism or adherence to codes. Like *Robinson Crusoe*, the novel which is cited in 'La Solitude' and which recapitulates the historical process (the move from isolation to community and to the beginnings of a commercial order), the *Petits Poèmes en prose* situate the urban experience at the heart of a more profound psychological dichotomy between solitude and populousness, individuality and conformism.[7]

In doing so, they multiply and prolong resonances with earlier writing on the *multitude/solitude topos*, sometimes overtly, as with the references to *Robinson Crusoe*, to Pascal and to La Bruyère in 'La Solitude', or to Vauvenargues in 'Les Veuves', sometimes implicitly as with the indirect allusions to Rousseau in 'La Solitude' and 'Le Gâteau'.[8] Such poems might be read on one level as themselves paradoxically illustrating the fact that the apparently solitary activity of the poet is in fact itself a form of 'universelle communion'. In this way, 'Les Foules' might be read as a celebration of intertextuality:

Multitude, solitude: termes égaux et convertibles par le poete actif et fécond. Qui ne sait pas peupler sa solitude, ne sait pas non plus être seul dans une foule affairée.[9]

However, writers, or more precisely texts, do not coexist in a state of stasis, a masonic fraternity speaking a different, higher language within an alternative community of their own. Each new text rewrites the common *topos* and depends for its effect precisely on those areas of discrepancy or anomaly by which it differs from and interrogates those texts which have gone before. The references to masonry and secret hieroglyphics in poems such as 'Les Bons Chiens' and 'Le Crépuscule du soir' do not suggest the existence of a superior community of artists and poets speaking their own private language, but invite a different reading, perhaps as allusions to the reading process. Baudelaire's writings elsewhere suggest a more dynamic relationship between the individual text and its literary 'fraternity'. For example, in 'Richard Wagner et *Tannhäuser* à Paris' it is forcefully argued that 'il est impossible qu'un poète ne contienne un critique'.[10]

Against the background, then, of a massive, awe-inspiring image of conformity to the code, and the pressures of the collectivity, Baudelaire goes on to show how madness, like literature, and precisely *because* its private systems of paradigmatic association are at variance with the norm (the 'mass' perception), by disturbing or 'jarring' conventional assumptions and perceptions of the relationship between the signifier and the signified lays bare the arbitrariness of that relationship. The common ground of madness and literature can be viewed as lying in their mutual function of interrogating received perceptions and the very basis of language itself (which is convention). In other words both madness and poetry serve, by virtue of their very *exceptionality*, to defamiliarise existing codes which control and condition our everyday behaviour and thinking. The prominence of the madness theme seems then to be entirely consistent with the project of writing a work which would adapt itself to 'les soubresauts de la conscience'. Its importance cannot be overstated, both because it lies at the heart of the 'discussion' about poetic language which is going on throughout the *Petits Poèmes en prose*, and because it involves so many of the poems. If we look more closely at a number of examples we can explore the connection between madness, caprice and the poetics of the whole collection.

Of all the poems, 'Chacun sa chimère' offers the most striking and sombre depiction of madness. And, because it figures amongst the opening poems in the collection, it sets a precedent for those that follow. The scene it evokes is stark and barren, a vision of absolute desolation which bears no obvious superficial relation to the spectacle of the populous city. But it encapsulates a perspective on the human condition which is reiterated in many of the other poems. This symbolic picture of men bowed down by the weight of their monstrous chimera portrays a weary and serious humanity constantly burdened with illusion and madness. By suggesting that madness is universal ('Chacun sa chimère') it problematises it as a category and sabotages our conventional assumptions as to what constitutes the norm and what constitutes deviance. The poem provides the collection with a bleak backcloth which undermines and further ironises the relativism of collective 'sanity' and individual folly adumbrated in several of the other poems ('Le Fou et la Vénus', 'La Femme sauvage et la petite-maîtresse', 'Le Crépuscule du soir', 'Déjà!', 'Mademoiselle Bistouri'). With its funereal description of individuals proceeding beneath a grey sky, across an empty plain, bent double beneath the grotesque beast–masks of their personal obsessions and each quite unconscious of the peculiarity of his or her condition, 'Chacun sa chimère' offers a despairing vision of humankind's collective frailty: the prison-house of 'idées fixes'.

The terrible inevitability of this, the anti-vital, obsessional face of human madness, is suggested again in 'Mademoiselle Bistouri', a poem which explores the problem of divine judgement and the defining of good and evil, madness and sanity.

CAPRICIOUS ASSOCIATION AND FANTASY

However, the tragedy of internment, whether within the restrictions of invisible mental and psychological shackles or by incarceration behind the iron bars of a cage or an asylum, is contrasted in the *Petits poèmes* with another kind of *folie* which offers *an exact inversion of the first*: that is, the crazy, capricious play of whimsical and volatile fancy, the exuberance of the rhapsodical imagination. This form of *folie*, the delight of boundless metaphoricity, is associated with unrestraint and *vagabondage* and with poetry ('L'Etranger', 'Les Foules', 'Un Hémisphère dans une chevelure', 'L'Invitation au voyage', 'Les Projets', 'Les Vocations', 'Déjà!', 'Les Bienfaits de la lune', 'Le Port', 'La Soupe et les nuages').

Jean Prévost saw 'Chacun sa chimère' as a response to the Goya *Capricho* 'Tu que no puedes', which depicts two men struggling to carry monstrous asses. And indeed one can see that the association with Goya's subversive collection of 'moral poems' may be taken still further.[11] For the entire collection of *Caprichos*, like the *Petits poèmes en prose*, chart the dangerous waters of the relationship between creative artistic fantasy and 'clinical' insanity, as Goya's remark on his original title leaf testifies:

La fantasia abondanada de la razon, produce monstruos imposibles: unida con ella, es madre de las artas y origen de sus marabillas.
(Imagination abandoned by reason produces impossible monsters: united with her, she is mother of the arts and the source of their wonders.)[12]

Goya's initial intention was to foreground this theme in the opening plate (he originally intended for this position Plate 43, captioned 'The sleep of reason produces monsters'). Certainly, like a number of the prose poems ('Un plaisant', 'Les Chimères' and 'Les Bons Chiens') the *Caprichos* thematise unreason (often symbolised by asses or monkeys) in a complex network of equivalences and reversals. From the spectacle of unreason and irrational conventional prejudice both works derive a bitter comedy or *raillerie*. In the case of both the *Caprichos* and *Le Spleen de Paris* configurations of the monstrous can be seen as thematic manifestations of the work's own exceptional status, as well as of a profound socio-political alienation and black humour.

Like the prose poems, one *Capricho* often reflects on to another, exploiting effects of echo or inversion. Certain plates invoke puns (for example numbers 26 and 36). Here, too – and this is an important feature of Goya's 'moralités' – the artist portraying the human beast is in no way presented as superior or as exempt from the condition he portrays: the ass sits for his portrait but the portraitist is himself an ape (*Capricho* 41, 'Ni màs ni menos'); or, to give another example, the ape artist, this time a musician, is portrayed entertaining the ass with his violin (*Capricho* 38). One is reminded of 'Mademoiselle Bistouri', where the monstrous obsessiveness of the narrator–portraitist parallels that of his subject, the prostitute. Moreover, as is the case with *Le Spleen de Paris*, the structure of Goya's collection is based on a system of recurrences, and in this respect it resembles the obsessional quality of the 'pathological' imagination. Characteristically, just as he was to draw particular attention to the workings of the leitmotif in Wagnerian opera, so Baudelaire focused on this very distinctive feature of the *Caprichos* in his 1857 article on Goya's masterpiece:

...il y a dans les œuvres issues des profondes individualités quelque chose qui ressemble à ces rêves périodiques ou chroniquent qui assiègent regulièrement notre sommeil. C'est là ce qui marque le véritable artiste, toujours durable et vivace même dans ces œuvres fugitives, pour ainsi dire suspendues aux événements...[13]

LUNAR REFLECTIONS

Caprichos, caprices, capriciousness... The prose poems themselves thematise in the same terms the principle of capriciousness that Goya foregrounds in his work's title and which Diderot highlights in his epigraph quotation from Horace: 'Vertumnis quotquot sunt, natus iniquis' (*Le Neveu de Rameau*). In 'Les Bienfaits de la lune' the strategic platitude of the poem's opening words ('La Lune qui est le caprice même') draws attention to the poetics linking the whole collection of poems, a poetics which it shares intertextually with Goya's exceptional collection of engravings, with Diderot's equally anomalous satire, and with Sterne's hobby-horsical narrative. By asserting that the moon *is* capriciousness, the poem promotes it as the very emblem of the arabesque, the spiral, the leitmotif. At the same time, the emphasis in 'Les Bienfaits de la lune' on reflection ('le reflet de la redoutable divinité') serves as a reminder that in Western literature the moon has traditionally been associated with 'the poetry of mirrors', with reflexivity, with intertextuality and with the recognition of literary heritage. For as well as being a clichéd *topos* of love poetry, the moon, shining with the 'borrowed' light of the sun, is of course above all an image of reflection, and allusions to the moon as a mirror echo back at least as far as Lucan and Aristophanes.[14] In a work as 'hypertextual' as *Le Spleen de Paris* it comes as no surprise to find a 'lunar' motif prolonging echoes with other, earlier, self-conscious texts such as Sterne's *Tristram Shandy* and Bertrand's *Gaspard de la nuit*, which themselves offer tongue-in-cheek reworkings of the lunar *topos*. (The moon is cited in *Tristram Shandy* as the power behind the 'hobby-horse', whether it takes the form of Uncle Toby's gentle lunacy, the obsession with military fortification, or 'mad-cap' Tristram's[15] own wildly careering 'steed', the narrative progression itself. Tristram at one point dedicates his book to the moon, which he sees as having 'most power to set my work agoing, and to make the world run mad after it'.)[16]

In the period between 1857 and 1861 Baudelaire thought of entitling his emerging collection of prose poems *Poèmes nocturnes*.

This would undoubtedly have drawn attention to the thematic points of comparison with *Gaspard de la nuit*, the book which set Baudelaire a precedent in the genre, and whose allusions to night, to madness and to the black arts offer similarities with the *Petits Poèmes en prose*. In recent years, readings of Bertrand's work by Max Milner and Kathryn Slott[17] have done much to illuminate the interest and importance of *Gaspard de la nuit* and to further our understanding of why Baudelaire should have cited as a model a work at one time virtually excluded from the critical canon. However 'singulièrement différent' Baudelaire perceived his own collection of prose poetry to be, *Gaspard de la nuit* is nevertheless recalled, prominently, in the dedication to Arsène Houssaye which stands as a declaration of intent, a mysterious and esoteric poetics of the work that is to follow.

Bertrand's work is contrasted with Baudelaire's own collection because it is more 'pittoresque', less abstract. But thematically the parallels are obvious. At least thirty of the sixty-seven poems in Bertrand's text evoke a nocturnal atmosphere. As Max Milner has shown, a web of references to the nocturnal, to madness and to magic links such poems as 'Le Fou', 'Le Clair de lune', 'La Ronde sous la cloche', 'Les Gueux de nuit', 'La Cellule', 'Les Deux Juifs', and 'L'Ange et la fée'. More dramatically and memorably, *Gaspard de la nuit* presents *itself* as the madman's book of the last poem (dedicated to Sainte-Beuve and later to Nodier). With a movingly terse evocation of art as the madman's currency, a counter, or stake, in the game of life at which we are all ultimately losers, Bertrand concludes his work with the following lines:

L'homme est un balancier qui frappe sa monnaie à son coin. La quadruple porte l'empreinte de l'empereur, la médaille du pape, le jeton du fou.
 Je marque mon jeton à ce jeu de la vie où nous perdons coup sur coup et où le diable, pour en finir, râfle joueurs, dés, et tapis vert.
 L'empereur dicte des ordres à ses capitaines, le pape adresse des bulles à la chrétienté, et le fou écrit un livre.
 Mon livre, le voilà tel que je l'ai fait et tel qu'on doit le lire, avant que les commentateurs ne l'obscurcissent de leurs éclaircissements.

'Le Joueur généreux' and 'La Fausse Monnaie' can both be read as offering ironic reworkings of similar themes which foreground the monetary image and highlight its significance in the context of a modern capitalist society.

Gaspard de la nuit's disposition towards intertextuality, parody and self-parody has been the subject of detailed study by Kathryn Slott,[18] who suggests that Bertrand's 'Clair de lune' parodies a Romantic convention and that its title announces its filiation from such poems as Hugo's 'Clair de lune' in *Les Orientales* and Musset's 'Ballade à la lune' in *Contes d'Espagne et d'Italie*. A series of clichés in *Gaspard de la nuit* centres on the phrase 'La lune, grimant sa face... tir[e] sa langue comme un pendu!'

Another instance of the 'hypertextuality' of the lunacy motif is drawn attention to in 'Le Désir de peindre', when an allusion is made to Lucan's *Pharsalia*, linking it to the literary cliché of the 'soleil noir':

Elle est belle, et plus que belle; elle est surprenante. En elle le noir abonde: et tout ce qu'elle inspire est nocturne et profond... Je la comparerais à une soleil noir, si l'on pouvait concevoir un astre noir versant la lumière et le bonheur. Mais elle fait plus volontiers penser à la lune, qui sans doute l'a marquée de sa redoutable influence; non pas la lune blanche des idylles, qui ressemble à une froide mariée, mais la lune sinistre et enivrante, suspendue au fond d'une nuit orageuse et bousculée par les nuées qui courent; non pas la lune paisible et discrète visitant le sommeil des hommes purs, mais la lune arrachée du ciel, vaincue et révoltée, que les sorcières thessaliennes contraignent durement à danser sur l'herbe terrifiée! (*Oc* I, 340)

The allusion to Thessalian witches here recalls a passage in Book VI of the *Pharsalia* which describes magical rites and witchcraft in Thessaly, where the legendary King Ionos first smelted metal into ingots, and, by making it possible to count wealth, first led mankind into the evil of war. Lucan tells that it was there that witches 'brought down the stars from the swiftly-moving sky; and the clear moon, beset by dread incantations, grew dim and burned with a dark and earthy light'.[19] The passage directly precedes Lucan's dramatic account of Pompey's visit to the witch Erictho to request her prophecy of the outcome of the war. In 'Le Désir de peindre' the description of the artist's ideal subject in terms of a 'soleil noir' and the reference to Thessalian witches not only prepare the reader for the next poem, 'Les Bienfaits de la lune' with its celebration of a similar ideal of nocturnal beauty, but also, by recalling the necromantic powers of the witch Erictho, contribute to the theme of metamorphosis and magic associated with the powers of the artist in 'Les Foules' and 'Le Joueur généreux'. Had Baudelaire completed the planned prose poem 'Les Derniers Chants de Lucain' mentioned in his *Listes de projets*[20] the intertextual links between *Le Spleen de Paris* and the *Pharsalia* would undoubtedly have been more fully developed.

Clearly, Lucan and Aloysius Bertrand were very real presences for Baudelaire and for his more informed contemporaries, but doubtless more immediately apparent to the modern reader than the thematic echoes from such works as the *Pharsalia*, *Gaspard de la nuit*, the *Caprichos* or even *Le Neveu de Rameau* or *Tristram Shandy* are the reverberations within and between all the different poems in *Le Spleen de Paris* which explore the themes of capriciousness and lunacy. For example, the portrait of the poet as a worshipper of the principle of capriciousness ('Les Bienfaits de la lune') confirms the association between madness and creative fantasy already prominent in 'Le Crépuscule du soir'. A further poem, 'Le Thyrse', evokes both types of capriciousness by its use of the verb 'folâtrer':

Autour de ce bâton, dans des méandres capricieux, se jouent et folâtrent des tiges et des fleurs...

This movement of the flowers around the thyrsus wand is compared later in the poem to 'la promenade de votre fantaisie autour de votre volonté'. The subject addressed here is Liszt and the poem can be viewed on one level as a tribute to the musician's genius, but, as has often been observed, the description may also be read as referring to the composition of the prose poems themselves and to their own 'musical' structure.

In other words, by self-consciously combining the 'linearity' of the *moralité* with a capricious mobile potential for contingency and rhapsodic association, the poems, as we have seen, present themselves as offering a 'solution' to the problem of sententiousness and rectitude inherent in the ineluctable succession which characterises the novel. The 'volonté rétif' of the reader is respected, as the poet points out in the dedication. The reading of the prose poem is *not* an exercise in 'tutelage'.

The '*promenade* de la fantaisie', which appears in 'Le Thyrse' merely as a metaphor, is narrativised in 'L'Invitation au voyage', 'Les Projets', 'Un Hémisphère dans une chevelure' and 'Les Vocations' (where the bohemian life of 'vagabondage' is associated with the sort of gypsy music which would have appealed to Liszt). Again, the association of physical and imaginative travelling with madness and caprice in 'Les Vocations' is echoed in 'Les Bienfaits de la lune', where 'lunatiques' such as the poet–narrator are described as loving 'le lieu où ils ne sont pas'.

Madness, escapism or creativity? The poet-figures in *Le Spleen de Paris* are repeatedly associated with monstrosity, and with a social ostracism which is seen as a necessary corollary of the creative intensity of the individual imagination. A number of symptoms which were fundamental to the contemporary nineteenth-century perception and classification of insanity are clearly demonstrated.[21] The first of these is melancholia, often associated with the love of solitude ('La Solitude', 'A une heure du matin', 'Anywhere out of the World', 'Les Chimères'). A second is hysteria ('Le Mauvais Vitrier', 'Assommons les pauvres!', 'Le Vieux Saltimbanque'), and a third is satanism ('Le Joueur généreux', 'Le Joujou du pauvre', and the *Epilogue*). The poet's 'inévitable et impitoyable Muse' is also associated with madness, especially hysteria ('La Soupe et les nuages', 'Laquelle est la vraie?', 'Les Bienfaits de la lune').

The association between the 'lunatique' poet and the sea in 'Les Bienfaits de la lune' and 'Le Crépuscule du soir' recalls a traditional association between madness and water, and the description in 'Déjà!' evokes the powerful fifteenth-century image of the *Nef des fous*. Like 'Le Crépuscule du soir', 'Déjà!' also suggests that there is a necessary association between the poet's eccentricity, his social exclusion, and the infinite vitality of his solitary dialogue with beauty, the freedom of the private imagination which allows him to experience 'les humeurs, les agonies et les extases de toutes les âmes qui ont vécu, qui vivent et qui vivront!' Similarly, the knowledge of how to be *alone* in a busy crowd presents itself as the same prerequisite for the orgy of the imagination in 'Les Foules'.

The imaginary spectacle of the circus wild woman in 'La Femme sauvage et la petite-maîtresse' serves both as a representation of a historically familiar sight, the commercially exploited public display of madness, and as a *mise en abyme* of the poet-figure's sadistic relationship with the addressee. As we have seen, the poet-figure presents himself as the counterpart of 'the other monster', the brutal husband, and the inner spectacle provides an ironic dramatisation of his own sadism. In 'Mademoiselle Bistouri', the narrator-figure draws a still more explicit parallel between the prostitute's 'monstrous' condition and his own:

La ville fourmille de monstres innocents. – Seigneur, mon Dieu! Vous, le Créateur, vous la Maître, vous qui avez fait la Loi et la Liberté; vous le Souverain qui laissez faire, vous, le juge qui pardonnez; vous qui êtes pleins de motifs et de causes, et qui avez peut-être mis dans mon esprit le goût de l'horreur pour convertir mon coeur, comme la guérison au bout d'une lame; Seigneur, ayez pitié des fous et des folles! Ô Créateur! peut-il exister des monstres aux yeux de Celui-là seul qui sait pourquoi ils existent, comment ils *se sont faits* et comment ils auraient pu *ne pas se faire*? (*Oc* I, 355–6)

Another public display of 'madness', the last performance of the 'buffon' Fancioulle in 'Une Mort héroïque', is engineered by a *capricious* despot whose rule corresponds in some respects to that of the husband and poet in 'La Femme sauvage'. Here too the sadist is a 'monster':

les efforts bizarres qu'il faisait pour fuir ou pour vaincre ce tyran du monde (l'Ennui) lui auraient certainement attiré, de la part d'un historien sévère, l'epithète de 'monstre' (*Oc* I, 320)

In other words, the narrator-figure's periphrasis strategically draws attention to the presence of the leitmotif.

The poet of 'Le Crépuscule du soir' distances himself from the insane, whose minds are clouded by the advent of the night

Poetry and madness

('la nuit qui mettait ses ténèbres dans leur esprit, fait la lumière dans le mien') and he contrasts his own sanity with the behaviour of two of his friends. However, as we shall see in the next chapter, the 'mad' behaviour of the first friend is legitimised by analogy with another poem ('La Femme sauvage'). Also, the second madman is described in terms which call to mind a third poem, 'A une heure du matin', thereby encouraging the reader to regard that poem as illustrating a form of lunacy:

L'autre, un ambitieux blessé, devenait, à mesure que le jour baissait, plus aigre, plus sombre, plus taquin. Indulgent et sociable encore pendant la journée, il était impitoyable le soir; et ce n'était pas seulement sur autrui, mais aussi sur lui-même, que s'exerçait rageusement sa manie crépusculeuse.
(II) porte en lui l'inquiétude d'un malaise perpétuel, et fût-il gratifié de tous les honneurs que peuvent conférer les républiques et les princes, je crois que le crépuscule allumerait encore en lui la brûlante envie de distinctions imaginaires. ('Le Crépuscule du soir', I, 311–22)

Enfin! seul!... Enfin! la tyrannie de la face humaine a disparu, et je ne souffrirai plus que par moi-même. Enfin! il m'est donc permis de me délasser dans un bain de ténèbres!... Horrible vie! Horrible ville!... Mécontent de tous et mécontent de moi, je voudrais bien me racheter et m'enorgueillir un peu dans le silence et la solitude de la nuit. Ames de ceux que j'ai aimés, âmes de ceux que j'ai chantés, fortifiez-moi, soutenez-moi, éloignez de moi le mensonge et les vapeurs corruptrices du monde, et vous, Seigneur mon Dieu! accordez-moi la grace de produire quelques beaux vers qui me prouvent à moi-même que je ne suis pas le dernier des hommes, que je ne suis pas inférieur à ceux que je méprise! ('A une heure du matin', *Oc* I, 287–8)

The poet of 'Le Crépuscule', despite his disclaimer to the contrary, is associated with the 'lunatiques' by virtue of the fact that he belongs to the night rather than the day. Like the moon-worshippers of 'Les Bienfaits de la lune', and the poet of 'Le Désir de peindre', he is fascinated by the phenomenon of light in darkness. The natural effects of sunset and stars and the artificial phantasmagoria of the lights of a modern city ('explosion des lanternes...feu d'artifice de la déesse Liberté') are alike in that they provide an image of the imagination itself:

On dirait encore une de ces robes de danseuses, où une gaze transparente et sombre laisse entrevoir les splendeurs amorties d'une jupe éclatante, comme sous le noir présent transperce le délicieux passé; et les étoiles vacillantes d'or et d'argent dont elle est semée, représentent ces feux de la fantaisie qui ne s'allument bien que sous le deuil profond de la Nuit. (*Oc* I, 312)

BREAKING THE LAW: 'ASSOMMONS LES PAUVRES!' AND 'LE NEVEU DE RAMEAU'

As though presenting an ironic response, or counterpart, to the ambitions of the poet in 'A une heure du matin', whose prayer seems to illustrate the 'brûlante envie de distinctions imaginaires' of the madman described in 'Le Crépuscule du soir', a third poem, 'Assommons les pauvres!', reveals the poet-figure proudly laying claim to a 'brevet de folie' (the only honour which his republic can bestow on him). The poet of 'Assommons les pauvres!' self-consciously aligns himself with an intertextual portrait gallery of mad geniuses which includes Socrates:

j'entendis une voix qui chuchotait à mon oreille, une voix que je reconnus bien: c'était celle d'un bon Ange, ou d'un bon Démon, qui m'accompagne partout. Puisque Socrate avait son bon Démon, pourquoi n'aurais-je pas mon bon Ange, et pourquoi n'aurais-je pas l'honneur, comme Socrate, d'obtenir mon brevet de folie, signé du subtil Lélut et du bien avisé Baillarger? (*Oc* I, 358)

The allusion also calls to mind the words of Rameau's nephew, that other 'grand fou' who cites the case of Socrates and whose own madness is conditioned by social context, a 'brevet' awarded by a society which thereby indicts itself. The argument is the Nephew's own:

Celui qui serait sage n'aurait point de fou; celui donc qui a un fou n'est pas sage; s'il n'est pas sage, il est fou; et peut-être, fût-il roi, le fou de son fou.[22]

Although, as in the cases of 'Le Thyrse' and 'Le Joueur généreux', there is no explicitly acknowledged link with Diderot's text, 'Assommons les pauvres!' offers a number of parallels with a passage in *Le Neveu de Rameau* in which the social value of men of genius is debated. A further intertextual digression thus presents itself, and may briefly be examined here. The debate about madness in *Le Neveu de Rameau* is occasioned by the philosopher's enquiry about the nephew's relationship with his uncle Rameau, the famous musician. The discussion focusses on the problem of distinguishing between eccentricity, genius, and socially unacceptable deviance from the norm:

LUI
Il faut des hommes: mais pour des hommes de génie: point. Non, ma foi, il n'en faut point. Ce sont eux qui changent la face du globe... Si je savais l'histoire, je vous montrerais que le mal est toujours venu ici-bas par quelque homme de génie... J'étais un jour à la table d'un ministre du roi de France qui a de l'esprit comme quatre; eh bien, il nous démontra clair comme un et un font deux, que rien n'était plus utile aux peuples que le mensonge; rien de plus nuisible que la vérité... il s'ensuivait évidemment que les gens de génie sont détestables, et que si un enfant apportait en naissant, sur son front, la caractéristique de ce dangereux présent de la nature, il faudrait ou l'étouffer, ou le jeter au cagnard...

MOI
...Tout en convenant avec vous que les hommes de génie sont communément singuliers, ou comme dit le proverbe, qu'il n'y a pas de génie sans un grain de folie, on n'en reviendra pas. On méprisera les siècles qui n'en auront pas produit... L'homme de génie qui décrie une erreur générale, ou qui accrédite une grande vérité, est toujours digne de notre vénération. Il peut y arriver que cet être soit la victime du préjugé et des lois; mais il y a deux sortes de lois, les unes d'une équité, d'une généralité absolue; d'autres bizarres qui ne doivent leur sanction qu'à l'aveuglement des circonstances. Celles-ci ne couvrent le coupable qui les enfreint que d'une ignominie passagère; ignominie que le temps renverse sur les juges et sur les nations, pour y rester à jamais. De Socrate, ou du magistrat qui lui fit boire la ciguë, quel est aujourd'hui le déshonoré?[23]

In both 'Assommons les pauvres!' and the Diderot passage the example of Socrates serves as a model of misunderstood genius, and the concepts of madness and evil genius figure importantly in both texts. In the prose poem the reference to Socrates and his 'brevet de folie, signé du subtil Lélut et du bien-avisé Baillarger'[24] immediately precedes an account of the poet-figure's attack on an old beggar, an incident which illustrates the poet's own evil genius or 'madness', and which seems to suggest (like the description of the children in 'Le Joujou du pauvre') that the only real fraternity lies in the satanic equality of a shared sadism.

In Diderot's text the Philosopher manoeuvres his way uneasily around the unpalatable concept of evil genius. By contrast, the poet-figure in 'Assommons les pauvres!' defends the use of violence in humorously uncompromising terms. Diderot's Philosopher refuses to confront the problem fully and contents himself with referring to behaviour which is audacious and bizarre, but which is not completely at variance with conventional morality. Moreover it becomes apparent that his own bourgeois values, and, in particular, his assertion that there exist 'deux sortes de lois', allow him to tolerate relatively brutal social doctrines. This becomes clear in the course of the ensuing discussion about the social values of the man of genius as compared with the man of good sense. Throughout this discussion Rameau defends the conformist man of good sense, because he thinks that such a man has the potential to become a rich benefactor, and as a social parasite he values such individuals. Although his own defence of the man of genius runs counter to Rameau's argument, the Philosopher cannot find fault with the social contribution of the bourgeois man of good sense. However, with humorous innuendo regarding the Nephew's own 'parasitic' status, the philosopher makes the proviso that the shopkeeper would only be truly laudable if he were to free himself of parasites:

MOI
pourvu qu'il n'eût pas employé d'une façon déshonnête l'opulence qu'il aurait acquise par un commerce légitime; qu'il eût éloigné de sa maison tous ces joueurs; tous ces parasites; tous ces fades complaisants; tous ces fainéants, tous ces pervers inutiles; et qu'il eût fait assommer à coups de bâton, par ces garçons de boutique, l'homme officieux...[25]

The ugly side of bourgeois morality is revealed here, and Rameau does not allow the remark to pass unnoticed. His excited reaction to the idea that the parasite should be 'assommé à coups de bâton', and his amusing assertion that the law would not stand for it (a comment which of course reminds the reader of the Philosopher's preceding statement that there are two kinds of laws), all contribute to give emphasis to the passage:

LUI
Assommer! monsieur, assommer! on n'assomme personne dans une ville bien policée.[26]

A number of further parallels may be drawn. The slightly unusual choice of the verb 'assommer' in Diderot's passage may be compared with Baudelaire's use of the term in 'Assommons les pauvres!' Reference is made in the prose poem, as in the Diderot passage, to the agents of the law, thereby calling attention to the arbitrary, relativist character of the 'laying down of the law'. Baudelaire's poet–philosopher glances carefully around to ensure that no police officer is in the vicinity when he attempts to test the validity of his own social theories:

Je dois avouer que j'avais préalablement inspecté les environs d'une coup d'oeil, et que j'avais vérifié que dans cette banlieue déserte je me trouvais, pour un assez long temps, hors de la portée de tout agent de police. (*Oc* I, 359)

If one reads 'Assommons les pauvres!' in the light of Diderot's text, the attack on the social 'parasite' in the prose poem appears amusingly to belie Rameau's assertion that 'on n'assomme personne dans une ville bien policée', whilst at the same time, by a strategy of exaggeration, it brings into ridicule the legal double standard and the anti-parasite theories of the Philosopher.[27]

On one level, then, 'Assommons les pauvres!' can be read as a variation and development of the motif of evil genius already dramatised in 'Le Joueur généreux', a poem which Yoichi Sumi has shown constitutes a 'tribute' to *Le Neveu de Rameau*.[28] It can be seen to extend the play of intertextuality between the prose poems and *Le Neveu de Rameau* and to add a further dimension to that network of relations between Diderot's text and 'Le Thyrse' and 'Le Joueur généreux' (which has been cogently analysed by Yoichi Sumi). The association of the 'brevet de folie' with evil genius and with satanism allows the reader of 'Assommons les pauvres!' to embark on a dual process of digression which comprises the reconsideration of other poems in the collection and the intertextual reappraisal of Diderot's text. Whatever the complexity of this exercise in digression, it is intrinsic to the act of reading the prose poems. Here again, echoing Sterne's words in *Tristram Shandy*, one can say that the digression *is* the work itself ('Non enim excursus hic est, sed opus ipsum est').[29] 'Capricious' association is fundamental to the experience of this poetry, and it is no coincidence that both Baudelaire and Diderot depict the imaginative and creative impulse of the mind itself under the rule of capricious deities (Vertumnis in *Le Neveu de Rameau*, the moon goddess in *Le Spleen de Paris*).

Le Spleen de Paris situates itself, then, in the tradition of texts which themselves 'break the law', or interrogate the conventions of existing literary and philosophical genres. Like *Le Neveu de Rameau, Le Spleen de Paris* is a text which is *hors-série* and which calls into question the codes commonly operating in philosophical discourse and in the novel. In its problematising of the whole arena of 'laying down the law' it follows in the same radical and provocative tradition as *Le Neveu*. Again, like the Diderot text, it has a particular appeal for readers of our own postmodern era at a time when 'serious' literature has largely abandoned the quest to offer law-like explanations of human character and actions.

Madness or badness, *hystérie* or *satanisme*? The prose poems reopen the fundamental moral issues already addressed in Diderot's text. In a passage in 'Le Mauvais Vitrier' which is itself a provocative example of digression and of the subversion of narrative continuity (at a moment of mock suspense), the reader is invited to speculate as to the nature of the very lunacy and capriciousness which the digression itself ironically illustrates on the formal level of the discourse. The reader is reminded that the same mood which governs the capricious behaviour of the 'mad' sadist ('ivre de (sa) folie') also lies behind the 'esprit de mystification', or formal capriciousness, of the poet–narrator:

Un matin je m'étais levé maussade, triste, fatigué d'oisiveté, et poussé, me semblait-il, à faire quelque chose de grand, une action d'éclat; et j'ouvris la fenêtre, hélas!

(Observez, je vous prie, que l'esprit de mystification qui, chez quelques personnes, n'est pas le résultat d'un travail ou d'une combinaison, mais d'une inspiration fortuite, participe beaucoup, ne fût-ce par l'ardeur du désir, de cette humeur, hystérique selon les médecins, satanique selon ceux qui pensent un peu mieux que les médecins, qui nous pousse sans résistance vers une foule d'actions dangereuses ou inconvenantes.) (*Oc* I, 286)

The impulse to 'faire...une action d'éclat', which is here translated literally into the *mise en éclats* of the glazier's merchandise, recalls the 'brûlante envie de distinctions imaginaires' which is treated ironically in 'Le Crépuscule du soir' and 'Perte d'auréole'. It also echoes the lyrical effusion in 'A une heure du matin', and the thirst for distinction which encourages the poet-figure in 'Assommons les pauvres!' to listen to his 'bon Démon' and undertake an action which will earn him, like Socrates, a 'brevet', even if it is only a 'brevet de folie'. If the dividing line between madness and badness is in question, then once one of these terms is invalidated, or appears only as a warrant accorded by society to the exceptional individual who deviates from an arbitrary code, the other term is made problematic as well.

Who decides the laws which determine good and evil, sanity and insanity? The question raised by Diderot's Philosopher when he argues that there are two types of laws, the good ones (with which one agrees) and the bad ones (with which one disagrees), remains a vital issue in *Le Spleen de Paris*. Are such categories as madness and monstrosity God-given, or are they merely the markers of deviance from the community and the codes and conventions which unite and define it? In a profoundly challenging conclusion to 'Mademoiselle Bistouri', the poet-figure, after recalling that God is supposedly the creator, law-giver and judge, 'pleins de motifs et de causes', questions the bases of moral judgement and conventional psychology:

O Créateur! peut-il exister des monstres aux yeux de Celui-là seul qui sait pourquoi ils existent, comment ils *se sont faits* et comment ils auraient pu *ne pas se faire*? (*Oc* I, 356)

Baudelaire's 'moralité' here appears to subvert and to expose the conventions of the genre itself, rather in the same way that the prose poems serve, as Barbara Johnson has shown, to interrogate the poetics of *Les Fleurs de mal*, and explicitly to reflect on the functioning of poetic language itself.

One is tempted to add as a postscript that, given the nature of the 'lunacy' motif in the *Petits Poèmes en prose*, it is not without a sense of irony that one notes the popularity of critical studies on the theme *Baudelaire malade*, *La Folie de Charles Baudelaire*, *La Maladie de Baudelaire*, and so on. The poet's own acquisition of a 'brevet de folie' was astutely predicted, as literary history has borne witness.

1 Goya, *Capricho* 43: 'The sleep of reason produces monsters.'
La fantasia abandonada de la razon, produce monstruos imposibles: unida con ella, es madre de las artes y origen de sus marabillas.
Imagination abandoned by reason produces impossible monsters: united with her, she is the mother of the arts and the source of their wonders.

2 Goya, *Capricho* 37: 'Might not the pupil know more?'
No se sabe si sabra mas ō menos lo cierto es qᵉ. el maestro es el personage mas grabe qᵉ. se ha podido encontrar.
One cannot say whether he knows more or less; what is certain is that the master is the most serious-looking person who could possibly be found.

3   Goya, *Capricho* 38: 'Bravo!'
Si para entenderlo bastan las orejas nadie habra mas intelligente; pero es de temer q.ᵉ aplauda lo q.ᵉ no suena.
If ears were all that were needed to appreciate it, no one could listen more intelligently; but it is to be feared that he is applauding what is soundless.

De que mal morira?

4 Goya, *Capricho* 40: 'of what ill will he die?'
El medico es excel.^{te} meditabundo, reflexibo, pausado serio. Que mas hay q.^{e} pedir?
The doctor is excellent, pensive, considerate, calm, serious. What more can one ask for?

5 Goya, *Capricho* 41: 'Neither more nor less.'
Hace muy bien en retratarse: asi sabran quien es los q.ᵉ no le conozcan ni ayan visto.
He is quite right to have his portrait painted: thus those who do not know
him and have not seen him will know who he is.

6 Goya, *Capricho* 42: 'Thou who canst not.'
Quien no dira que estos dos caballeros son caballerias?
Who could not say that these two cavaliers are cavalry (riding beasts)?

7 Goya, *Capricho* 63: 'Look how solemn they are!'
La estampa indica q.ᵉ estos son dos brujos de conbeniencias y autor.ᵈ q.ᵉ han salido à hacer un poco de exercicio a caballo.
The print shows that these are two witches of means and position who have gone out to take a little exercise on horseback.

CHAPTER 6

Poetic cookery

Vous pouvez vivre trois jours sans pain;...sans poésie, jamais...
Salon de 1846

Digressions, incontestably, are the sunshine; – they are the life, the soul of reading... all the dexterity is in the good cookery and management of them.
Sterne, *Tristram Shandy*

Un valet, se levant le chapeau de la teste,

Nous vint dire tout haut que la souppe estoit preste

Je cogneu qu'il est vray ce qu'Homère en escrit,

Qu'il n'est rien qui si fort nous resveille l'esprit;

Car j'eus, au son des piats, l'âme plus altéré,

Que ne l'auroit un chien au son de la curée.
Maturin Régnier, *Satyre x: Le Souper ridicule*[1]

There is a puzzling passage in 'Le Crépuscule du soir' in which the poet describes the effect which twilight produces on madmen, and in which he compares the system of thought of one insane or *lunatique* 'friend' of his to hieroglyphic writing, that is writing which is secret or enigmatic, difficult to make out:

Le crépuscule excite les fous. – Je me souviens que j'ai eu deux amis que le crépuscule rendait tout malades. L'un méconnaissait alors tous les rapports d'amitié et de politesse, et maltraitait, comme un sauvage, le premier venu. Je l'ai vu jeter à la tête d'un maître d'hotel un excellent poulet, dans lequel il croyait voir je ne sais quel insultant hiéroglyphe. Le soir, précurseur des voluptés profondes, lui gâtait les choses les plus succulentes. (*Oc* I, 311)

Two types of pleasure and desire are compared here: the satisfaction of the gourmet, and the 'voluptés profondes' associated with the night itself. Even when reading the isolated poem the reader is encouraged to associate nocturnal 'voluptés' with the activity of the poetic imagination, the 'fête intérieure' evoked later in the poem. But it is only when the poem is read in the light of the surrounding collection that one is fully sensitised to the fact that the pleasures of the flesh, however 'excellent' or well cooked the cuisine, are presented as degraded, even disgusting, by comparison with the imaginative elixir associated with the night and with poetic inspiration. Symbolising the arousal of those appetites which attach the poet to the earth and distract him from the realm of the imagination, the invitation to consume an excellent chicken allows itself to be interpreted by the reader of the larger poetic unit, as by the poet's 'friend', as an insult. The reader is manipulated into this position by the logic of the collection as a whole, and encouraged to recognise a radical and disturbing affinity between the arcane processes of paradigmatic association inherent in reading poetry and the 'lunatique' and whimsical mental processes of the insane.[2] How does this come about? Let us pursue for a moment the capricious movements of association which seem to be invited by the insulting hieroglyph of the restaurant chicken.

In 'L'Invitation au voyage' the poet evokes for his 'vieille amie' a paradisal land which can boast, amongst other delights, a 'cuisine...poétique' which resembles the addressee, being both 'grasse et excitante à la fois'. The analogy constitutes a departure from the preceding clichéd description of the 'pays de rêve' and there is a momentary suggestion of irony. If the 'vieille amie' is interpreted as being the poet's mistress, the vulgar comparison of that mistress to a 'cuisine...grasse et excitante à la fois' upsets all conventional expectations of gallant love poetry. However, the addressee of 'L'Invitation au voyage' invites comparison with another 'vieille amie' or 'excitante' described in 'La Chambre double': 'la fiole de laudanum; une vieille et terrible amie'. Later in 'L'Invitation au voyage' the poet compares the different forms of 'rêverie' which the reader may associate with the two poems (the naturally induced mental journey and the artificial one):

Des rêves: toujours des rêves! et plus l'âme est ambitieuse et délicate, plus les rêves l'éloignent du possible. Chaque homme porte en lui sa dose d'opium naturel.

The comparison between 'vieille amie' and 'cuisine', as well as suggesting a comparison between poetry and drugs, particularly focusses the reader's attention on the unusual association of the two words 'cuisine' and 'poétique'. A second culinary reference later in the poem acts as a mnemonic trigger reinforcing the first: the paradisal land, whose superiority is like that of Art over Nature, is described as 'riche, propre et luisant...comme une magnifique batterie de cuisine'. This repeated association between poetry and cookery has brought a mixed response from Baudelaire's critics, ranging from Suzanne Bernard's scornful 'Eh quoi! c'était tout cela, le rêve de beauté voluptueuse de Baudelaire. Une vie confortable et tranquille, une cuisine "grasse et excitante"!' to Barbara Johnson's comment that such culinary images illustrate 'l'incursion du code romanesque dans un contexte "poétique"', demonstrating the 'lutte de codes' which characterises prose poetry as a genre.[3]

However, ingestion is of course a time-honoured self-reflexive *topos*, and the references to food in the prose poems remind us that *Le Spleen de Paris* owes as much to its associations with prose precedents such as Cervantes' *Chien Berganza* or *The Golden Ass* of Apuleius as to its self-differentiation from conventional lyric poetry. The echoes between different poems within the *Spleen de Paris* collection are anyway richly suggestive, even if we leave aside for the moment the intertextual resonances with other works. The association between poetry and food recurs several times in such poems as 'Le Chien et le flacon', 'Le Gâteau', 'Le Crépuscule du soir', 'Assommons les pauvres!', 'Les Tentations' and 'La Soupe et les nuages'. The forms of appropriation which are involved fall into two contrasting categories which may be crudely summarised as 'poetic' or superior, and 'anti-poetic' or degraded.

'Assommons les pauvres!', for example, opens with a reference to a degraded category of cuisine associated with inferior literature, the work of naive moralists who ignore the complexity of life and who believe in universal panaceas. The poet–narrator describes how he spent a fortnight absorbed in reading these treatises only to find that, like badly cooked food, they might be swallowed but were indigestible:

Pendant quinze jours je m'étais confiné dans ma chambre, et je m'étais entouré des livres à la mode dans ce temps-la (il y a seize ou dix-sept ans); je veux parler des livres ou il est traité de l'art de rendre les peuples heureux, sages et riches, en vingt-quatre heures. J'avais donc digéré, – avalé, veux-je dire, toutes les élucubrations de tous ces entrepreneurs de bonheur public (*Oc* I, 357)

When, later in the poem, the narrator-figure reveals his own moral philosophy, the reader is predisposed to be on the alert for ironic innuendo. Describing his own master-remedy for human suffering and poverty, the narrator assumes the guise of a conscientious philosopher chef who is bent on rendering his dish tender and appetising, and he describes the 'medication' which he applies to a beggar as follows:

je me saisis d'une grosse branche d'arbre qui traînait à terre, et je le battis *avec l'énérgie obstinée des cuisiniers qui veulent attendrir un beefsteak* (*Oc* I, 359; my italics)

This gastronomic comparison, by bringing to mind the earlier reference to indigestible literature, puts the stooge narrator's punitive sententiousness into a ridiculous light whilst at the same time it seems to parody the culinary symbolism which one finds elsewhere in the collection. As we saw earlier, far from seriously advocating the thrashing of the poor, as over-hasty readers have often mistakenly suggested, the poem is here parodying a specific genre of hypocritical cure-all *moralité* with its naive recipes for solving human problems.[4]

In 'Perte d'auréole', aggression towards inferior poets is tempered with self-mockery, with the poet-figure being dubbed, again in gastronomic terms: 'le buveur de quintessences, le mangeur d'ambroisie'. But the irony takes a more savage turn in 'Le Chien et le flacon', where bad literature is equated with a 'paquet d'excrément', the favourite diet of the poet's dog, and, by association, of the undiscriminating public.

Although in 'Assommons les pauvres!' bad cookery is associated with inferior literature, this is not the case in all the poems. In some, a degraded form of alimentation suggests a carnal dimension which contrasts with the spiritual realm of poetry. This is true, of course, of the example we have already looked at, of the excellent chicken in 'Le Crépuscule du soir'. But also two very similar passages in 'Le Gâteau' and 'Le Joujou du pauvre' prolong the comparison between the two categories of 'cuisine'. In 'Le Gâteau' the poet–narrator finds himself in a land neighbouring the clouds, a landscape which, besides ironically recalling a Rousseauist ideal, also echoes the escapist aerial dream evoked in 'L'Etranger', 'La Soupe et les nuages' and 'Les Vocations'.[5] As in the case of 'La Soupe et les nuages' the poem oscillates between two poles: the poetic or ethereal and the carnal, here the alpine utopia and the fratricidal battle over a piece of bread. The description of the seizing of the poet's bread by the 'petit sauvage' invites comparison with a similar passage in 'Le Joujou du pauvre', where the poet-figure describes the reaction which the reader might observe were he or she to offer toys to the children of the poor:

Et je l'entendis soupirer, d'une voix basse et rauque, le mot: gâteau! Je ne pus m'empêcher de rire en entendant l'appellation dont on voulait bien honorer mon pain presque blanc, et j'en coupai pour lui une belle tranche que je lui offris. Lentement il se rapprocha, ne quittant plus des yeux l'objet de sa convoitise; puis, happant le morceau avec sa main, se recula vivement, comme s'il eût craint que mon offre ne fut pas sincère ou que je n'en repentisse déjà. ('Le Gâteau', *Oc* I, 298)

Vous verrez leurs yeux s'agrandir démesurément. D'abord ils n'oseront pas prendre; ils douteront de leur bonheur. Puis leurs mains agripperont vivement le cadeau, et ils s'enfuiront comme font les chats qui vont manger loin de vous le morceau que vous leur avez donné, ayant appris à se défier de l'homme. ('Le Joujou du pauvre', *Oc* 1, 304)

In both passages there is a repetition of the same initial gesture (the seizing of the 'gâteau' and the seizing of the 'cadeau'), and both are accompanied by an identical movement of flight and mistrustful caution. In both there is an allusion to food (in the first, the child seizing the bread, in the second the reference to cats when they are given scraps). The toy, one infers, would feed the child's imagination just as the 'cake' would satisfy the physical appetite of the small savage. Comparison of the two commodities is encouraged by their phonetic similarity: 'cadeau', 'gâteau'. The description of the little savage's voice ('basse et rauque') suggests that the word which the narrator takes as being 'gâteau' can be interpreted as a phonetically corrupted version of 'cadeau'.[6] A symbolic dichotomy becomes apparent when the conclusions of the two poems are compared, for whilst the 'gâteau' of the first poem 'suffit pour engendrer une guerre parfaitement fratricide', the 'cadeau' of the second poem, which is given to the poor child by his parents, unites the two children in fraternal, if sadistic, delight. Whilst the toy, the 'poetic' sustenance, appears as a commodity which can be endlessly shared and never exhausted, the carnal food, symbolised by the cake, appears as a source of strife, for it can only be consumed once and all are eager to have as much as possible of the limited stock.

An equally conspicuous reference to eating in 'Les Tentations' further extends the play of associations. The second devil spurned by the poet-figure in this poem is the glutton Plutus, whose distorted belly is illustrated with images of human deprivation and suffering, and when the glutton slaps his stomach he provokes a metallic rattle which finishes in the vague moaning of many human voices. There are echoes of Goya's *Cronos Devouring his Children*, but in a much lighter vein. Certainly, Gluttony has here become a symbol of all forms of materialism, and in an inversion of the clichéd contemporary usage which is highlighted in other poems, *sauvagerie* (here cannibalism) is identified with the dominant ideology of the day.

A less conspicuous reference to ingestion in 'Les Yeux des pauvres' further broadens the network of allusions. In this poem the cheap splendour of a new cafe dazzles the impoverished trio who contemplate it from the evening darkness of the street outside. Immediately, the detailed description of the cafe implies a judgement on the 'civilisation' it represents, just as Poe's description of American interiors in *The Philosophy of Furniture* had revealed the corruption of taste associated with the dollar-manufacture (see Baudelaire's *Présentation de Philosophie d'ameublement*).[7] The shiny gilt ornamentation inspired by Classical mythology and the clichéd images of a more graceful aristocratic past provoke a wry comment on the fate of culture in the new Paris: 'toute l'histoire et tout la mythologie mises au service de la goinfrerie'.

However, in other poems the references suggest a duality which is more timeless and fundamental and which goes beyond a limited reaction to local historical circumstance. For example, a degraded form of food is frequently associated in the *Petits Poèmes* with women, and in such instances women represent everything that is natural, instinctive and bestial in humanity. This is particularly true of the references to young women, whose sexual attractiveness makes them a threat to the poet questing less earthly pleasures. The references to older women often provide a contrast, suggesting that it is not the female sex as such which is antipathetic so much as the type of desire provoked by young women. In 'La Femme sauvage et la petite-maîtresse', for example, the opening references to deprived and hungry old women, 'les glaneuses sexagénaires' and the 'vieilles mendiantes', recall the sympathy for the poor expressed or implied in 'Les Yeux des pauvres', 'Le Gâteau' and 'Les Tentations', where the extravagances of the few are shown to depend on the exclusion of the many. Old women are placed in a different category from the sensual younger women. Their experience of 'l'indispensable douleur', 'la fertilisante douleur'[8] (described in 'Le Désespoir de la vieille' and in 'Les Veuves'), enables them to accede to the realm of 'rêverie', and for this reason they are associated with the poor and with the poet.

In 'Les Veuves', for example, the solitary widow whose physical desires are poorly satisfied, lunching miserably in some third-rate café, is animated by the private and powerful interest of her reading material:

Je ne sais dans quel misérable café et de quelle façon elle déjeuna. Je la suivis au cabinet de lecture; et je l'épiai longtemps pendant qu'elle cherchait dans les gazettes, avec des yeux actifs, jadis brûlés par les larmes, des nouvelles d'un intérêt puissant et personnel. (*Oc* I, 293)

Even if her reading-matter, like her mourning-dress, reflects 'une absence d'harmonie qui le rend plus navrant', the widow's capacity to 'peupler sa solitude' suggests that she belongs to a special category. The two forms of ingestion, eating and reading, are conspicuously contrasted here. On the other hand, the poet–narrator of 'La Femme sauvage et la petite-maîtresse' reproaches his well-fed mistress in the following terms:

on dirait, à vous entendre soupirer, que vous souffrez plus que les glaneuses sexagénaires et que les vieilles mendiantes qui ramassent des croûtes de pain à la porte des cabarets... vous qui... ne mangez que de la viande cuite, et pour qui un domestique habile prende soin de découper les morceaux... (*Oc* I, 289)

As we have seen, in the course of the poem this mistress comes to be associated with the fairground wild woman her lover takes her to observe. The paradigmatic organisation of the prose poems is such that the repugnant account of this woman's animalistic consumption of living fowl in 'La Femme sauvage' can contribute to the reader's interpretation of the insulting hieroglyph in 'Le Crépuscule du soir'. Reading across the two poems, one is aware that the refined restaurant-goer who enjoys an excellent chicken resembles the 'petite-maîtresse' who eats only cooked meat skilfully carved by a servant; both can be associated with the 'monstre poilu', the caged woman of the fairground. The bizarre reaction of the poet's friend at the sight of the chicken, inexplicable in terms of conventional bourgeois reasoning and appearing as a sign of lunacy, can be seen in the context of the network of associations which link the different poems to conform to a consistent poetic logic.

The resemblance between 'petite-maîtresse' and 'femme sauvage' is underscored in a later poem, 'Portraits de maîtresses', by an anecdote about an astonishing woman who consumed food at such a rate that her ex-lover reflects:

J'y aurais pu faire ma fortune en la montrant dans les foires comme *monstre polyphage*.

The expression 'monstre polyphage' alerts the attentive reader to the parallel between 'Portraits de maîtresses' and 'La Femme sauvage et la petite-maîtresse'. The 'phénomène vivante' of 'Portraits de maîtresses' brings together the characteristics of the two women in the earlier poem. Like the wild woman, 'elle mangeait, mâchait, broyait, dévorait, engloutissait...', and like the girlfriend, 'elle avait une manière douce, rêveuse, anglaise et romanesque'. Moreover, her lover's ability at conjuring up for her special supplies of food 'par quelque tour de bâton à lui connu' may remind the reader of the husband of 'La Femme sauvage' and his sadistic 'tours de bâton'. The figure of speech of one poem becomes the extended narrative of another.[9] In both poems the associations between ingestion and sexual receptiveness are flagrantly and humorously underscored.

Not all the descriptions of young women in the poems involve a negative association with an inferior sustenance. In poems such as 'L'Invitation au voyage' and 'Un Hémisphère dans une chevelure' the woman is celebrated as a source of poetic inspiration rather than a distraction from poetry, although as we have seen with the description of the 'cuisine poétique' and the 'magnifique batterie de cuisine' in 'L'Invitation au voyage' the culinary comparisons here too draw attention to themselves by their incongruity in the context of what might at first sight pass as a traditional exercise in gallant love poetry. The imaginative appropriation of not just the woman but the whole world of associations which she triggers is prized as a higher goal than the 'natural' objective of writing gallant poetry as a means towards achieving her physical seduction.

In 'La Belle Dorothée', on the other hand, the description of cooking seems less to echo the association between ingestion and sexuality than to draw attention to the artistry of a civilisation deemed primitive by Europeans. The attractive description of the interior of Dorothée's cabin contrasts with the account of the slum dwelling of a European prostitute like Mademoiselle Bistouri, whilst the description of Dorothée's exotic ragoût of crab and saffron rice offers itself for comparison with the description of the saltimbank's broth in 'Les Bons Chiens'. The contrasting contexts of these two examples of 'cuisine poétique' reflect ironically on the situation of beauty and art in Western civilisation.

In 'Un Hémisphère dans une chevelure' the poet concludes the address to his lover as follows:

Laisse-moi mordre longtemps tes tresses lourdes et noires. Quand je mordille tes cheveux élastiques et rebelles, il me semble que je mange des souvenirs. (*Oc* I, 301)

The statement, as Barbara Johnson has observed in her excellent meditation on the nature of poetic language (*Défigurations du langage poétique*), violates the reader's conditioned expectations of traditional lyric poetry.[10] The blunt, unmediated juxtaposition of the concrete verb 'manger' and the abstract noun 'souvenirs' is perceived by the reader as anomalous, and it has provoked a number of extreme, and often conflicting, reactions from critics. Whether or not we read the poem as Johnson proposes as 'une lecture déconstructrice' of the verse 'Chevelure', it is plain that this particularly conspicuous association of poetic inspiration ('des souvenirs') with ingestion ('je mordille', 'je mange') acts as an encouragement to situate it in the context of the other allusions to ingestion which proliferate in the wider collection. More than just gesturing to the other 'Chevelure' poem in a self-conscious affirmation of its own 'anatomical' difference, 'Un Hémisphère' is also vitally enriched by its contextual relationship with the rest of *Le Spleen de Paris*.

Whereas in 'Un Hémisphère' a superior form of ingestion or appropriation is linked with the wanderings of imaginative association dependent on memory, in 'La Soupe et les nuages', conversely, food is associated with the material world and stands in antithesis to the phantasmagoria which absorbs the poet. As in 'Le Gâteau' the oscillation in 'La Soupe et les nuages' between the spiritual and the secular is associated with violence and with a reaction of shock on the part of the poet-figure ('tout à coup je reçus un violent coup de poing dans le dos').

The last poem in the collection, 'Les Bons Chiens', lends concluding emphasis to the *topos* of 'ingestion'. An opening invocation to Sterne, and the mention of an incident from *Tristram Shandy* involving Tristram's benevolent gesture of offering a macaroon to an ass, prepares the reader for further reference to charity meals later in the poem. It is soon revealed that some of the 'chiens calamiteux' celebrated by the poet sup at the doors of a Palais-Royal kitchen, whilst others eat food provided by old women. But, the poet insists, the most 'civilisé' enjoy the 'soupe puissante et solide' prepared in the room of a saltimbank. In Sterne's novel Tristram's relationship with the ass parodies the relationship between the narrator and the reader, as Baudelaire clearly acknowledges in a reference to *Tristram Shandy* in *Le Salon de 1859* when he draws attention to a painting by Legros which depicts the awkwardness of a poor child as he tastes in God's temple the wonders of an otherworldly realm. The child reminds the poet of Sterne's ass, and he associates these two examples of an artist depicting the act of reception of a superior or spiritual 'food':

> Par une association mystérieuse que les esprits délicats comprendront, l'enfant grotesquement habillé qui tortille avec gaucherie sa casquette dans le temple de Dieu, m'a fait penser à *l'âne de Sterne et à ses macarons*. Que l'âne soit comique en mangeant un gâteau, cela ne diminue rien de la sensation d'attendrissement qu'on éprouve en voyant le misérable esclave de la ferme cueillir quelques douceurs dans la main d'un philosophe. Ainsi, l'enfant du pauvre, tout embarrassé de sa contenance, goûte, en tremblant, aux confitures célestes. (*Oc* II, 630)

But whereas in *Tristram Shandy* it is the narrator-figure himself who feeds the ass, in 'Les Bons Chiens' the benefactor is absent from the scene. The saltimbank is absent and the culinary masterpiece is termed '*l'œuvre sans nom*': both are mysterious. On another occasion in *Le Spleen de Paris* the narrator of 'Le

Vieux Saltimbanque' compares a saltimbank to a man of letters who has outlived success and who is left destitute. The absent saltimbank of 'Les Bons Chiens' thus indirectly invites association with the implied author of the prose poems: eternally elusive and beyond reach. If we make a connection between the two poems it may appear that the miserable hut to which we have been denied access in 'Le Vieux Saltimbanque' is thrown open to us in 'Les Bons Chiens'.

'Le Vieux Saltimbanque' is not the only other poem in the collection which can influence our reading of 'Les Bons Chiens'. The description in this last poem of the 'soupe puissante' also invites comparison with 'La Soupe et les nuages', as well as recalling fleetingly the maritime imagery of 'Le Port' and 'L'Invitation au voyage':

Mais regardez... ces deux personnages intelligents... qui surveillent, avec une attention de sorciers, *l'oeuvre sans nom* qui mitonne sur le poêle allumeé, et au centre de laquelle une longue cuillère se dresse, plantée comme un de ces mâts aériens qui annoncent que la maçonnerie est achevée. (*Oc* I, 362)

The motif of both clouds and architecture links 'Le Port' and 'La Soupe et les nuages', whilst allusions to architecture and soup are common to both 'La Soupe et les nuages' and 'Les Bons Chiens'. The spoon is compared to 'un de ces mâts aériens' and the adjective 'aériens' suggests that the masts penetrate high into the sky, or neighbour the clouds, those 'merveilleuses constructions de l'impalpable', which are also described in 'La Soupe et les nuages' as 'les mouvantes architectures que Dieu fait avec les vapeurs'. But whereas in 'La Soupe et les nuages' the architectural metaphor stands in antithesis to the soup, the degraded cuisine served up by the poet's mistress, in 'Les Bons Chiens' the soup is equated with the 'maçonnerie': 'maçonnerie' again suggesting architecture and the construction of an important edifice, but also signifying the combining and articulating of a number of varied elements (echoing the Dedication to Arsène Houssaye with its emphasis on 'combinaison'). Also the conspiratorial associations of the term 'maçonnerie', the suggestion of a secret understanding between people of like interests, reinforces the impression already made on the reader by their clandestine introduction into the absent saltimbank's room. An aura of mystery surrounds the episode, encouraging the reader to interpret it as a model of their own relationship with the esoteric text itself.

The dog sorcerers seem to have much in common with the poet, but the sorcery can be taken as applying as much to the imaginative recreation of the text as to its original composition.[11] The 'bad' dogs already dismissed by the poet earlier in the poem provide an indication of the possible identity of the *good* dogs, that is, the poor *flâneurs* that the poet surveys with a 'fraternal' eye. There is the dog which is too lively, 'turbulent comme un enfant', recalling the child who accompanies the lonely widow in 'Les Veuves' and who cannot serve as a confidant, 'car l'enfant est turbulent, égoiste...et il ne peut même pas, comme le pur animal, comme le chien et le chat, servir de confident aux douleurs solitaires' (*Oc* I, 294). Then there is the type of dog which is described as a four-legged serpent, the type of dog which is unintelligent and which cannot follow a friend's trail, '[ceux] qui ne logent même pas dans leur museau pointu assez de flair pour suivre le piste d'un ami, ni dans leur tête aplatie assez d'intelligence pour jouer au domino'. By implication it would seem that the 'good' dogs will serve as confidants and will be adept at following a friend's trail, however sinuous and digressive it may be. However, readers, like dogs, have a rough time in *Le Spleen de Paris* if they come to the text expecting facile morality and attractive bouquets. One remembers the savage and complex aside in the opening lines of the moral fable 'La Fausse Monnaie':

> Nous fîmes le rencontre d'un pauvre qui nous tendit sa casquette en tremblant. – Je ne connais rien de plus inquiétant que l'éloquence muette de ces yeux suppliants, qui contiennent à la fois, pour l'homme sensible que sait y lire, tant d'humilité, tant de reproches. Il y trouve quelque chose approchant cette profondeur de sentiment compliqué, dans les yeux larmoyants des chiens qu'on fouette.

– lines which in their turn call to mind the poem 'Le Chien et le flacon' and the conflicting tastes which some dogs/readers might bring to the poet's offering. For the general public, we are reminded, should never be presented with 'des parfums délicats qui l'exaspèrent, mais des ordures soigneusement choisies'. A parcel of excrement would be more to their taste. However, the 'good' dogs of the last poem have a more discerning palate. They concentrate all their attention on the simmering broth and hope to consume some of it. The reader understands that it has been prepared by the shadowy 'saltimbanque': 'saltimbanque' signifying 'showman' or 'acrobat', but also, in colloquial terms, 'charlatan' or 'trickster', that is to say a spiritual brother to Laurence Sterne, lauded earlier in the poem as a 'sentimental farceur, farceur incomparable'.

The '*œuvre sans nom*' which simmers on the saltimbank's stove is open to being read as a metaphor for the *Petits Poèmes en prose* themselves, the ultimate example of poetic cookery. The metaphoric indirection seems to be acknowledged in the expression itself: '*œuvre sans nom*', an extraordinary or unspeakable work, but also an unnamed or deliberately anonymous work, one whose identity the reader has to deduce. Read in this light, the spoon mast appears as a metaphoric beacon, announcing that the dish is perfectly cooked, the edifice completed, and the secret, quasi-masonic understanding between poet and reader is at an end. Of all the prose poems it is arguable that 'Les Bons Chiens' alone must be read in the order of presentation, at the end of the collection.[12] But the end of the poem, and of the collection, is not a moment of closure: by sending the reader back to earlier references to alimentation elsewhere in *Le Spleen de Paris*, the saltimbank's broth illustrates well the 'retroactive' forces operating throughout the collection. From broth or soup to macaroon, to cake, to ambrosia, to beefsteak, to excrement, to restaurant chicken – we are continually reminded that this *hotch-potch* of a collection is one in which 'tout est à la fois tête et queue'.

Ingestion, appropriation and self-aggrandisement. All have been seen as manifestations of Eros or the driving force of Desire, which can be viewed as powering the hunger for food, for sex and for that poetic *totalising* of experience which allows the kaleidoscopic concentration of *Le Spleen de Paris* to claim a rivalry with *La Comédie humaine* ('cela vaut mieux qu'une intrigue de 6,000 pages').[13] It is the jewel-like compactness and density of the inter-reflections (or digressions) between its constituent parts which made this possible. This 'cuisine poétique' is indeed also a 'bijouterie bariolée'.

But not only can *Le Spleen de Paris* be seen as presenting itself, as in 'Les Bons Chiens', as a delicious soup, an *œuvre-aliment*, it also situates itself more ironically as an *œuvre alimentaire* or *pot-boiler*, just another form of merchandise in the insatiable market-place of a consumerist society. The further thematising of this mercantilist ethos will be illustrated in the next chapter.

CHAPTER 7

The poet as savage: rewriting cliché

> Laissez les génies tranquilles dans leur originalité. Il y a du sauvage dans ces civilisateurs mystérieux. Même dans leur comédie, même dans leur bouffonnerie, même dans leur rire, même dans leur sourire, il y a de l'inconnu.
>
> Hugo, *William Shakespeare*

In the last chapter I drew attention to the passage in 'Le Crépuscule du soir' about a character who is so excited by the approach of the night that he is described as being sick, or insane. His madness is illustrated by the fact that he once rejected a fine chicken brought to him in a restaurant. The behaviour of this man is paradigmatically legitimised by the anecdote of 'La Femme sauvage et la petite-maîtresse', in which even the most refined bourgeois meat-eater is equated with the carnivorous 'wild woman' who tears apart squawking fowl with her bare teeth. The chicken in 'Le Crépuscule du soir' is open to interpretation as a 'hieroglyph', then, not only by the madman but also by the reader, whose attention is likely to be attracted by this allusion to a form of writing whose enigmatic character resembles that of the text they are reading.

The narrator describes the 'madman' of his story using a clichéd figure of speech: 'il méconnaissait... tous les rapports d'amitié et de politesse, et maltraitait, *comme un sauvage*, le premier venu' (my italics). The word 'sauvage' might easily pass unnoticed, but if readers remember 'La Femme sauvage et la petite-maîtresse', they may be struck by the fact that the gesture which earns the man this epithet is precisely what distinguishes him from the 'femme sauvage' of the earlier poem. The irony is only apparent when the poem is considered retrospectively in the wider context of the whole collection where both 'sauvagerie' and madness seem to offer themselves as types of social ungrammaticality which invite a hermeneutic or metaphorical reading.

With the word 'sauvage' the reader is confronted with a cliché whose meaning becomes increasingly problematic. A situation is created in which, paradoxically, every time the stereotype recurs in the collection it no longer produces an automatic response but instead provokes a movement of reaction and comparison. No longer ossified in its ritual gesture towards an established social prejudice, the expression becomes problematic and dynamic, inviting contrary interpretations.[1]

As well as meaning 'savage' the word 'sauvage' also, idiomatically, suggests a recluse, an unsociable or anti-social individual. In 'Le Crépuscule du soir' the expression therefore also applies, implicitly, to the second 'madman':

L'autre, un ambitieux blessé, devenait, à mesure que le jour baissait, plus aigre, plus sombre, plus taquin. Indulgent et sociable encore pendant la journée, il était impitoyable le soir; et ce n'était pas seulement sur autrui, mais aussi sur lui-même, que s'exerçait rageusement sa manie crépusculeuse. (*Oc* I, 311–12)

The description of this second *sauvage* recalls elements from 'A une heure du matin', where the poet–narrator himself seems to invite condemnation by society, and by the conventional reader, because of his extreme unsociableness. Does the metropolis epitomise and distil *civilisation* or *barbarousness*? Is the anti-social citizen 'sauvage' manifesting symptoms of his urban condition? Does he reveal his *naturalness*? Or demonstrate superior, more 'civilised' perception of life's values? Is the *barbarism* of rejecting the restaurant dish a way of interrogating standard behaviour, just as the observation of 'barbarian' or *different* cultures offers a way of questioning of one's own civilisation?[2] Conventionally, a metropolis is usually seen as constituting a quintessence of a particular civilisation or culture. That which a culture rejects as 'barbarian' is also what helps to define that culture. In the prose poems, whenever *sauvagerie* is mentioned, whether it refers to individual behaviour which violates society's unwritten codes or whether it serves as a way of designating an exotic, alien culture, it *always* furthers the central project of interrogating the values of contemporary nineteenth-century Paris.

Western civilisation is typified in the prose poems by such 'solemnities' as the city fair evoked in 'Le Vieux Saltimbanque': 'C'était une de ces solennités sur lesquelles... comptent les saltimbanques, les faiseurs de tours, les montreurs d'animaux et les boutiquiers ambulants, pour compenser les mauvais temps de l'année.' The only incense floating about this modern Parisian crowd (which, it is implied, has lost all sense of the sacred) is the heavy odour of frying fat (evidence even in the nineteenth century of a degraded Western cuisine). The saltimbank, like the madmen of 'Le Crépuscule du soir', invites comparison with the poet, and like the first madman and the poet he is also associated with savages:

Au bout, à l'extrême bout de la rangée de baraques, comme si, honteux, il s'était exilé lui-même de toutes ces splendeurs, je vis un pauvre saltimbanque, voûté, caduc, décrépit, une ruine d'homme, adossé contre un des poteaux de sa cahute; *une cahute plus misérable que celle du sauvage le plus abruti.* (my italics; *Oc* I, 296)

Baudelaire's comment in *Mon Cœur mis à nu*, 'Le commerce est *naturel, donc* il est *infame*',[3] is well illustrated by this archetypal metropolitan scene, metaphorically assimilated to unreasoning nature rather than culture. The description of the antics of the fairground Herculeses flaunting their ape-like physiques, and the reference to 'les faiseurs de tours, les montreurs d'animaux', recall 'La Femme sauvage et la petite-maîtresse', which appears a little earlier in the collection and which also illustrates a world where material and physical preoccupations have left little space for other values. It provides a further example of the degradation to which the subjects of civilised France will submit for the sake of a few sous. The description of the saltimbank's hut and the clichéd reference to brutish savages ('une cahute plus misérable que celle du sauvage le plus abruti'), coming as it does in the midst of this humane yet unsentimental account of the sordidness of Western civilisation, only underlines the fatuous pretentiousness of the unthinking members of 'La

Civilisation du Progrès'. (One recalls the relativism of Baudelaire's comment in 1855 on the buildings characteristic of distant lands: 'tout peuple est académique en jugeant les autres, tout peuple est barbare quand il est jugé'.)[4]

Various parallels between the two poems encourage comparison of the scene in 'Le Vieux Saltimbanque' with the escapist setting of 'La Belle Dorothée' (a poem which, although published in 1862, a year later than 'Le Vieux Saltimbanque', was written in 1860). The conventional Parisian notion of the miserable shacks belonging to primitives, as expressed in 'Le Vieux Saltimbanque', contrasts with the attractive picture of Dorothée's artistically arranged cabin, where beauty is not a function of price: 'sa petite case si coquettement arrangée dont les fleurs et les nattes font à si peu de frais un parfait boudoir'. The metaphor of the sea provides a second parallel between the two scenes, and underlines the fundamental contrast between the 'civilised' and the 'savage' worlds. For whilst the saltimbank's hut is surrounded by the discordant sea of the Parisian crowd ('un mélange de cris, de détonations de cuivre et d'explosions de fusées'), Dorothée's cabin is set beside the monotonous and rhythmic ocean which breaks against the beach at a distance of a few yards.

Even if, in 'Les Projets', the primitivist ideal is ironically acknowledged to be little more than a pipe-dream, it nevertheless serves in the opening paragraphs of 'La Belle Dorothée' as a means of contrast with degraded Parisian reality. Dorothée's name, like other fictional names in the prose poems, is suggestive in itself. It paronomastically encapsulates the word 'or' (gold), implying an ideal, and also the homonym 'thé', suggesting the importance of a specific colouring (we know from Baudelaire's correspondence that he originally intended to subtitle the poem 'Idéal de la beauté noire', echoing once again the cliché of the 'soleil noir').[5]

The early Romantic myth of the pure savage, the Rousseauist belief that 'l'homme est né bon', which is attacked in 'Le Gâteau',[6] is treated both ironically and nostalgically in 'La Belle Dorothée'. This is the myth propounded by the 'dorloteurs et endormeurs' of the human race whom Baudelaire attacks so vehemently in his *Notes nouvelles sur Edgar Poe* for 'feignant d'oublier...que nous sommes tous nés marquis par le mal!'[7] The opening description of 'La Belle Dorothée', which appears, at least initially, to be very much in this early Romantic vein, serves to pamper ('dorloter') the unwary reader, but only in order to leave him particularly vulnerable to the disturbing 'awakening' of the poem's conclusion with its aggressive reminder of colonial exploitation and of universal 'déchéance'. The luxurious semi-consciousness of the siesta evoked in the poem's first paragraph seems ironically to mirror the escapist reader's level of moral awareness. Theirs is the beatitude described in 'Le Joueur généreux': 'une béatitude sombre, analogue à celle que durent éprouver les mangeurs de lotus quand, débarquant dans une île enchantée, éclairée des lueurs d'une éternelle après-midi, ils sentirent naître en eux, aux sons assoupissants des mélodieuses cascades, le désir de ne jamais revoir leur pénates, leurs femmes, leurs enfants'. The escapist illusion of the good savage is qualified not only by the conclusion of 'La Belle Dorothée' but also by its ironic echoing in 'Le Joueur généreux', where the reader is in effect reminded that 'la plus belle des ruses du Diable' is that of persuading mankind that he does not exist.

Just as in *Pauvre Belgique!* what begins as an unfavourable comparison of the Belgians to the French becomes a critique of the human condition, regardless of national boundaries, so the contrast in the prose poems between civilised and primitive man suggests a more general despair as to the human condition. Baudelaire's sentiments were more directly formulated in the *Journaux Intimes*:

Quoi de plus absurde que le Progrès, puisque l'homme, comme cela est prouvé par le fait journalier, est toujours semblable et égal à l'homme, c'est-à-dire toujours à l'état sauvage. (*Oc* I, 663)

Dorothée is described as 'souriant d'un blanc sourire, comme si elle apercevait au loin dans l'espace un miroir reflétant sa démarche et sa beauté'; and although, read in isolation, the image of the brilliant whiteness of the teeth contrasting with the darkness of her complexion can be taken as a clichéd detail of realistic description, in the context of a series of allusions occurring in different poems in the *Spleen de Paris* the 'blanc sourire' offers another significance. For although this most self-conscious of images might evoke a beautiful picture such as that of the woman described in 'Le Désir de peindre' ('le rire d'une grande bouche, rouge et blanche, et délicieuse, qui fait rêver au miracle d'une superbe fleur éclose dans un terrain volcanique') rather than reminding the reader of the teeth of the 'Femme sauvage' festooned with the entrails of her 'prey', both these other women are characterised by 'la volonté tenace et l'amour de la proie' ('Le Désir de peindre').[8] The whiteness of Dorothée's smile is also rendered problematic by the emphasis on the whiteness of the children's teeth in 'Le Joujou du pauvre', where, in a striking reversal of conventional Western colour symbolism, whiteness seems to be the stamp of savagery, the underlying savagery which is common to all human beings regardless of race or class: 'Et les deux enfants se riaient l'un à l'autre fraternellement, avec des dents d'une égale blancheur' (*Oc* I, 305). In the prose poems, only age breaks the association between femininity and carnality, and the old woman of 'Le Désespoir de la vieille', whose toothlessness is like that of the baby she admires, is presented no less sympathetically than the majestic and aristocratic old beauty of 'Les Veuves'.

The conclusion of 'Les Bons Chiens' suggests that Baudelaire's familiarity with Montaigne's arguments in 'Des Cannibales' encouraged him to view with irony Swedenborg's geography of a paradise in which cultural and racial boundaries would be maintained:

Et que de fois j'ai pensé qu'il y avait peut-être quelque part (qui sait, après tout?), pour récompenser tant de courage, tant de patience et de labeur, un paradis spécial pour les bons chiens, les pauvres chiens, les chiens crottés et désolés. Swedenborg affirme bien qu'il y en a un pour les Turcs et un pour les Hollandais! (*Oc* I, 362)

The coyly clichéd '(qui sait aprés tout?)' and the exclamatory 'un pour les Turcs et un pour les Hollandais!' would leave the reader in little doubt as to the irony even if this poem were read in isolation.

However, although the escapist ideal of 'La Belle Dorothée' is undermined when we are reminded of the commercial influence of Western civilisation even in the most exotic of settings, the description of Dorothée, a 'real' savage (according to conventional Parisian perception), nevertheless makes a striking contrast with the picture of her Western namesake in 'La Femme sauvage et la petite-maîtresse'. Whilst the fairground fake lunges around her cage and shakes the bars like an orang-utan, Dorothée is 'forte et fière comme le soleil'. Whilst the one is in chains, the other moves freely: the harmony of her movements is completely untrammelled, she does not even wear shoes. The frenzy of the metropolis contrasts with the peacefulness of the exotic land; the disgusting offal devoured by the 'wild woman' could not be more unlike Dorothée's skilfully prepared cuisine. Whilst one woman is publicly beaten by her husband–master, the other is 'admirée et choyée de tous' (although this admiration is, of course, not mentioned without ironic innuendo). In Europe a beauty such as Dorothée's could only be found immured in a museum (an unobtrusive parenthesis draws attention to the poem's significance within the wider context of the *Spleen de Paris*):

et son pied, pareil aux pieds des déesses de marbre que l'Europe enferme dans ses musées, imprime fidèlement sa forme sur le sable fin. (*Oc* 1, 316)

The beauties of Europe, and Paris, are sterile and inaccessible, and this brief allusion calls to mind the emotional climate of 'Le Fou et la Vénus'. The nearest living European equivalent to Dorothée might be the mistress described in 'Un Cheval de race' (the ideal beauty of 'Le Désir de peindre' is not located in a specifically Parisian context). But the beauty of the Parisienne has been marked by her existence; the perfume of her hair may evoke the vitality of the south of France but her charm is a heroic and paradoxical vestige of an anterior and more perfect beauty. Time may not have destroyed the harmony of her walk, but it is 'une harmonie pétillante', quite different from the easy grace of Dorothée 'balançant mollement son torse si mince sur ses hanches si larges'. There is something brittle and precarious about the Western mistress whose silhouette seems to have been eroded by time, and who is all elegance and 'armature'. She is associated with images of death and interment, suggesting the Fall ('elle est fourmi, araignée, si vous voulez, squelette même'). The comparison with the thoroughbred horse, and the stridently 'chauvinist' stance of her poet lover (indicated by such phrases as 'l'œil du véritable amateur'), make it clear that this woman's existence is closer to that of the caged 'femme sauvage' than to that of 'la belle Dorothée':

Usée peut-être, mais non fatiguée, et toujours héroique, elle fait penser à ces chevaux de grande race que l'œil du véritable amateur reconnaît, même attelés à un carosse de louage ou à un lourd chariot. (*Oc* I, 343)

Although she may represent an absolute authority as well as a miraculous chemical force ('breuvage, magistère, sorcellerie!'), her power is over the imagination of the poet, not over her own existence. In other respects she shares the fate of the animals in the metropolis, and the metaphor of the 'cheval de race' (another contemporary cliché recorded uncritically by Balzac in *Le Père Goriot*)[9] may be compared with the description of Belgian cart-dogs in 'Les Bons Chiens' and of the ass in 'Un Plaisant' ('harcelé par un malotru armé d'un fouet'). The irony is, of course, that in the Paris of the *Petits Poèmes en prose* men too, albeit often unconsciously, are shown to share the same condition. In 'Un Plaisant' the smart city-dweller who mocks the ass is himself half choked by his elegant attire, imprisoned by the very symbols of his civilisation ('un beau monsieur ganté, verni, cruellement cravaté et emprisonné dans des habits tout neufs'). The exotic, escapist ideal of harmony, dignity and unrestraint contrasts with images of physical and psychological constriction associated with daytime city life.

The man who rejects the psychological restraints and conventions of the metropolis is associated with the savage (the madman of 'Le Crépuscule du soir' or the saltimbank). In the city the 'sauvage' is defined by his marginality, by the fact that he is rejected by the group, and also by the fact that he is seeking some form of freedom. This freedom may be associated with solitude or unsociability ('un double tour à la serrure'),[10] with drugs ('la fiole de laudanum; une vieille et terrible amie'),[11] with travel ('mon plaisir serait d'aller toujours droit devant moi, sans savoir où'),[12] with artistic inspiration ('feu d'artifice de la déesse Liberté'),[13] or with death.

In 'La Corde', the child who finds his habitual escape route denied when his patron refuses him his customary intoxicants seeks evasion in death. On discovering the child's corpse, the painter calls for help from his neighbours, but to no avail:

J'ai négligé de vous dire que j'avais vivement appelé au secours; mais *tous mes voisins avaient refusé de me venir en aide, fidèles en cela aux habitudes de l'homme civilisé, qui ne veut jamais,* je ne sais pourquoi, *se mêler des affaires d'un pendu.* (my italics; *Oc* I, 330)

Even if we leave aside the implied association between the child's suicide and the poetic vocation, it is clear that the suicide victim and the 'sauvage' are comparable in so far as both are antipathetic to 'l'homme civilisé'. The irony of 'La Corde' is complete when it is revealed that the 'civilised' neighbours, who refuse to involve themselves in the case of someone who has hanged himself, have no scruples over exploiting the *commercial* potential of the situation. The behaviour of the child's mother, which destroys one of the painter's most fundamental and clichéd illusions about the reality of human nature, is the most radical expression of the code observed by the painter's neighbours. It is they rather than the child suicide who represent the truly *natural* – that is, as so often for Baudelaire, *infamous*[14] – specimens of humanity. The discussion of human nature is introduced in the first paragraph of the poem, and the conclusion vehemently underlines the iconoclastic moral of the tale by the juxtaposition of the words 'commerce' and 'consoler', with alliteration dramatically calling attention to the ironic subversion of the conventional illusion:

Et alors, soudainement, une lueur se fit dans mon cerveau, et je compris pourquoi la mère tenait tant à m'arracher la ficelle et par quel commerce elle entendait se consoler. (*Oc* I, 331)

Here, as in 'La Femme sauvage' and 'Laquelle est la vraie?', stereotyped perceptions of 'nature' and 'reality' are once again questioned. Maternal love is perceived as 'l'illusion la plus naturelle'.

But it is in 'Les Vocations' that 'sauvagerie' is most clearly associated with artistic values in contrast to materialism. Of the four boys described in the poem, one particularly excites the sympathy of the poet–narrator. This child tells the others of his longing to travel, and he recounts how at a village fair he once saw three wandering musicians. Theirs is the way of life which he would like to emulate when he grows up.

The first details of the boy's description of the musicians recall aspects of the portrait of 'La Belle Dorothée'. They are 'grands, presque noirs et très fiers quoique en guenilles, avec l'air de n'avoir besoin de personne'. They possess the same pride and personal dignity as Dorothée, as well as a certain physical poise, and they also share her colouring to some extent. But the qualification '*presque* noirs', more than just constituting a realistic reference to racial identity or to the effects of constant exposure to the sun, also suggests something which falls just short of an absolute. If the passage is interpreted in the context of the wider collection of poems it appears that the musicians in fact fail to attain to the ideal which was ironically evoked in the original sub-title to 'La Belle Dorothée' ('Idéal de la beauté noire') and which is associated in 'Le Désir de peindre' with artistic inspiration itself. Like the mistress in 'Un Cheval de race', they are tarnished by their contact (albeit marginal) with modern French society. But although the three players, like other artists in the prose poems, are degraded by their financial dependence on the public (they only 'appear' to be independent), they are nevertheless motivated by other than purely economic considerations, for they enjoy their music-making so much that they continue playing after their audience has dispersed. It is perhaps not surprising, then, that they too are linked with the notion of *sauvagerie*:

Ils étaient si contents d'eux-mêmes qu'ils ont continué longtemps à jouer *leur musique de sauvages*, même après que la foule s'est dispersée. (my italics; *Oc* I, 334)

Here, too, a poet–narrator is associated with 'sauvages', this time through his identification with the child, who in turn identifies with the musicians. Once again, an apparently 'realist' descriptive detail, the reference to the musicians' 'primitive' gypsy music, gains ironic significance from its context in the wider collection of poems. The musicians are likened to savages precisely because of their art, that art which in his *Journaux intimes* Baudelaire was to describe, after Castagnary, as 'un agent civilisateur'.[15]

For only art could make possible the miraculous conjunction of dream and reality, and introduce that element of beauty and fantasy which was so lacking in a France preoccupied with public affairs and commerce. In 'L'Invitation au voyage' the poet offers, as Georges Blin has shown,[16] an evocation of a land which is synonymous with art, and, at the same time, an ironical rewriting of the portrait of mercantile Holland which was a commonplace of contemporary French literature. As Robert Kopp has remarked, the writings of authors as various as Bernardin de Sainte-Pierre, Diderot, Louis Veuillot, Gautier and Champfleury abound in descriptions associating Holland and China.[17] But in the context of the many variants on the motif of 'sauvages' and of barbarisms the clichéd evocation of this idyllic 'pays de Cocagne' takes on a special significance. For the land which is described here as a metaphor for Art itself, this paradoxical '*Orient de l'Occident*', this hub of commercialism and world exchange, is also the region where the exotic or 'barbarian' and the Western or 'civilised' worlds come together.

CHAPTER 8

Musicality

> cette musique était *la mienne*
> (Letter to Wagner, 17 February 1860)
>
> le miracle d'une prose poétique, musicale sans rythme et sans rime, assez souple et assez heurtée pour s'adapter aux mouvements lyriques de l'âme, aux ondulations de la rêverie, aux soubresauts de la conscience
> (Dedication to Arsène Houssaye)

THE EXAMPLE OF WAGNER: LEITMOTIF

Although Mallarmé's remarks about music and poetry have attracted a considerable body of commentary, Baudelaire's statement in his dedication to Houssaye about a musical prose poetry has intrigued generations of readers but has not provoked as much formal discussion as might perhaps have been expected. When the subject *has* been broached, all too frequently insufficient attention has been paid to the fact that Baudelaire specifically excludes effects of rhythm and rhyme from his comparison of prose poetry with music, and, curiously, there have been a number of studies of rhythmic effects in the prose poems. A more rewarding approach might lie in the close examination of Baudelaire's article 'Richard Wagner et *Tannhäuser* à Paris' and its postscript 'Encore quelques mots', which were contemporaneous with the composition of the *Petits Poèmes en prose* (the article on *Tannhäuser* was published in the *Revue européenne* in April 1861). What light do Baudelaire's reactions to Wagner's music shed on his comments about the miracle of a 'musical' prose poetry? Are there any parallels between the new musical structures created by Wagner and Baudelaire's revolutionary collection of prose poems?

The whole question of analogies between the arts is, of course, a problematic one, and this no doubt partly explains the relative silence which has fallen over the question of Baudelaire's affinity with Wagner, and his interest in such innovative musical developments as the *leitmotif* and Wagner's dissonant harmonies. Whilst such caution is understandable, Baudelaire's writings on Wagner so well illuminate our understanding of his use of the word 'musical' that we would be ill-advised to ignore them completely.

In the past, critics have sometimes been misled by the exaggerated modesty with which Baudelaire occasionally referred to his own ignorance of music (notable in his letter to Wagner, 17 February, 1860, although is it hard to imagine Baudelaire being so insensitive as to adopt any other posture when writing to a great professional musician).[1] However, Baudelaire's perceptiveness is increasingly recognised by students of his music criticism who have drawn attention to his awareness of the novelty of Wagnerian *leitmotif* and dissonant harmony.[2] Another noteworthy feature of his writings on Wagner is the awareness that they reveal of the new demands which such music placed on its audience's powers of concentration and its memory. In what ways, if any, might these demands resemble those implicit in his own *Petits Poèmes en prose*?

If we look more closely at the article 'Richard Wagner et *Tannhäuser* à Paris' we find that Baudelaire returns again and again to the subject of the *leitmotif*:

Dans ce que j'avais éprouvé, il entrait sans doute beaucoup de ce que Weber et Beethoven m'avaient déjà fait reconnaître, mais aussi quelque chose de nouveau que j'étais impuissant à définir... (*Oc* II, 785)

Cependant, des répétitions fréquentes des mêmes phrases mélodiques, dans des morceaux tirés du même opéra, impliquaient des intentions mystérieuses et une méthode qui m'étaient inconnues. Je résolus de m'informer du pourquoi, et de transformer ma volupté en connaissance... (786)

l'ouverture... résume... la pensée du drame par deux chants... cette ouverture contient non seulement l'idée mère, la dualité psychique constituant le drame, mais encore les formules principales, nettement accentuées, destinées à peindre les sentiments généraux exprimés dans la suite de l'œuvre, ainsi que la démontrent les retours forcés de la mélodie diaboliquement voluptueuse et du motif religieux ou *Chant des pèlerins*, toutes les fois que l'action le demande. (*Oc* II, 794, 797)

J'ai déjà parlé de certaines phrases mélodiques dont le retour assidu, dans différents morceaux tirés de la même œuvre, avait vivement intrigué mon oreille... Nous avons observer que dans *Tannhäuser* la récurrence de deux thèmes principaux, le motif religieux et le chant de volupté, servait à réveiller l'attention du public... Dans *Lohengrin*, ce système mnemonique est appliqué beaucoup plus minutieusement. Chaque personnage est, pour ainsi dire, blasonné par la mélodie qui représente son caractère moral et le rôle qu'il est appelé à jouer dans la fable... (*Oc* II, 801)

He quotes a passage from Franz Liszt's study in which Liszt contrasts Wagner's *leitmotifs* to traditional operatic structures where the listener might expect to find '[des] morceaux détachées... engrenés l'un après l'autre sur le fil de quelque intrigue':

Wagner, forçant notre méditation et notre mémoire à un si constant exercise, arrache, par cela seul, l'action de la musique au domaine des vagues attendrissements et ajoute à ses charmes quelques-uns des plaisirs de l'esprit. Par cette méthode qui complique les faciles jouissances procurées par *une série de chants rarement apparentées entre eux*, il demande une singulière attention du public; mais en même temps il prépare de plus parfaites émotions à ceux qui savent les goûter. Ses mélodies sont en quelque sorte des personnifications d'idées... Il est des phrases... qui traversent l'opéra comme un serpent venimeux... Il en est... qui ne reviennent que rarement, avec les suprêmes et divines révélations... (*Oc*, II, 802)

Liszt's 'aristocratic' emphasis on the difficulty of Wagner's music and the superior concentration required from its audience must have caught Baudelaire's attention at a time when he was himself increasingly interested in the idea of a species of aristocracy and in the problem of making allowance for the limited concentration span of the mass of readers.[3] His fascination with Wagner's 'système mnemonique' has implications with regard to his own preoccupation with the problem of writing a modern epic like Hugo's *Légende*. In his dedication to Houssaye Baudelaire uses the same serpent metaphor as Liszt, but he uses it slightly differently. Rather than the intensely demanding and, for many, inaccessible play of Wagnerian leitmotif (the 'serpent venimeux' described by Liszt) Baudelaire implies that his own *Petits Poèmes* will offer their audience the dual possibility of individual 'tronçons' or 'serpent tout entier'. By catering for two different levels or stages of reception he may have hoped that the collection might protect itself from the naively hostile reception that the contemporary French public had reserved for Wagner's music.

Equally significantly, Baudelaire chooses to quote the passage in which Liszt points to the fact that Wagnerian *leitmotif* is accompanied by a weakening of narrative: the plot no longer, as in traditional opera, imposes a rigidly consecutive succession of melodies. Again we can see an analogy with the *Petits Poèmes en prose*, where the poet warns us that 'tout est à la fois tête et queue' and at the same time declares 'je ne suspends pas la volonté rétive du lecteur au fil interminable d'une intrigue superflue'. And again the writings on Wagner reveal Baudelaire's increasing recognition that a work of art is never completed by its composer, and an emphasis on the creative role of the reader or listener:

Dans la musique, comme dans la peinture et même dans la parole écrite, qui est cependant le plus positif des arts, il y a toujours une lacune complétée par l'imagination de l'auditeur. (*Oc* II, 781–2)

Immediately after quoting Liszt's description of Wagner's leitmotifs Baudelaire comments on the 'poetic' quality of Wagner's opera. His comparison with poetry is founded on a principle of internal cohesion, the reciprocity of elements making up the whole:

En effet, sans poésie, la musique de Wagner serait encore une œuvre poétique, étant douée de toutes les qualités qui constituent une poésie bien faite; explicative par elle-même, tant toutes choses y sont bien unies, conjointes, réciproquement adaptées, et, s'il est permis de faire un barbarisme pour exprimer le superlatif d'une qualité, prudemment *concaténés*. (*Oc* II, 803)

Baudelaire's insistence on the importance of combination or selection as a quality complementing the digressive force of the leitmotif, the spiral of association, helps to explain the bitterness of his attack on Jules Janin's *Gâteaux des rois*, a work which paraded itself as musical under the sub-title 'Symphonie fantastique'. Baudelaire's scathing comments in the *Lettre à Jules Janin* (1865) reveal his impatience with a work where the spiral of capricious association is never complemented by the controlling rod of the author's effort at selection and combination, an effort which demands so much personal energy and concentration from the greatest artists:

> Vous n'aimez pas les combinaisons... tout cela exige qu'on prenne trop de soins pour l'obtenir. (*Oc* II, 233)

> Vous aimez les musiques qu'on peut entendre sans les écouter. (*Oc* II, 234)

Baudelaire's outburst may initially have been provoked by Janin's criticism of Heine and other 'satanic' modern foreign poets, but his assertion that Janin would never be able to appreciate Wagner seems to be founded as much on the argument about combination, difficulty and *maîtrise* as on the fact that Janin would not appreciate the dissonant elements in such music (although for Baudelaire the two qualities were related). This is clear if we look at the fragment of an article on Janin (1848):

> *Le Gâteau des rois*, espèce de *Christmas*, ou livre de Noel, était surtout une prétention clairement affirmée de tirer de la langue tous les effets qu'un instrumentaliste transcendant tire de son instrument – jouer des variations infinies sur le dictionnaire! Déplacement de forces! erreur d'esprit faible! Dans cet étrange livre, les idées se succédaient à la hâte, filaient avec la rapidité du son, s'appuyant au hasard sur des rapports infiniment ténus. Elles s'associent entre elles par un fil excessivement frêle... vaste courant d'idées involontaires, course au clocher, abnégation de la volonté. Ce singulier tour de force fut exécuté par l'homme que vous savez, dont l'unique et spéciale faculté est de n'être pas maître de lui, l'homme aux rencontres et aux *bonheurs*. (*Oc* II, 24)

Baudelaire's writings on Wagner draw attention, then, to the internal coherence of a work which, despite its length, seems to work together as one whole whose elements are all reciprocally adapted to one another.

He describes Wagner's opera as 'une œuvre poétique', and consequently the problem of its length and the way in which it taxes the listener's memory by the use of leitmotif may be compared to problems associated with the epic or long poem which he discusses in his *Notes nouvelles sur Edgar Poe* and in his essay on Hugo.

In his discussion of Wagnerian leitmotif, Baudelaire points to the way in which it can take on an analytical or self-reflexive function. He writes of how the overture to *Tannhäuser* contains in a condensed form the substance of the whole drama: 'L'ouverture...résume...la pensée du drame.' It seems that Baudelaire is here identifying an effect which today we might term *mise en abyme*.[4] It is an effect which invites comparison with certain passages in the *Petits Poèmes en prose*, where the literal organisation of the collection as a whole appears to be reflected. Most of these emblematic passages involve reference to inter-reflecting light (recalling the *jeu de miroirs* of a kaleidoscope) or to music, and sometimes the two are directly associated. For example, the 'pays singulier' of 'L'Invitation au voyage' (a land deemed to be 'supérieur aux autres comme l'Art est à la Nature') is characterised by the description of an interior crowded with reflecting surfaces. The visual effect of correspondences and inter-reflections between the different elements in this interior is compared to music:

Les miroirs, les métaux, les étoffes, l'orfèvrerie et la faience y jouent pour les yeux une symphonie muette et mystérieuses...Un vrai pays de Cocagne, te dis-je, où tout est riche, propre, luisant, comme une belle conscience, comme une magnifique batterie de cuisine, comme une splendide orfèvrerie, comme une bijouterie bariolée!

The symphony is silent, an important paradox which recalls the statement in the dedication about an ideal prose poetry whose musicality would not depend on euphony ('musical sans rythme et sans rime'). The comparison with the multi-coloured treasure-house or 'bijouterie bariolée', given emphasis by the use of alliteration and by its position at the end of the sentence, leaves the reader with a metatextual image very similar to the one of the kaleidoscope.

Again, the description of a public concert in 'Les Veuves' brings together a similar play of sparkling inter-reflections and associates these with music and with a privileged interiority (although, of course, on this occasion the music is audible):

l'orchestre jette à travers la nuit ces chants de fête, de triomphe ou de volupté. Les robes traînent en miroitant; les regards se croisent... Ici rien que de riche, d'heureux... excepté l'aspect de cette tourbe qui s'appuie là-bas sur la barrière extérieure, attrapant gratis, au gré du vent, un lambeau du musique, et regardant l'étincelante fournaise intérieure. (*Oc* I, 293)

Elsewhere, the mobility of this play of inter-reflections is what catches the reader's attention, as in 'Le Port', where the paradoxical description of the clouds' *mobile architecture* is associated with the changing colours of the sea and the glittering, revolving light of the lighthouse beacons:

Un port est un séjour charmant pour une âme fatiguée des luttes de la vie. L'ampleur du ciel, l'architecture mobile des nuages, les colorations changeantes de la mer, le scintillement des phares, sont un prisme merveilleusement propre à amuser les yeux sans jamais les lasser. (*Oc* I, 344)

The reference in the dedication to the interconnecting ways in a great city is echoed and expanded in the opening paragraph of 'Un Plaisant', where the image of a crazy world of mud and snow traversed by a thousand carriages is associated with a sparkling effect (here of toys and sweets, rather than, say, the 'bijouterie bariolée' of 'L'Invitation au voyage' or the shimmering of sea and beacon in 'Le Port'):

C'était l'explosion du nouvel an : chaos de boue et de neige, traversé de mille carosses, étincelant de joujoux et de cupidités et de bonbons, grouillant de cupidités et de désespoirs, délire officiel d'une grande ville fait pour troubler le cerveau du solitaire le plus fort.

The *mises en abyme* which I have mentioned are important in helping to show the reader how the collection should be read (i.e. as an inter-reflecting whole). Yet, paradoxically, it is only *after* one has realised that the collection may be read in this way that it is possible to recognise that such passages are small models of the whole work. In other words, the detection of these instances of self-representation involves a hermeneutic circle. This is one of the paradoxes inherent in such varieties of *mise en abyme* which reflect the overall literal organisation of a text, a paradox explained by Lucien Dallenbach in his pioneering study of *Le Récit spéculaire*. Dallenbach writes that this type of *mise en abyme* 'suppose une précomprehension destinée à être validée, rectifiée ou affinée par la compréhension qu'elle aura permise'.[5] In the case of the *Petits Poèmes en prose* one can see that the prior understanding which Dallenbach mentions is encouraged by the inclusion of the Dedication to Arsène Houssaye, with its mention of an ideal, musical prose poetry, and its comparison of this musical ideal to the pattern of interconnections within great cities ('le croisement de leurs innombrables rapports').

In Wagner's music the melodies of the overture may at times be only fleetingly echoed in later passages, and in a similar manner in the *Petits Poèmes en prose* the *mises en abyme* of a musical or inter-reflecting source of entertainment are sometimes only partially echoed in other brief references, for example to music, to the moving architecture of clouds, and to the reflection of light in eyes or mirrors (the latter often relating to the idea of 'dédoublement' inherent in Romantic irony, and to the notion that the prose poems are a description of '*une* vie moderne').[6]

The presence of these and other *mises en abyme* helps to alert the reader to the play of interconnections linking the different poems in the collection. As the comparisons with the kaleidoscope and with the network of relations in a city would suggest, the number of such inter-reflections operating within the collection seems to be 'innumerable' and in this book I have focussed on a selection which is necessarily arbitrary and limited. The *mises en abyme* which I have been discussing help to draw attention to this fact, but at the same time they also perhaps reflect Baudelaire's uncertainty about the reception which would be reserved for a work whose originality or 'singularité' might provoke the sort of response that Wagner's music had already elicited. Lucien Dallenbach has noted that the *mise en abyme* is 'the most powerful textual symbol and aid to readability',[7] but that 'in resorting to *mise en abyme*, texts manifest their fears about their own readability'.[8] The *mise en abyme* helps to ensure a 'minimum of readability', lessening the basic ambiguity of the text by way of a form of *surcodage*.[9] In the case of the kaleidoscope or musical models in the *Petits Poèmes en prose* this *surcodage* encourages readers to be aware of their chance to participate in exploring and creating the plurivocality of the text. However, here as in some of the examples cited by Dallenbach, the *mise en abyme* may also be 'symptomatic of a public whose horizon of expectation is being questioned'.[10]

DISSONANT HARMONY

We have seen how Baudelaire particularly emphasises Wagner's talent for combination or assemblage of all the elements within his operas, and that it is this aspect of his work which, for Baudelaire, makes it 'une œuvre poétique'. It is important to recognise this when one considers the question of Wagnerian harmony and attempts to assess whether the effects of 'soubresaut' in the *Petits Poèmes en prose* may usefully be compared to musical dissonance.

It is difficult to use a musical term such as 'dissonance' in the description of a work of literature, not least because in music dissonance implies more than just a break of sequence (which might be effected by a *false* note as well as by a dissonant note) and suggests a change of direction, a progression in the melody. For this reason, and in order to avoid some of the confusions which can arise from the transference of terminology from one art to another, it may be more appropriate to compare the *effects* produced in music by dissonance with those produced semantically in the prose poems by a strategy of irresolution or sabotage of conditioned expectations. In this way it may be possible to investigate functional correspondences between Wagner's music and Baudelaire's poetry, whilst still recognising the enormous diversity involved in the practice of different media.

My analysis of this problem owes much to Gisèle Brelet's

study of Wagner's music in *Le Temps musical: Essai d'une esthétique nouvelle de la musique*, and to Umberto Eco's discussion of Leonard Meyer's *Emotion and Meaning in Music*, a later work which like Brelet's book is heavily influenced by the Gestaltist tradition.[11]

Although the notions of consonance and dissonance may be infinitely variable and may change as cultural expectations are modified by each new piece of music that is heard, the basic principle underlying their contrast does not change: the one is always associated with resolution and fulfilment, the other with movement and anxiety. The aspiration for consonance and calm which is provoked by dissonance is satisfied in classical music, Brelet argues, but constantly frustrated by Wagner's music. Here any resolution is only relative: one dissonant chord is resolved by another, the sense of irresolution being continually reborn.

If one considers how Baudelaire, for his part, disturbs his reader's conditioned expectations, one conspicuous device which springs to mind is his use of the oxymoron.[12] The oxymoron might at first sight appear to create an effect comparable to that produced by musical dissonance, but on closer consideration this hypothesis is not very convincing. The use of oxymoron in Baudelaire's prose poems does not in itself seem sufficient to explain the poet's emphasis on the 'soubresauts de la conscience' in the *Dédicace*. Oxymorons are no more prevalent in the *Petits Poèmes en prose* than in *Les Fleurs du mal*. Although the oxymoron does subvert unwritten semantic norms and thus creates an effect of surprise, such terms as 'délire officiel', 'magnifique imbécile', 'langue muette', 'étoiles noires', 'démon bienvieillant', 'écrasantes chimères' and 'sainte prostitution' tend to be expanded and explained in the poems (thus tending, if anything, towards *resolution* rather than towards the more profound *irresolution* of Wagnerian dissonance). They provide a focus for an investigation of the medium itself and draw attention to the materiality of the language. However, the oxymorons do not produce a lasting sense of hesitation or uncertainty, and above all they do not seriously complicate or impede interpretation of the passage. The oxymoron is just one of a number of instances of semantic inappropriateness in the prose poems. For example, the 'pays de rêve' evoked in 'L'Invitation au voyage', a dreamland synonymous with art itself, is described as 'l'Orient de l'Occident' – a perfect 'coincidentia oppositorum' where paradoxically the poetic ideal may be realised in the utilitarian and materialist West. Elsewhere the accumulation of contradictory epithets creates similar paradoxical effects, as in 'maudite chère enfant gâtée', or 'sa chère, délicieuse et exécrable femme'.

But in addition to this, and more seriously complicating the process of interpretation, there are certain effects of open-ended irony which leave the reader puzzling over a variety of possible readings and associations, unable to 'resolve' the poem, in the sense of settling on one closed interpretation. This type of irony produces an effect perhaps more comparable to Wagner's unresolved dissonances. The reader experiences a sense of anxiety rather than the satisfaction or beatitude which Baudelaire associates with classical art in his essay on Banville: no single interpretation of the ironic statement will suffice. Like *Tannhäuser*, the *Petits Poèmes en prose* derive their effects from a dialectic of the expected and the unexpected. This is true of all effects in art, as Leonard Meyer observes in his analysis of patterns of culture in *Emotion and Meaning in Music*, but it remains true that the accent on the unexpected is greater in Wagner's music and in Baudelaire's prose poems. Irony, like musical dissonance, is only functional in relation to a contextual norm. For example, the reader's interpretation of the words of the quasi-scientific narrator of 'Les Veuves', claiming a 'Balzacian' penetration of his subjects' hearts, will be influenced by the reading of 'Les Fenêtres' and 'Mademoiselle Bistouri', where the infallibility of such powers of perception is cast in doubt. But the 'soubresauts' of irony in the prose poems often go beyond a simple inversion of meaning and produce an effect of irresolution. For example, the italicised words '*capital*' and '*faveur*' in 'Une Mort héroïque' or '*égale*' in 'Le Joujou du pauvre' are an invitation to speculation. Irony is here close to its original etymological meaning of eirona or interrogation.[13]

When Baudelaire writes to Wagner in February 1860 to express his appreciation of his work and gratitude for '*la plus grande jouissance musicale que j'ai jamais éprouvée*', he describes how on first hearing Wagner he had the strange impression that he recognised the music ('il me semblait que cette musique était *la mienne, et je la reconnaissais comme tout homme reconnaît les choses qu'il est destiné à aimer*') and he comments: 'Généralement ces profondes harmonies me paraissaient ressembler à ces excitants qui accélèrent le pouls de l'imagination.' The complexity or what Baudelaire terms the *profundity* of Wagnerian harmony offers the poet a dazzling artistic model of the sort of harmonic complexity which he sees as reflecting modern experience. His own prose poetry is inspired by 'la fréquentation des villes énormes...[le] croisement de leurs innombrables rapports', and he writes in *Le Peintre de le vie moderne* of 'l'étonnante harmonie de la vie dans les capitales, harmonie si providentiellement maintenue dans le tumulte de la liberté humaine'.[14] If the *Petits Poèmes en prose* are inspired by the notion of an overall harmony, it is a harmony that must accommodate the internal contradictions of a modern personality, the 'soubresauts de la conscience', as well as echoing in their own manner the complexity and the discordant characteristics of a modern city environment. Whatever the shades of irony or malice which may or may not be implied in the poet's reference to Houssaye's 'Chanson du vitrier', Baudelaire's comment in the *Dédicace à Arsène Houssaye* draws our attention to the paradox of incorporating a discordant cry into a song. It seems unlikely that Baudelaire meant to ridicule this ambition in itself, whatever he may have thought of the inadequacies of Houssaye's poem:

Vous-même, mon cher ami, n'avez-vous pas tenté de traduire en une *chanson* le cri strident du *Vitrier*, et d'exprimer dans une prose lyrique toutes les désolantes suggestions que ce cri envoie jusqu'aux mansardes, à travers les plus hautes brumes de la rue? (*Oc* I, 276)

Baudelaire's understanding of the term *harmony* seems on the whole to have been close to the original Greek sense of the word as *assemblage*. But this notion of combination implicit in harmony has frequently been neglected by critics of the *Petits poèmes* who have loosely opposed 'harmony' to 'dissonance' as though the two were antithetical. Whilst this approach may partly be justified by common usage it does not contribute to a clear understanding of the prose poems. In musical terms harmony does not preclude dissonance, being concerned with the relationship between several superimposed notes, including concords and discords.

Whilst it would be wrong to convey the impression that Baudelaire's statements about harmony at different periods in his career are all perfectly consistent,[15] it is equally misguided to suggest that the sudden shifts of tone so frequent in his later works imply an outright contradiction of his earlier theories. Compositional harmony was not always equated by the poet with uniformity and consonance, as Suzanne Bernard misleadingly suggested when she wrote of the jarring notes in the prose poems:

De telles dissonances...ne contredisent-elles pas à la 'grande loi d'harmonie générale' posée par Baudelaire lui-même et qui devrait, en poésie comme en peinture, répandre sur toutes les teintes du tableau l'unité d'une 'atmosphère dominante'?[16]

The emphasis on consonant or dissonant harmony varies over the course of Baudelaire's career, but his concern with subtle combination remains consistent. His original 1846 theory of harmonic composition which emphasised the importance of the individual imagination could easily accommodate a new stress on dissonance – which would reflect the satanic quality of the modern artist's temperament.[17] The decision to write poetry in prose does not suggest that the poet is disregarding the criterion of harmony, although it does suggest that he no longer associates harmony with uniformity and consonance (as he had on occasions in the past). The use of prose enables Baudelaire to introduce new elements into the overall harmony in a way which is analogous to that by which Wagner enriched and complicated musical harmony with new dimensions of dissonance.

Baudelaire's interest in the importance of regularity and symmetry is well known, but it should not be forgotten that he stressed the equal importance of harmonic complexity:

la régularité et... la symétrie... sont des besoins primordiaux de l'esprit humain, au même degré que la complication et l'harmonie. (*Oc* I, 663)

His criticisms of Hégésippe Moreau's verse, in the article of 1862, show that he was sensitive to the dangers of excessive symmetry and lack of variety in verse.[18] Similarly, in *Fusées* he writes of the necessary *irregularity* of beauty:

Ce qui n'est pas légèrement difforme a l'air insensible; – d'où il suit que l'irrégularité, c'est-à-dire l'inattendu, la surprise, l'étonnement sont une partie essentielle et la caractéristique de la beauté. (*Oc* I, 656)

This emphasis on the bizarre and the unexpected was characteristic of the poet's later writings, but as early as 1846 he had criticised Hugo's cold and excessive exploitations of the devices of symmetry and antithesis.[19] In the article of 1852 'Edgar Poe, sa vie et ses ouvrages' he contrasts the harmonic complexity of Poe's poetry with the more facile forms of Musset and Lamartine.[20] The reference here is to Poe's verse poetry and not to his prose. Clearly it would be wrong to suggest that for Baudelaire the verse form excluded the possibility of complexity. Indeed a statement in the *Projets de préface* for *Les Fleurs du mal* makes it clear that this was far from being his view (if any clarification were needed other than the example of his poetry itself):

le rythme et la rime répondent dans l'homme aux immortels besoins de monotonie, de symétrie et de surprise. (*Oc* I, 182)

This implies that verse need not preclude an element of surprise, the unexpected resolution of a process. Complexity was possible in verse poetry, as Edgar Allan Poe had demonstrated. However, although he admired the complexity of Poe's own verse, Baudelaire was familiar with Poe's argument in 'The Rationale of Verse' regarding the relative lack of complexity in verse as compared to music. Poe had described verse as 'an inferior or less capable Music' where 'there is happily less chance for complexity', and had described the varying degrees of complexity possible in verse, citing as an 'ultimatum of complexity' triple-rhymed, natural dactylic lines'.[21] Poe only seems to have thought to compare the sound qualities of poetry and music, and therefore, understandably, he argued that verse poetry lacked the potential to rival music's complexity.

In the light of Poe's argument, the logic of Baudelaire's disclaimer regarding the sound qualities in prose poetry ('sans rythme et sans rime') becomes apparent. If poetry, even in verse form, could not vie with music in terms of sound qualities, then in order to be termed 'musical' prose poetry must find for itself an alternative but equivalent complexity which would not be dependent on rhythm and rhyme. This complexity could be achieved through leitmotif, and also, I would argue, through a semantic approximation to Wagnerian dissonance.

If one considers the manner in which the *Petits Poèmes en prose* might reconcile the contrasting demands of symmetry and surprise, one finds that one of the commonest patterns in the individual poems resolves this tension perfectly. The pattern is that of semantic inversion, an organising and shaping principle which governs even some of the poems which have been criticised for being excessively 'rhapsodic'.

In his short chapter on prose poetry in *Les Genres du discours* Tzvetan Todorov notes that Baudelaire's prose poems are characterised by 'une thématique de la dualité' which he sees as corresponding to the 'rencontre des contraires' of prose poetry as a genre. He isolates three different figures of duality, 'l'invraisemblance', 'l'ambivalence' and 'l'antithèse', and argues that it is this confrontation of opposites in a work where 'l'antithèse est nappée dans un système de correspondances' which gives *Le Spleen de Paris* its unity.[22] In order to appreciate the significance of the many examples of duality cited by Todorov it is helpful to situate the discussion within the wider context of a number of statements made by Baudelaire about poetry and music. Many of the examples of duality instanced by Todorov involve poems which pivot on an ironic inversion which is more dynamic than his word 'antithesis' might suggest. 'Le Gâteau', 'Assommons les pauvres!', 'Le Chien et le flacon' and 'Le Fou et la Vénus', to name just a few examples, involve an element of surprise which is not accounted for in Todorov's expression 'juxtaposition antithétique'. Whereas the straightforward use of symmetry and antithesis would produce a static effect, these poems, on the contrary, effectively exploit a system of probabilities and expectations of the kind described by Leonard Meyer in terms of Gestalt theory. By providing *unexpected* solutions to the circle *stimulus – crisis – expectation – satisfaction – re-establishment of order* they produce a more intense pleasure for the reader.

In this way ironic inversion could contribute to that element of proportion or symmetry which Baudelaire considered to be of such importance, whilst still avoiding the trap of excessive predictability. At the same time the shifts of tone in the prose poems contribute towards making the reading process more complex and less predictable. In *Fusées* Baudelaire makes a loose analogy between the literary effect of mixing different moral registers and the musical effect produced by what he calls 'les discordances':

Le mélange du grotesque et du tragique est agréable à l'esprit comme les discordances aux oreilles blasées. (*Oc* I, 661)

The terms 'discordance' and 'dissonance' were frequently confused by writers of the period, as Jean-Marc Bailbé shows in *Le Roman et la musique en France sous la monarchie de juillet*.[23] The above passage seems to illustrate this confusion, and Baudelaire here seems to use the term 'discordance' as a synonym for 'dissonance', as in the English language. The statement does not make sense if the word 'discordance' is interpreted as a quality intrinsically disagreeable to the ear (its true sense in the French language).

Baudelaire's comparison of musical dissonance with the mixture of registers in literature suggests that it was perhaps the influence of Victor Hugo that made him receptive to Wagner's music. In the *Préface de Cromwell* Hugo had advocated the principle of variety and contrast in art, and had argued that modern poetry should imitate nature by mixing light and dark, the grotesque and the sublime. The theatre of Shakespeare represented an ideal towards which modern poetry might tend. Hugo's writings on the mixture of genres and on Shakespeare's drama seem to have been in Baudelaire's mind when he was writing the article 'Richard Wagner et *Tannhäuser* à Paris'. One particular passage describing an episode in *Tannhäuser* shows the possible process of association:

il y a une puissance de contraste qui agit irrésistiblement sur l'esprit et qui fait penser à la manière large et aisée de Shakespeare. (*Oc* II, 795)

In the *Préface de Cromwell* Baudelaire would have read that 'la poésie vraie, la poésie complète, est dans l'harmonie des contraires'.[24] Hugo had expressed a delight in complex dramatic harmony, and writing of the superiority of the grotesque genre he had asserted:

enfin il [the grotesque] peut sans discordance, même dans la scène du roi Lear et son fou, mêler sa voix criarde aux plus lugubres, aux plus rêveuses musiques de l'âme.[25]

Hugo's statement perhaps finds its echo in the idea of a prose poetry which might adapt itself 'aux mouvements lyriques de l'âme, aux ondulations de la rêverie, aux soubresauts de la conscience'.

In his article on Théodore de Banville Baudelaire emphasises the heterogeneity of modern poetry and its consequent complexity. He suggests that Banville's art is not characteristic of the age because it is not satanic:

Comme l'art antique, il n'exprime que ce qui est beau, joyeux, noble, grand, rythmique. Aussi, dans ses œuvres, vous n'entendrez pas les dissonances, les discordances des musiques du sabbat, non plus que les glapissements de l'ironie, cette vengeance du vaincu. (*Oc* II, 168)

Modern poems, and thus by implication Baudelaire's own *Petits Poèmes en prose*, are suggested to be characterised by *dissonance*, which is here assimilated to irony. Baudelaire also seems to suggest that modern art is not naturally concerned with that which is rhythmic, since he associates rhythm with the expression of beautiful, joyful and noble themes such as those which are to be found in Classical art. This is consistent with the fact that he omits Poe's definition of poetry as 'the rhythmical creation of beauty' when he describes the American poet's theories in his *Notes nouvelles sur Edgar Poe*.[26] If Baudelaire is inspired in the writing of *Le Spleen de Paris* by the idea of a prose poetry which would be 'musicale sans rythme et sans rime' we can see that such a music would have to be radically *modern* in character, balancing effects of novelty, surprise and irresolution (analogous to those he recognised in Wagner) against the conditioned cultural expectation of a certain symmetry and proportion, coupling the *éternel* and the *transitoire*.

CHAPTER 9

Straight lines and arabesques

> Il faut considérer la déclamation comme une ligne, et le chant comme une autre ligne qui serpenterait sur la première.
>
> Diderot, *Le Neveu de Rameau*[1]

> Could a historiographer drive on his history, as a muleteer drives on his mule, – straight forward... he might venture to foretell you to an hour when he should get to his journey's end; – but the thing is, morally speaking, impossible: For if he is a man of the least spirit he will have fifty deviations from a straight line to make as he goes along.
>
> ...in my opinion, to write a book is for all the world like humming a song...
>
> Sterne, *Tristram Shandy*[2]

> Il est des phrases... qui traversent l'opéra comme un serpent venimeux.
>
> Liszt, quoted by Baudelaire, 'Richard Wagner et *Tannhäuser* à Paris'[3]

In addition to the initial statement of intent, the evocation in the dedication to Houssaye of a musical model, there is, of course, one particular prose poem which enigmatically, but nevertheless conspicuously, invites consideration in relation to an ideal of musicality, and that is 'Le Thyrse', with its dedication to Franz Liszt and its tribute to his genius.

If, as we have seen, Baudelaire quoted at length Liszt's analysis of the structure of Wagnerian opera in his famous article 'Richard Wagner et *Tannhäuser* à Paris', it was precisely in order to foreground Liszt's discussion of the way in which Wagner had moved away from the tradition of offering a series of pieces *in succession* along a narrative thread ('morceaux détachées...engrenés l'un après l'autre sur le fil de quelque intrigue').[4] The image used by Liszt and quoted by Baudelaire to evoke Wagner's practice is that of a venomous serpent, a metaphor for the effects of *leitmotif* in Wagnerian opera. The image offers an obvious similarity to Baudelaire's description of his own collection of prose poems as a snake in the dedication to Houssaye. Also, as we saw earlier, the dedication to Houssaye with its discussion of the *lack* of concentration required of the readers of *Le Spleen de Paris* recalls Liszt's discussion of the level of concentration that Wagner's music solicited from its audience. This passage in Baudelaire's dedication can be read as a typically facetious example of ironic inversion, where in fact what is being signalled is the very opposite to what is stated: the reader's memory and powers of concentration will be taxed to the full. However, the snake image also offers itself for comparison with the image of the sinuous vine which is presented as one of the two elements making up the thyrsus, one of the aspects of that astonishing and glorious *duality* which constitutes the musical genius of Liszt. If we read the prose poem, as many critics have done, as offering a *mise en abyme* of the poetics of *Le Spleen de Paris*, then the snake-like, sinuous, capricious, feminine element of the vine emerges, equally, as representing one half of their own '*étonnante dualité*'.

XXXII
LE THYRSE
A Franz Liszt

Qu'est-ce qu'un thyrse? Selon le sens moral et poétique, c'est un emblème sacerdotal dans la main des prêtres ou prêtresses célébrant la divinité dont ils sont les interprètes et les serviteurs. Mais physiquement ce n'est qu'un bâton, un pur bâton, perche à houblon, tuteur de vigne, sec, dur et droit. Autour de ce bâton, dans des méandres capricieux, se jouent et folâtrent des tiges et des fleurs, celles-ci sinueuses et fuyardes, celles-là penchées comme des cloches ou des coupes renversées. Et une gloire étonnante jaillit de cette complexité de lignes et de couleurs, tendres ou éclatantes. Ne dirait-on pas que la ligne courbe et la spirale font leur cour à la ligne droite et dansent autour dans une muette adoration ? Ne dirait-on pas que toutes ces corolles délicates, tous ces calices, explosions de senteurs et de couleurs, exécutent un mystique fandango autour du bâton hiératique ? Et quel est, cependant, le mortel imprudent qui osera décider si les fleurs et les pampres ont été faits pour le bâton, ou si le bâton n'est que le prétexte pour montrer la beauté des pampres et des fleurs ? Le thyrse est la représentation de votre étonnante dualité, maître puissant et vénéré, cher Bacchant de la Beauté mystérieuse et passionnée. Jamais nymphe exaspérée par l'invincible Bacchus ne secoua son thyrse sur les têtes de ses compagnes affolées avec autant d'énergie et de caprice que vous agitez votre génie sur les cœurs de vos frères. – Le bâton, c'est votre volonté, droite, ferme et inébranlable ; les fleurs, c'est la promenade de votre fantaisie autour de votre volonté ; c'est l'élément féminin exécutant autour du mâle ses prestigieuses pirouettes. Ligne droite et ligne arabesque, intention et expression, roideur de la volonté, sinuosité du verbe, unité du but, variété des moyens, amalgame tout-puissant et indivisible du génie, quel analyste aura le détestable courage de vous diviser et de vous séparer ?

Cher Liszt, à travers les brumes, par delà les fleuves, par-dessus les villes où les pianos chantent votre gloire, où l'imprimerie traduit votre sagesse, en quelque lieu que vous soyez, dans les splendeurs de la ville éternelle ou dans les brumes des pays rêveurs que console Cambrinus, improvisant des chants de délectation ou d'ineffable douleur, ou confiant au papier vos méditations abstruses, chantre de la Volupté et de l'Angoisse éternelles, philosophe, poète et artiste, je vous salue en l'immortalité ![5]

The symbol of the thyrsus, like so many of the *topoi* raised in the prose poems, is a literary cliché, an intertextual nexus which itself touches precisely on the subject of intertextuality and all lateral associations within the text. Critics have noted in particular the echoing of a passage from De Quincey's *Suspiria*, which is also paraphrased by Baudelaire at the beginning and at the conclusion of 'Un Mangeur d'opium'.[6] The similarity between some aspects of 'Le Thyrse' and another text, the Nephew's description of the 'model of song' in *Le Neveu de Rameau*, also invites consideration. On the most obvious level, both texts are concerned with an ideal of musicality and both raise the possibility of this ideal's application to poetry.

Le chant est une imitation...ou par la voix ou par l'instrument des bruits physiques ou des accents de la passion...en changeant là-dedans les choses à changer, la définition conviendrait exactement à la peinture, à l'eloquence, à la sculpture, et à la poésie...

Quel est le modèle du musicien du chant? C'est la déclamation... Il faut considérer la déclamation comme une ligne, et le chant comme une autre ligne qui serpenterait sur la première. Plus cette déclamation, type du chant, sera forte et vraie, plus le chant qui s'y conforme la coupera en un plus grand nombre de points; plus le chant sera vrai; et plus il sera beau...

L'accent est la pépinière de la mélodie. Jugez de là de quelle difficulté et de quelle importance il est de savoir bien faire le récitatif. Il n'y a pas de bel air, dont on ne puisse faire un beau récitatif, et point de beau récitatif, dont un habile homme ne puisse tirer un bel air... je serais surpris que celui qui chante bien, ne sut pas bien réciter.[7]

The immediate analogy between this passage and 'Le Thyrse' rests on a simple graphic image: the emblem of the serpentine line which spirals around the first line, continually intersecting it. This image constitutes the essence of the musical model put forward by Diderot's Nephew as a model not only for opera, but also for other art forms, including poetry. The relationship between 'Le Thyrse' and *Le Neveu de Rameau* has been discussed at length by Yoichi Sumi in his admirable study *Le Neveu de Rameau: Caprices et logiques du jeu*.[8] In a discussion of the significance of intertextual allusion in poetic works, Sumi makes the case for reading the two prose poems 'Le Thyrse' and 'Le Joueur généreux' (which he also discusses in detail) as two variations on Diderot's text, two interpretations or tacit 'hommages' to *Le Neveu de Rameau*:

La poésie, même en prose, réalise l'intégration absolue de ses éléments dans son unité structurale; de telle sorte que le moindre emprunt ou la moindre allusion à l'ouvrage d'autrui, si dérisoires qu'ils puissent paraître à la première vue, réveillent la conscience du lecteur vigilant et l'invitent à réfléchir sur le rôle qui leur est donné à jouer respectivement dans l'ensemble significatif de l'œuvre. L'influence du *Neveu de Rameau* sur l'auteur du *Joueur généreux* et du *Thyrse* est un fait plus qu'épisodique, et c'est de ce point de vue que les deux poèmes en prose devraient être tenus pour deux variations possibles sur le roman de Diderot, ou mieux, pour deux interprétations du dialogue, en un mot, pour deux 'hommages' sinon formels, du moins tacites, rendus par Baudelaire au *Neveu de Rameau*.[9]

Straight lines and arabesques

One can refine on this by arguing, with Judith Still and Michael Worton in their excellent recent study of intertextuality, as follows:

> in each encounter with a quotation, the reader perceives that, while there is an obvious conflict between sameness or identity and difference, there is also a covert fusion of differences *within* the single textual utterance... Every quotation is a metaphor which speaks of that which is absent and which engages the reader in a speculative activity.[10]

Sumi offers a fascinating and persuasive reading of 'Le Thyrse' as a reformulation of the dualities explored in *Le Neveu de Rameau*, foregrounding the semantic fields of *hierarchy* (master and servant, divinity and worshippers) *galanterie* (the masculine element and the feminine element, *libertinage*) and *poetics* (centring on the graphic image of the straight line and the serpentine line).[11] By drawing inferences from the reversibility of the master/servant, divinity/worshippers hierarchy of the rod and the flowers in the poetics of 'Le Thyrse', Sumi gains insight into *Le Neveu de Rameau* and the interchangeable relationship between *sagesse* and *folie*, *maître* and *serviteur* which operates with regard to the semantic fields of the aesthetic (the model of song) and of morality in that text:

> Et quel est, cependant, le mortel imprudent qui osera décider si les fleurs et les pampres ont été faits pour le bâton, ou si le bâton n'est que le prétexte pour montrer la beauté des pampres et des fleurs? (*Oc* I, 336)

In other words, it is suggested that the *thematics of rectitude* (straight lines, control, *volonté*, and rational deductive 'moral' argument) *versus irregularity* (caprice, *folie*, servility and fantasy) which permeates every level of *Le Neveu de Rameau* is reformulated in 'Le Thyrse'. My own reading of such *topoi* as conformity (civilisation) and individuality (*sauvagerie*), conventional wisdom and madness, sententiousness and facetiousness, in *Le Spleen de Paris* suggests that the resonances between *Le Neveu de Rameau* and *Le Spleen de Paris* are even more extensive and fundamental than Yoichi Sumi has indicated in his readings of 'Le Thyrse' and 'Le Joueur généreux'. For example, as we saw above in Chapter 3, the thematising of controlling, phallic rod or stick and 'feminine' subservient vine in 'Le Thyrse' resonates in the context of a number of other poems in which the 'Argument of the Stick', the traditional discourse of the moral fable, and perhaps, by extension, the sententiousness of linear (predominantly syntagmatic) prose itself, is held up for comparison with the arabesque lateral freedoms of an unsententious, facetious, ironic mode, with its play of inversion, and the spiral openness of metaphoric (predominantly paradigmatic) poetic discourse. If we consider 'Le Thyrse' in the light of this whole network of allusions in poems such as 'Le Femme sauvage et la petite-maîtresse', 'Assommons les pauvres!' and 'Portraits de maîtresses', to cite only the most obvious examples, one reading which the poem allows is *both* as a model of *musicality and* as an ideal of prose poetry which exploits the dual potentialities of both poetry and prose: 'feminine' sinuosity and 'masculine' rectitude, the paradigmatic/metaphoric and the syntagmatic/metonymic axes of language itself.

In Baudelaire's article 'Richard Wagner et *Tannhäuser* à Paris' an allusion is made to passages in which Diderot wrote about music, passages which Baudelaire appears to interpret as justifying Wagner's conception of lyrical or musical drama:

En feuilletant la *Lettre sur la musique*, je sentais revivre dans mon esprit, comme par un phénomène d'écho mnémonique, différents passages de Diderot qui affirment que la vraie musique dramatique ne peut pas être autre chose que le cri ou le soupir de la passion noté et rythmé. Les mêmes problèmes scientifiques, poétiques, artistiques se reproduisent sans cesse à travers les âges, et Wagner ne se donne pas pour un inventeur, mais simplement pour confirmateur d'une ancienne idée... (*Oc* II, 788)

Baudelaire goes on to note Wagner's interest in the drama of the Ancient Greeks, and he quotes a passage from a letter by Wagner to Berlioz where he describes drama as the art form in which the *idea* might be most clearly intelligible to the audience. In the passage quoted by Baudelaire, Wagner writes of how, when thinking of the popularity and success of Ancient Greek drama, he had been struck by the perfect concurrence of art forms contributing to the whole ('l'alliance de tous les arts concourant ensemble au même but'). It was then, he writes, that he had been led to consider the relationship between music and poetry:

> Je reconnus, en effet, que précisément là où l'un de ces arts atteignait à des limites infranchissables commençait aussitôt, avec la plus rigoureuse exactitude, la sphère de l'autre; que, conséquemment, par l'union intime de ces deux arts, on exprimerait avec la clarté la plus satisfaisante ce que ne pouvait exprimer chacun d'eux isolément; que par contraire, *toute tentative de rendre avec les moyens de l'un d'eux ce qui ne saurait être rendu que par les deux ensemble, devait fatalement conduire à l'obscurité, à la confusion* d'abord, et ensuite *à la dégénérescence et à la corruption de chaque art en particulier*. (my italics; *Oc* II, 789)

What might have been the significance for Baudelaire of such a meditation on the confluence of different art forms ('l'union intime de deux arts') by a genius in the creation of *musical drama* or opera, itself a hybrid genre? Baudelaire too was facing the challenge of exploiting to the full the potentialities of what had traditionally been seen as generically distinct forms (poetry and prose). With his concern to achieve 'le miracle d'une prose poétique, musicale sans rythme et sans rime' he was seeking to achieve the perfect complementary amalgam of prose (with its disposition towards metonymic sententiousness, its linearity/law of succession) and poetry (with its disposition towards lateral, paradigmatic association, the spiral freedoms and gratuitousness of metaphor and its arabesques). Might Baudelaire have read in Wagner's letter to Berlioz a message of direct relevance to his own project? Perhaps the lesson that prose poetry might most successfully achieve the combined ends of *moralité* and poem? In other words, that the combining of the two forms into a new genre was preferable, say, to trying to make either verse poetry or the moral fable do alone what they could not properly do individually?

Baudelaire's description of the success of Wagner's 'totalité d'effet' and of the perfect confluence of words and music, decor and *mise en scène* recalls the passage in *Le Neveu de Rameau* in which the Nephew puts forward his 'model of song' as an ideal which might equally apply to other art forms such as poetry, painting and even sculpture:

Ce goût absolu, despotique, d'un idéal dramatique, où tout, depuis une déclamation notée et soulignée par la musique avec tant de soin qu'il est impossible au chanteur de s'en écarter en aucune syllabe, véritable arabesque de sons dessinée par la passion, jusqu'au soins les plus minutieux relatifs aux décors et à la mise en scène, où tous les détails, dis-je, doivent sans cesse concourir à une totalité d'effet, a fait la destinée de Wagner. (*Oc* II, 790)

If we consider this indirect echoing of Diderot's 'model of song' passage alongside Baudelaire's explicit statement, quoted earlier, that when reading Wagner's *Lettre sur la musique* he recalled 'différents passages de Diderot qui affirment que la vraie musique dramatique ne peut être que le cri ou le soupir de la passion noté et rythmé', then it appears that the 'model of song' is being used by Baudelaire as a means of accounting for Wagner's success in achieving a perfect union of different art forms into a new hybrid.

Baudelaire is of his time in that, like Diderot and Wagner, he relates this 'success' to feelings and emotions. But whereas Diderot presents the criterion of fidelity to *sentiment* in terms of mimesis ('l'imitation... des accents de la passion'), Wagner focusses on the emotions of the audience:

L'arrangement rythmique et l'ornement (presque musical) de la rime sont pour le poète des moyens d'assurer au vers, à la phrase, une puissance qui captive comme par un charme et gouverne à son gré le sentiment. Essentielle au poète, cette tendance le conduit jusqu'à la limite de son art, limite qui touche immédiatement la musique, et, par conséquent, l'œuvre la plus complète du poète devrait être celle qui, dans son dernier achèvement, serait une parfaite musique. (*Oc* II, 791)

The 'musical' ideal of prose poetry evoked by Baudelaire in the Dedication to Houssaye is also, of course, measured in terms of its adaptation to human psychology, although here the gauge is one of a very subtle conformity to mental and emotional states ('mouvements lyriques de l'âme... ondulations de la rêverie... soubresauts de la conscience'). However strongly the element of *raillerie* was to be accentuated in Baudelaire's descriptions of *Le Spleen de Paris* and within the poems themselves, this *raillerie* was never to be coldly intellectual. The poet's academic 'mentor' was not to be Swift, the 'farceur froid',[12] but Sterne, the 'sentimental farceur, farceur incomparable'.[13]

This may seem circumvoluted and tortuous. But if we are to begin to make some meaning of Baudelaire's baffling and complex ideal of 'une prose poétique, musicale sans rythme et sans rime' it has to be by a reading which is itself circuitous. We are not given any clear 'explanation' of Baudelaire's meaning regarding the musical ideal which lay behind the creation of *Le Spleen de Paris*. However, whether by Baudelaire's conscious intention or not, the reader is nevertheless encouraged to make a series of associations and deductions based on the resonances between one prose poem and another, between Baudelaire's own different writings on music and the texts which he cites by Liszt, Wagner and Diderot.

The comparisons do not end with Diderot. *Le Neveu de Rameau* situates its own reformulation of the regularity/capriciousness duality in relation to Horace's Seventh Satire, which is cited in the epigraph to Diderot's text. The poetics of 'Le Thyrse', with its image of the duality of masculine power, organisation and oneness combined with feminine digressiveness and lateral association, may also call to mind Montaigne[14] and the references to the sexual hierarchy which structure his thinking on textuality.

In the last prose poem in *Le Spleen de Paris*, 'Les Bons Chiens', the poet–narrator opts to choose Laurence Sterne, rather than Buffon, as his academic muse. In doing so, he effectively invites the reader to consider 'Les Bons Chiens', and indeed the whole collection of prose poems, in the light of *Tristram Shandy*, a novel which itself repeatedly invites comparison with music and which contrasts the 'Argument of the Stick' (the *Argumentum Baculinum*) with the 'Argument of the player of a shepherd's pipe' (the *Argumentum Fistulatorium*), that is, the argument of *musical* indirection.[15]

Tristram Shandy also thematises the formula of the straight line and the arabesque. For example, the description of the brandishing of Corporal Trim's stick (an action which designates the joys of bachelor freedom) and the illustration of that action by a squiggly line on the white page implicitly echo the earlier description which I have quoted, in which Tristram's narrative is compared to a journey full of digressions and chance encounters pursued on the back of a mule. In *Tristram Shandy*, then, as in 'Le Thyrse' and *Le Neveu de Rameau*, the freedoms of the text's own arabesque of lateral associations (and intertextuality, like metaphor, should doubtless be seen as just one aspect of this dimension) are figured in terms of *galanterie* and contrasted with the linearity, or oneness, of celibacy. In Sterne's novel the gesture of flourishing the stick directly precedes a digression in which the 'edifying' bawdy story of Corporal Trim's brother Toby's marriage is paradigmatically 'rhapsodized'[16] into the narrative. The embedded story is itself an allegory of substitution (the paradigmatic), enabling Uncle Toby's state of arousal to be satisfied and that which was unwarily 'conjured up' to be conjured down again.[17] Uncle Toby's earnest glances towards his cottage and his bowling green, which follow close after Corporal Trim's flourishing of the stick, remind the reader of the *substitutional* connotations of Uncle Toby's favourite activity of pretend action in his toytown military 'fortifications', which stands in lieu of the 'fornication' advocated by Corporal Trim.

The obscurity of 'Les Bons Chiens', which has often been remarked upon by critics, has the effect of promoting the casual, 'conversational', apparently throwaway allusion to Sterne to the status of a signpost, an indication to the reader (and here I borrow the terminology of Michael Riffaterre) that only the intertext can complete the 'grammaticality' of the text before us.[18]

'Le Thyrse' and the whole *réseau* of allusions to the arabesque which it foregrounds serve as a conspicuous reminder of the complexity of the reading process solicited by the prose poems. Far from presenting their audience with an easy task which will tax neither their powers of concentration nor their memories, they in fact ask of us the 'impossible' task of a reading which not only strives to take account of the connections between the constituent poems but, also, one which must attempt to integrate within its frames of reference the implications of the wealth of intertextual allusion embedded in the text. By allowing us to glimpse the idea of such a reading, *Le Spleen de Paris*, in its jewel-like compactness, comes close to suggesting that ultimate Baudelairean ideal of 'l'Infini dans le fini...le rêve'.[19]

Conclusion

Since their publication the *Petits Poèmes en prose* have stimulated discussion about differences of genre and about the nature of poetic discourse. In Baudelaire's day the association of *poetry* and *prose*, so long held to be discrete and mutually exclusive categories, was surprising and challenging, if not a wholly novel departure. Voltaire's orthodox insistence on genre distinctions ('on confond toutes les idées, on transpose les limites des Arts quand on donne le nom de Poème à la Prose')[1] had provided a new generation of nineteenth-century artists with a set of assumptions against which to react; and, although the concept of prose poetry had been advanced before by such writers as Boileau and the Abbé du Bos in connection with certain novels, it was in the 1830s that the term was given a new immediacy by the work of artists such as Aloysius Bertrand and Maurice de Guérin.[2]

Although today the notion of prose poetry no longer arouses indignation or surprise, Baudelaire's prose poems still provoke speculation about the nature of poetic discourse, although, as Barbara Johnson has commented, the line of demarcation has shifted from the poetry/prose axis to the axis of ordinary language/poetic language.[3]

A number of critics have tried to assess the role of the *Petits Poèmes en prose* in respect to the historical development of prose poetry in France.[4] Others have attempted to formulate an ahistorical working definition of prose poetry.[5] Preoccupation with the question of genre used also to lead to debate as to whether all the pieces in *Le Spleen de Paris* in fact constituted prose poems.[6] Questions of chronology were at one time much debated, and the argument that certain poems were composed *after* their verse counterparts in *Les Fleurs du mal* was held by some critics to be an important indication of their artistic status.[7]

There have been several studies investigating the nature of the relationship between the prose poems and *Les Fleurs du mal*, and in particular some detailed comparisons of prose and verse poems have been made, particularly in cases where identity of title or simultaneity of publication seems to have invited comparison of the different versions.[8] Other critics, aware of a more broadly based pattern of correspondences between *Les Fleurs du mal* and the counterpart, or 'pendant', *Spleen de Paris*, have drawn up longer tables of corresponding verse and prose poems.[9]

Numerous critics have responded to what appears to be an open invitation to measure the *Petits Poèmes en prose* against the musical ideal evoked in Baudelaire's Dedication to Houssaye.[10] In particular, attention has tended to focus on the concept of the 'soubresaut'. Some have interpreted the term 'musicale' as referring to euphony; others have taken the qualifying phrase, 'sans rythme et sans rime', to be an indication that some other feature of music is being suggested.[11] Musicality has sometimes been associated with harmony and contrasted with the 'dissonance' of the 'soubresaut' (although there is little evidence to support the idea that Baudelaire believed that musical harmony and dissonance were antithetical – on the contrary, as I have argued, his admiration for Wagner suggests the very opposite).[12]

The preoccupation with identifying a poetic 'essence' and with comparing the *Petits Poèmes en prose* with other forms of poetry, and particularly with *Les Fleurs du mal*, has led to the comparative neglect of another, central feature of the prose poems: their relationship to other prose works and particularly to the works of writers such as Sterne, Diderot, Defoe, Chateaubriand, Rousseau, Pascal, Vauvenargues and others which are evoked in the text itself. Baudelaire's comments in the *1859 Salon* on the 'dangerous' role of fantasy in open-ended genres such as prose poetry and the novel suggest that he would have seen the relationship of *Le Spleen de Paris* to the novel as being as significant as, if not more significant than, its links with verse poetry.[13]

The thrust of my argument in this book has been to show that the role of the prose poems in offering a *mise en question* of the codes governing prose forms such as the novel and the moral fable or portrait is as important as their role in implicitly calling into question the conventions of lyric poetry. I have tried to draw attention to the wealth of intertextual allusion linking *Le Spleen de Paris* to earlier (for the most part *prose*) texts. Given the status of *Le Spleen de Paris* as 'literature', and still more as 'poetry', it is impossible to dismiss such allusions as marginal or tangential; instead the reader is encouraged to embark on the process of integrating such references within his or her understanding of the poem and of the collection. Such an endeavour implies some degree of rereading of the earlier text in an attempt to establish how that text is itself 'read' by the prose poem.

Amongst the relatively few existing studies of the intertextual links between the prose poems and other prose works, two stand out. One is Yoichi Sumi's substantial chapter on the relationship between 'Le Joueur généreux', 'Le Thyrse' and *Le Neveu de Rameau* in his book *Le Neveu de Rameau: Caprices et logiques de jeu*.[14] The other is Ross Chambers's article 'The Artist as Performing Dog', which offers a detailed and suggestive intertextual reading of the prose poem 'Les Bons Chiens' in the light of Cervantes's *Colloquio de los perros* and Hoffmann's *Chien Berganza*.[15] Both critics suggest that such prose poems constitute both a tribute and a critique of the earlier texts to which they refer. Other contributions by Jean Pommier, Robert Kopp, Melvin Zimmermann, Jean Thomas, Walter Benjamin, Rosemary Lloyd, Barbara Johnson and Graham Chesters have all helped to demonstrate that the relationship of *Le Spleen de Paris* to the prose tradition offers a fertile area for investigation and analysis.[16]

A new approach to the individual prose poems as examples of narrative is to be found in Marie Maclean's recent study, *Narrative as Performance: The Baudelairean Experiment*, which uses *Le Spleen de Paris* to pursue an investigation of narrative as interplay and enactment. This book is to be welcomed in that it encourages the reader to put aside the well-trodden and sometimes rather unfruitful and narrow approach of traditional genre study and to consider the relevance to the prose poems of a much broader spectrum of literary theory. Equally, the recent work of Nathaniel Wing in *The Limits of Narrative: Essays on Baudelaire, Flaubert, Rimbaud and Mallarmé* and his article in *Paragraph* (13 March 1990) provide some exciting new readings of the poems and a lucid explication of the relevance to Baudelaire's text of theoretical work by Jean-François Lyotard, Laclau and Mouffe, Jean-Joseph Goux and others. In my view, Nathaniel Wing overstates the case when he argues that the fragmented serpent image of Baudelaire's Dedication to Arsène Houssaye disrupts the 'ideal of totality presumed characteristic of all books'. In the same Dedication the poet's declared ambition to describe, if not modern life in its entirety, '*une* vie moderne et plus abstraite' suggests at least some vestige of the totalising ambition of his nineteenth-century contemporaries. But these are rich and thought-provoking studies which unquestionably constitute a major contribution to Baudelaire studies.[17]

The considerable body of writings on *Le Spleen de Paris* have included very few attempts to read the collection of poems as one artistic unit of which all the constituent parts are related. An exception might be made of the various psychocritical investigations of Baudelaire's *œuvre* which also comprise a more global interpretation of the *Petits Poèmes*. For example, Charles Mauron's *Dernier Baudelaire* traces the development of a number of themes in the *Petits Poèmes en prose*. However, his analysis of the prose poems overlaps with readings of Baudelaire's other writings and of *Les Fleurs du mal*, with the result that there emerges no clearly differentiated reading of *Le Spleen de Paris* as such.[18] The same holds true in the case of Leo Bersani's *Baudelaire and Freud*, despite its general value as a stimulating contribution to Baudelaire studies.[19] Max Milner's 1979 edition of the prose poems is exceptional in that it both directly addresses the question of reading the collection as a unit and briefly indicates some possible lines of approach for an overall reading of the whole text.[20]

Yet it seems to me that it is of the greatest importance that we do *not* feel obliged to restrict our reading of the prose poems to individual, discrete pieces. The images of 'kaleidoscopic' inter-reflection in 'Le Port' and 'L'Invitation au voyage' combine with the images of city ways and their complex arabesque of interconnections (*Dédicace à Arsène Houssaye*, 'Les Bons Chiens', 'Un Plaisant') to make up a series of passages which, in retrospect, the reader recognises as small models of the functioning of the text as one overall unit. If we accept the argument advanced by Lucien Dallenbach in his seminal study of reflexivity, *Le Récit spéculaire*, we can see that this type of *mise en abyme*, serving as a miniature emblem of the literal organisation of the whole, involves a hermeneutic circle since it presupposes a prior understanding ('précompréhension') which is then validated, rectified or refined upon as a result of the understanding which is has itself made possible.[21]

The wider intertext constitutes another stage in the reading process which helps to prolong and to refine upon the suggestions implicit in such emblematic passages. Thus, for example, the notion of the textual *carrefour* first evoked in the dedication to Houssaye, and furthered in the imagery of 'Un Plaisant' and 'Les Bons Chiens', is in a sense elliptically confirmed by the invocation of Sterne as a possible 'academic muse' in the last prose poem.

Sterne has Tristram, his narrator, boast of his powers to convert the empty plain of the blank page into a populous city as a result of the innumerable digressive encounters which he embarks upon *en route*.[22] Tristram discusses the dilemma of the 'hobby-horsical' or digressive writer who proceeds *analogically*: he does not know in which order to introduce his material. All the novelist's material, if analogous, is *equal*: there is no hierarchy of importance. One of the themes of *Tristram Shandy* is that the great is on a level with the trivial, the 'bagatelle'. The implications of this rejection of hierarchies of importance are far-reaching. The refusal to impose a hierarchy is paradoxical in any novel, given the inevitable sententiousness of narrative itself: its natural propensity to impose meaning and morality through the successiveness of fictional time and plot. (See my earlier discussion of the prose poems' parodying of sententiousness, in Chapter 3.) If the text is to be ruled by the principle of *analogy*, and the balance is to lie in favour of the *paradigmatic*, then clearly this will produce tensions. Tristram compares his dilemma over where and *in which order* to include his tale of Trim's accident (whether amongst the anecdotes of Toby's amours with Widow Wadman, or with Toby's campaigns on the bowling green) to a baffling *crossroads*:

O ye powers... which enable mortal man to tell a story worth the hearing... I beg and beseech you... that wherever... it falls out that three several roads meet in one point, as they have done here, – that at least you set up a guide-post in the centre of them, in mere charity to direct an uncertain devil which of the three he is to take.[23]

The facetiously satanic implications here of the rejection of hierarchy as such (the forking of the ways, the uncertain devil) also find their echo in both *Le Neveu du Rameau* and *Le Spleen de Paris*. In 'Le Joueur généreux' the poet's *chance encounter* with the mysterious satanic Being takes place in the throng of the boulevard, that is precisely amidst 'la fréquentation [de la] ville énorme, [le] croisement de [ses] innombrables rapports'.

The *lieu commun* or common ground of the city as *crossroads* can be interpreted, as I suggested in Chapter 1, as a figure of (inter)textuality itself. Despite the tongue-in-cheek dismissal of the 'academic muse' in 'Les Bons Chiens' (the poet has just invoked Sterne), it is, of course, the case that the preferred, democratic, vulgar muse ('la citadine, la vivante') is as much a creature of the 'academic' intertext as she is a vulgar embodiment of contemporary Parisian reality. The poet's muse is double, the product of a personal and painful experience of modern urban reality, and inevitably, of the cultural/textual heritage which controls Baudelaire's, and his reader's, *apprehension* of both city and text.

Despite the fact that *Le Spleen de Paris* was written well over a century ago, it clearly raises questions about the functions and limitations of plot in extended prose works which remain central in the experimental novels of our own time. The artifice of a plot which might provide a thread linking the whole, and with it the corollary artifice of beginnings and endings, is conspicuously drawn attention to in the dedication, only to be dismissed. As a *mobile* work, a work whose parts may be read out of sequence, *Le Spleen de Paris* pushes towards an ideal of non-linearity. By doing this, and although it is not a novel, it serves to problematise some of the novel's most basic and paradoxical conventions: the inevitable tensions between, for example, the functioning of plot, the artifice of beginnings and endings, and the necessary open-endedness of any work of art which purports to respect the reader's own creative role. These issues constitute a major preoccupation in postmodernist novels, which habitually begin with explicit discussion of the arbitrary nature of beginnings, and end either with a choice of endings, an indication that endings are impossible, or by offering a pastiche or parody of a conventional ending.[24]

It is a truism to say that *Le Spleen de Paris* is not a novel. Of course it is not a novel. But the mere pigeon-holing of the work in a tidy genre classification is in itself an exercise of limited interest. What is of interest, and what is particularly striking, is the way in which this text is so exceptionally effective as a vehicle for problematising those genres to which it does not belong. As we have seen, the *Petits Poèmes en prose* directly invite comparison with Balzac and with the Sternean novel, but for the modern reader the significance of *Le Spleen de Paris* in relation to modernist and postmodern narratives is often equally thought-provoking. One obvious affinity lies in the abandonment or parodying of the realist (Balzacian) quest to offer law-like explanations of human behaviour. We have seen that in the case of *Le Spleen de Paris* there emerges a logical connection between the hostility towards 'the laying down of the law' and the refusal to impose a narrative thread, to impose a beginning and an ending.[25] Again, like many modernist and postmodern texts, and despite the pseudo-conclusion of 'Les Bons Chiens' with its paradoxical 'Sternean' device of putting the dedication, or invocation of the muse, at the *end*, the collection *does not convey a sense of completion*, presenting itself instead as inherently 'abandoned' rather than 'finished':

Nous pouvons couper où nous voulons, moi ma rêverie, vous le manuscrit, le lecteur sa lecture. (Dedication to Arsène Houssaye)

Again, as in both modernist and postmodern narratives the relationship between text and world is characterised by epistemological doubt. Of all the prose poems 'Les Fenêtres' offers perhaps the most obvious example of the abandonment of the pretension that the text describes the world or that its explanations are more than an approximation of truth:

Peut-être me direz-vous: 'Es-tu sûr que cette légende soit la vraie?' Qu'importe ce que peut être la réalité placée hors de moi, si elle m'a aidé à vivre, à sentir que je suis et ce que je suis?

Given this tendency it is doubtless unsurprising that another shared characteristic is the prominence of self-reflexivity. The metaphor of the kaleidoscope, for example, which Baudelaire favoured in his draft notes for the Dedication to Arsène Houssaye, has had a particular following amongst modernist and postmodern writers such as Proust, Musil, Carry Van Bruggen, Italo Calvino and Claude Simon. Moreover, such self-reflexive metaphors or *topoi* as, for example, the labyrinth, the journey without destination, mirrors, sexual penetration and capitalist financial speculation have figured repeatedly in modernist and postmodern narratives, as in *Le Spleen de Paris*. Intertextuality, too, is a particularly conspicuous feature of many postmodern works, and the metaphor of the palimpsest (which Baudelaire discusses in terms of 'la mnémotechnie du beau' in 'Un Mangeur d'opium')[26] has been a recurrent feature in postmodern writing.

With *Le Spleen de Paris* there is less confidence in the narrator's role than was to be found, say, in Sterne's novels. The contrasting and often contradictory voices in the different prose poems are at a far remove from the single narratorial voice of Sterne's Tristram, who so consistently elicits the smiles and good humour of his readers. In this, Baudelaire's text resembles more closely the metafictional works of twentieth-century writers like Nabokov, Barth and Beckett, who, as Inger Christensen comments, 'have a waning belief in the narrator's role and nourish few illusions of being understood by the world at large'.[27]

The prose poems pay tribute to the emotional attractiveness of Sterne's humour, its appeal to both the head and the heart of its audience ('sentimental farceur, farceur incomparable'). But, despite the loss of confidence in communication which is suggested in so many of the prose poems, there is nevertheless the tongue-in-cheek implication of a belief in communication with a chosen few ('les bons chiens'). Sterne's narrator wants to promote laughter as a way of establishing contact with the readers and of making them forget life's hard realities. In *Le Spleen de Paris* the element of *raillerie* which was so prized by Baudelaire and which his correspondence reveals him as striving so hard to maintain does not promote an analogous atmosphere of easy-going optimism, and on occasions it more clearly resembles the black humour of the more modern metafictionists. However, this is a text which still presents itself as striving for a broad psychological appeal, a conformity to both '[les] mouvements lyriques de l'âme', 'les ondulations de la rêverie', and to the 'soubresauts de la conscience'.

There are other areas in which the prose poems differ more strikingly from postmodernist works. For example, it is a characteristic of postmodern texts to subvert the reader's predisposition to look for textual coherence. In the case of *Le Spleen de Paris*, by contrast, although the readers are encouraged to pick up the book or to interrupt their reading as and when they feel like it, they are nevertheless explicitly encouraged from the outset to seek out evidence of textual coherence, since they are forewarned that 'tout y est à la fois tête et queue, alternativement et réciproquement'.

Another difference, and one which reveals *Le Spleen de Paris*'s links with Romantic and Humanist tradition, lies in the way Baudelaire's text signals the idea that a species of totality may be extrapolated from an individual world view. In the dedication the poet indicates his intention to embark upon 'la description de la vie moderne, ou plutôt d'*une* vie moderne et plus abstraite'. This passage has little in common with postmodernism, but it does call to mind Victor Hugo's

Conclusion

exhortations to the reader of the Preface to *Les Contemplations*, where the readers are urged to find their own soul's mirror in a book which is presented as the distillation of a life's experience and sufferings, a work which is at once single or personal and universal or multiple.

Clearly, it would be wrong to suggest that *Le Spleen de Paris* is simply a text which was 'ahead of its time', and which we should class alongside works of our own postmodern era, our own *fin de siècle*. But, as Baudelaire himself insisted in his article on Wagner, there are problems to which writers and artists perennially return ('Les mêmes problèmes scientifiques, poétiques, artistiques, se reproduisent sans cesse à travers les âges').[28] *Le Spleen de Paris* raises its share of such problems. Problems which go to the heart of our thinking about the tensions between paradigmatic and metonymic tendencies in literary texts, the balance between analogy and progression, metaphor and plot; about the role of morality or moral argument in works of art; or about the relationship between individuality/excentricity and conformity to preexisting codes, both in literature and in the world.

But above all the historical importance of *Petits Poèmes en prose* lies in the abandoning of a certain concept of poetic language. It is a concept which is well illustrated in the following passage taken from the *Petit Traité de poésie française* which was published by Banville in 1872 only a few years after Baudelaire's death:

Peut-il y avoir des poèmes en prose? Non, il ne peut y en avoir, malgré le *Télémaque* de Fénélon, les admirables *Poèmes en prose* de Charles Baudelaire et le *Gaspard de le Nuit* de Louis Bertrand; car il est impossible d'imaginer une prose, si parfaite qu'elle soit, à laquelle on ne puisse, avec un effort surhumain, rien ajouter ou rien retrancher; elle est toujours à faire, et par conséquent n'est jamais la chose faite.[29]

The poem is clearly seen here as a discrete, crystalline unit, from which nothing can be added and nothing taken away. It is 'la chose faite', a hallowed instance of perfection. Nothing could be further from the dynamic openness of Baudelaire's text and the opportunity for creative participation which it offers its readership; nothing could resemble less the awareness of (inter)textual continuity which informs every level of *Le Spleen de Paris*.

Notes

PREFACE

1 Charles Baudelaire, *Œuvres complètes* I, edited by Claude Pichois, (Paris, 1975), p. 1293. This is the edition to which I shall refer throughout.
2 See the article by Kathryn Slott, 'Le Texte e(s)t son double. *Gaspard de la nuit*: Intertextualité, parodie, auto-parodie', *French Forum*, 1 (1981), 28–35.
3 *Oc* II, 644.
4 Michel Butor, 'Le Roman et la poésie', *Répertoire* II (Paris, 1964), 20.
5 Barbara Johnson, *Défigurations du langage poétique* (Paris, 1979).
6 Roland Barthes, 'La Rochefoucauld: "Réflexions ou sentences et maximes"', in *Le Degré zéro de l'écriture* (Paris, 1972).
7 *Le Degré zéro de l'écriture*, 69.
8 *Oc* I, 276; *Correspondance* II (Paris, 1973), 301 and 473.

INTRODUCTION

1 See the account by Robert Kopp in his edition of the *Petits Poèmes en prose* (Paris, 1969), xxviii–lxxiii, and the *Listes de projets* in the *Reliquat du Spleen de Paris* (*Oc* I, 365–74).
2 See, for example, Marcel Ruff, *Baudelaire l'homme et l'œuvre* (Paris, 1955), 100–18; Max Milner, *Baudelaire: Enfer ou ciel qu'importe?* (Paris, 1967); C. Bruns, 'Architecture secrète', *Nottingham French Studies*, 5 (1966), 67. Others have commented further that *Les Fleurs du mal* were probably not written to conform to a rigid prior conception but that the 'cadre' must have evolved later: see Albert Feuillerat, 'L'Architecture des *Fleurs du mal*', in *Studies by Members of the French Department of Yale University*, edited by A. Feuillerat (New Haven and London, 1941), 223.
3 See Lévi-Strauss's description of the structural principle behind the kaleidoscope, *Le Pensée sauvage* (Paris, 1962), 49–50.

4 Hugo, *Œuvres complètes*, ed. Jean Massin (Paris, 1967), IV, 144. I have drawn here on the argument of K. K. Ruthven in his *Critical Assumptions* (Cambridge, 1979), 28.
5 *Oc* II, 493–6.
6 Léon Cellier makes this suggestion in *Baudelaire et Hugo* (Paris, 1970), 285.
7 *Oc* II, 139. See also his comment in 'Richard Wagner et *Tannhäuser* à Paris' that 'chacun est le diminutif de tout le monde, comme l'histoire d'un cerveau individuel représente en petit l'histoire du cerveau universel' (II, 793).
8 Michael Riffaterre, *Semiotics of Poetry* (Bloomington and London, 1978).
9 Joseph Frank, 'Spatial Form in Modern Literature', 73, in *Criticism: The Foundations of Modern Literary Judgement* (Berkeley and London, 1958), editors M. Schorer, J. Miles, and G. McKenzie.
10 See, for example, Paul de Man's discussion of 'Obsession' as a reading of *Correspondance*, *The Rhetoric of Romanticism* (New York, 1984), 243–62.
11 An exception is the argument advanced by Fernande de George, 'The Structure of Baudelaire's *Petits Poèmes en prose*', *L'Esprit créateur*, 12, 2 (1973), 144–53. This critic's description of a progressive oscillating structure is based on the, to my mind, reductive view that each poem contains one dominant theme and that the overall structure of the collection is plotted accordingly.
12 *Oc* II, 609.
13 Hugo, *Œuvres critiques*, 29 (Paris, 1969), 193–4.
14 Mallarmé, *Œuvres complètes* (Paris, 1945), 380. My comments in this paragraph are written partly in response to Gerald Brun's chapter on Mallarmé, in *Modern Poetry and the Idea of Language* (New Haven and London, 1974), 101–17.

1 THE CITY

1 See Victor Brombert, *Victor Hugo and the Visionary Novel* (Harvard, 1984), 1–15 and 49–85.
2 Victor Hugo, *Notre-Dame de Paris* (Paris, 1974), 113.
3 *Ibid.*, 170.
4 *Ibid.*, 115.
5 *Ibid.*, 123.
6 For example, through the references to 'maçonnerie' in 'Les Bons Chiens' and to cabalism in the *Canevas de la dédicace*.
7 *Notre-Dame*, 253.

8 *Ibid.*
9 Victor Brombert, 'Hugo: L'Edifice du livre', in *Romantisme*, 44 (1984), 52-3.
10 'Les Veuves' was, of course, a reworking of some of the themes in 'Petites Vieilles', the verse poem in *Tableaux Parisiens* which was dedicated to Hugo.
11 *Notre-Dame*, 191-2.
12 Balzac, *La Comédie Humaine*, V (Paris, 1977), 812-13. These examples were suggested to me by an open lecture on *Ferragus* by Jean Jacques Labia at Warwick University, November 1986.
13 Edgar Allan Poe, *A Tale of the Ragged Mountains*, in *Tales of Mystery and Imagination* (London and Paris, 1975), 25; Théophile Gautier, *Spirite*, in *Oeuvres complètes* IV (Geneva, 1978), 81.

Victor Hugo's contemporary description of the arabesque as a metaphor for fantasy illustrates the same preoccupation:

C'est la fantaisie, c'est l'arabesque.
L'arabesque dans l'Art est le même phénomène que la végétation dans la nature. L'arabesque pousse, croît... est incommensurable; elle a une puissance inouïe d'extension et d'agrandissement; elle emplit des horizons et elle en ouvre d'autres; elle intercepte les fonds lumineux par d'innombrables entre-croisements, et si vous mêtez à ce branchage la figure humaine, l'ensemble est vertigineux, c'est un saisissement... il se fait dans le fini une combinaison infini (*William Shakespeare*, in *Oeuvres complètes* XXIX, 137)

14 Laurence Sterne, *The Life and Opinions of Tristram Shandy, Gentleman* (Harmondsworth, 1970), 510-11.
15 Roland Barthes, 'De l'œuvre au texte', in *Revue d'esthétique*, 3 (1971), 17-24.
16 Jacques Derrida, *De la grammatologie* (Paris, 1967), 65.
17 These will be discussed in more detail in Chapter 4. On *Tristram Shandy*, see note 14 above.
18 Hugo, *William Shakespeare*, *Oeuvres complètes* XXIX, 18.
19 On the *flâneur* and the big city crowd, see Walter Benjamin, *Charles Baudelaire: A Lyric Poet in the Era of High Capitalism* (London, 1973), Part I, Chapter 2. See also the same book, Part II, Chapters 5 and 6 on the marginal status of the *flâneur* and the alienation produced by Haussmann's transformation of Paris.
20 Hugo, *William Shakespeare*, 61.
21 See Barbara Johnson's analysis of 'Le Galant Tireur', 'un texte qui... parle *explicitement*, en même temps que figurativement, de la figure', in *Défigurations*, 83-100.
22 Philippe Hamon in 'Texte et architecture', *Poétique*, 73 (1988), 3-26.

2 EXCHANGE CODES

1 *Oc* II, 125.
2 *Oc* I, 360.
3 Roland Barthes, *Essais critiques* (Paris, 1964), 91.
4 *Oc* I, 703.
5 *Oc* I, 439. See Barbara Johnson's detailed analysis of 'L'Invitation au voyage' highlighting the key notions of 'value', 'work' and 'economy' (*Défigurations*, 128–45).
6 Bertrand's 'jeton du fou' in the last piece of *Gaspard de la nuit* is a metaphor for his book itself:

> L'homme est un balancier qui frappe une monnaie à son coin. Le quadruple porte l'empreinte de l'empereur; la médaille, du pape: le jeton, du fou.
>
> Je marque mon jeton à ce jeu de la vie où nous perdons coup sur coup et où le diable, pour en finir, rafle joueurs, dés et tapis vert.
>
> L'empereur dicte ses ordres à ses capitaines, le pape adresse des bulles à la chrétienté, et le fou écrit un livre.

7 *Oc* I, 399.
8 Etienne Gilson, 'Baudelaire and the Muse', in Henri Peyre, *Baudelaire: A Collection of Critical Essays* (Englewood Cliffs, N.J., 1962), 82. See also Barbara Johnson's reading of this poem in *Défigurations*, 75–6.
9 *Oc* I, 1344.
10 See Barbara Johnson, *Défigurations*, 139–41 on the relationship in 'L'Invitation au voyage' between the priceless and the banal.
11 Walter Benjamin, *Charles Baudelaire*, 27–34.
12 Stendhal, *Le Rouge et le noir* (Paris, 1973), 273, in the chapter entitled 'Quelle est la décoration qui distingue?'
13 P. Arétin, *Œuvres choisies*, 'traduites de l'italien pour la première fois avec des notes par P.-L. Jacob, et précédées de la vie abrégée de l'auteur, par Dujardin, d'après Mazzuchelli' (Paris, 1845).
14 *Ibid.*, x–xi. Claude Pichois notes that Baudelaire had himself been termed 'a modern Aretino' (*Oc* I, 1353).
15 See Baudelaire's comparison of drug-taking to suicide in 'Le Poème du hachisch' (*Oc* I, 439).
16 Claude Pichois and Jean Ziegler, *Baudelaire* (Paris, 1987), 265–70.
17 *Correspondance* II, 453.
18 Claude Pichois and Jean Ziegler, *Baudelaire*, 496–7.

3 POETRY AND DESIRE

1 Peter Brooks, *Reading for the Plot: Design and Intention in Narrative* (Oxford, 1984), 37. See the whole of his Chapter 2, 'Narrative

Desire', for a fascinating illustration of Lacanien theory in its application to *La Peau de chagrin* and other narratives.
2 *Ibid.*, 37.
3 *Ibid.*, 39.
4 Laurence Sterne, *Tristram Shandy*, 83.
5 See Joan Joffe Hall's article, 'The Hobbyhorsical World of Tristram Shandy', *Modern Language Quarterly*, 24 (1963), 131–43.
6 Peter Brooks, *Reading for the Plot*, 60.
7 Diderot, *Le Neveu de Rameau et autres dialogues philosophiques* (Paris, 1972), 31.
8 Leo Bersani, *Baudelaire and Freud* (London, 1977), 12.
9 *Oc* I, 317.
10 *Oc* I, 355.
11 See especially his comments on the importance of imagination even in the art of portraiture and on the portrait as 'le drame naturel inhérent à tout homme'. The portraitist is described as a 'comédien'. *Oc* II, 655.
12 *Oc* I, 280.
13 Barbara Johnson, *Défigurations*, 44–8.
14 *Oc* I, 319.
15 Gérard de Nerval, *Œuvres*, edited by Albert Béguin and Jean Richer (Paris, 1974), I, 257–8.
16 Balzac, *Illusions perdues* (Paris, 1962), 385. For a description of the feminine qualities of the poet-figure Lucien de Rubempré, see for example pp. 34–5.
17 Quoted by Christopher Prendergast in *Balzac: Fiction and Melodrama* (London, 1978).

4 UNSENTENTIOUS MORALITIES

1 Geoffrey Bennington, *Sententiousness and the Novel: Laying down the Law in Eighteenth-Century French Fiction* (Cambridge, 1985), 62.
2 Quoted in *ibid.*, 62.
3 *Oc* I, 367, 368, 369.
4 See Geoffrey Bennington's lucid account in *Sententiousness and the Novel*, 21–5. Bennington's thoughts on the tensions between fragmentariness and totalisation in Vauvenargues and Chamfort are also of particular interest with regard to *Le Spleen de Paris*.
5 See the discussion of 'Le Rêve d'Alembert' by Jay Caplan, in *Framed Narratives: Diderot's Genealogy of the Beholder* (Manchester, 1986), 64–71.
6 *Notre-Dame de Paris*, Book XX, Chapter 4. The allusion to Rabelais early in Hugo's chapter alerts his readers to the play on intertextual parallels in *Gargantua*.

7 *Notre-Dame de Paris*, Gallimard, 1974, 525.
8 *Ibid.*
9 On the moon as a symbol of intertextuality see below, p. 81.
10 Just as in the contemporary text, *Le Peintre de la vie moderne*, it is the archetypal courtesan of a Guys study who is described as representing 'la sauvagerie dans la civilisation'. *Oc* II, 720.
11 See my article 'Laurence Sterne and *Le Spleen de Paris*', *French Studies*, 42 (1988), p. 171.
12 See *Tristram Shandy*, 92–3.
13 For a fascinating reading of 'Portraits de maîtresses' as a text in which 'narrative succession is used...as a form of symbolic execution', see Marie Maclean's chapter on 'Narrative Power and the Sexual/Textual nexus' in *Narrative as Performance: The Baudelairean Experiment* (London and New York, 1988), 125–40.
14 Margaret Gilman noted this in her article 'Baudelaire and Emerson' in *The Romanic Review*, 9 (1943), p. 222.
15 *Oc* II, 323.
16 'Le Marquis de ****, qui ne perd pas l'occasion de dire une méchanceté, disait hier, en parlant d'elle, que la maladie l'avait retournée, et qu'à présent son âme était sur sa figure. Malheureusement tout le monde trouva que l'expression était juste' (*Les Liaisons dangereuses* (Paris, 1958), 441).
17 See Edgar Allan Poe, *The Complete Works*, edited by James A. Harrison (New York, 1965), XVI, 161. Baudelaire's hostility to a certain breed of crude, hypocritical moralist is evident in a remark in *Les Paradis artificiels* (*Oc* I, 381): 'Quand je dis moralistes, j'entends pseudo-moralistes pharisiens.'
18 *Ibid.*, XVI, 166.
19 See the discussion of the 'madness' of the man of genius, *Le Neveu de Rameau*, 37 and the implied allusion to Pascal, *Le Neveu de Rameau*, 85:

> Celui qui serait sage n'aurait point de fou. Celui donc qui a un fou n'est pas sage; s'il n'est pas sage, il est fou; et peut-être, fût-il roi, le fou de son fou.

20 Shoshana Felman, *Writing and Madness* (New York, 1985), 252.
21 Barbara Johnson, *Défigurations*, 65.

5 POETRY AND MADNESS

1 Shoshana Felman, *Writing and Madness*.
2 *Los Caprichos by Francisco Goya y Lucientes*, edited with an introduction by Philip Hofer (New York, 1969), plate 43: 'The sleep of reason produces monsters'.

3 J. Cohen, 'Théorie de la figure', *Communications*, 16 (1970), 22.
4 M. Foucault, *Histoire de la folie à l'âge classique* (Paris, 1972), 365.
5 Blaise Pascal, *Pensées*, edited by Louis Lafuma (Paris, 1951), 232.
6 *Ibid.*, 94.
7 On *Robinson Crusoe* as 'one of our most important urban novels', see Richard Lehan, 'Urban Signs and Urban Literature: Literary Form and Historical Process', *New Literary History*, 18, 1 (1986), 99–113. Richard Lehan argues that *Robinson Crusoe*, despite appearing at first sight to have little or no connection to the city, is in fact 'one of our most important urban novels because it explains the cultural and historical process by which the commercial (that is, the modern) city came into being'.
8 On the allusions to Rousseau see Melvin Zimmermann, 'Trois études sur Baudelaire et Rousseau', *Etudes Baudelairiennes*, 9 (1981), 30–71.
9 *Oc* I, 291.
10 *Oc* II, 793.
11 The term used by an early critic, González Azaola, quoted by Nigel Glendinning, *Goya and his Critics* (New Haven and London, 1977), 61.
12 Reproduced in *Los Caprichos by Francisco Goya y Lucientes*, 43. See also Hofer's discussion (2–3) of the change of selection for the opening plate which he suggested may have been dictated by the political dangers of associating himself too closely with the name of Rousseau.
13 *Oc* II, 568.
14 See K. K. Ruthven, *Critical Assumptions* (Cambridge, 1979), 112.
15 *Tristram Shandy*, 296–7.
16 *Ibid.*, 46.
17 Aloysius Bertrand, *Gaspard de la nuit: Fantaisies à la manière de Rembrandt et de Callot*, edited by Max Milner (Paris, 1980); Kathryn Slott, 'Le Texte e(s)t son double. *Gaspard de la nuit*: intertextualité, parodie, auto-parodie', 28–35.
18 See note 10 above.
19 Lucan, *The Civil War (Pharsalia)*, with an English translation by J. D. Duff (Cambridge and London, 1969), VI, 341.
20 *Oc* I, 369, 370.
21 These classifications are demonstrated by Foucault in *Histoire de la folie à l'âge classique*.
22 *Le Neveu de Rameau*, 85.
23 *Ibid.*, 36–8.
24 *Oc* I, 358.
25 *Le Neveu de Rameau*, 39–40.

26 *Ibid.*, 40.
27 Baudelaire's allusion to Proudhon in a marginal note to 'Assommons les pauvres!' serves to remind one that, whatever his impatience with the economist's excessively direct formulations, and his lack of *dandysme*, long after 1851 he still retained his admiration for the theoretician and social reformer whose treatise on property represented a vigorous subversion of the values upheld by Diderot's Philosopher. In a letter to Ancelle of 8 February 1865 he writes as follows: 'S'il était question d'art... vous auriez raison de dire de Proudhon: Il est fou. – Mais en matière d'économie, il me paraît singulièrement respectable.' (The original manuscript comment, 'Qu'en dis-tu, citoyen Proudhon?', is also open to interpretation as drawing attention to the fact that the prose poem was a lesson in *dandysme* and the ironic register from which Proudhon might have profited.) See also Gretchen van Slyke, 'Dans l'intertexte de Baudelaire et de Proudhon: pourquoi faut-il assommer les pauvres?', *Romantisme*, 45 (1984), 57–77.
28 Yoichi Sumi, *Le Neveu de Rameau: Caprices et logiques du jeu* (Tokyo, 1975), 20.
29 The epigraph on the title-page of *Tristram Shandy*.

6 POETIC COOKERY

1 Maturin Régnier, *Satyre* x, '*Le Souper ridicule*', in *Œuvres complètes* (Paris, 1975).
2 See Chapter 9, below.
3 Suzanne Bernard, *Le poème en prose: De Baudelaire à nos jours* (Paris, 1959), 144, and Barbara Johnson, *Défigurations*, 106.
4 On the intertextual links between this passage and Diderot's *Neveu de Rameau*, see Chapter 5 above.
5 On the poem's implied subversion of the doctrine that 'l'homme est né bon' (attributed by Baudelaire to Rousseau), see Barbara Johnson, *Défigurations*, 77–9.
6 Baudelaire uses this type of phonetic corruption (substituting 'c' for 'g' and 'd' for 't') in his translation of Poe's *Angel of the Odd*, where it indicates the drunken enunciation of a curious personage who appears before the narrator one evening when he has been drinking. The small savages of 'Le Gâteau' similarly appear just after the narrator has taken a bottle of spirits from his pocket. Baudelaire wrote to E. Laumonier in January 1862 asking for a copy of this text to be sent to him as a matter of urgency. This was the year in which he published 'Le Gâteau'.
7 *Oc* II, 290–1.
8 *Oc* I, 444.

9 André Lebois drew attention to the way in which poems are invented from figures of speech such as 'voir la vie en beau', 'chacun sa chimère', 'la corde du pendu' and 'marchand de nuages' (*Prestiges et actualité des 'Petits Poèmes en prose'*, Archives des lettres modernes, 18 (1958), 20). To these might be added other examples such as 'manger son pain blanc le premier' ('Le Gâteau') and 'Ouvrir de grands yeux' ('Une mort héroïque', 'La Corde'). See also Barbara Johnson's analysis of the 'littéralisation' of the figure of speech 'tuer le temps' in 'Le Galant Tireur' (*Défigurations*, 83–100).

The prose poems share with the fantastic tale the characteristic of taking the figurative sense literally, and this affinity throws some light on Baudelaire's particular interest in the works of Hoffmann, Poe and Maturin. On this feature of the fantastic, see Tzvetan Todorov, *Introduction à la littérature fantastique* (Paris, 1970), 82–7.

10 *Défigurations*, 38–9 and 52–5.

11 On 'Les Bons Chiens' see Jean Starobinski, *Portrait de l'artiste en saltimbanque* (Geneva and Paris, 1970), and, especially, Ross Chambers, 'The Artist as Performing Dog', *Comparative Literature*, 23, 4 (1971), 312–24. Ross Chambers argues that the 'bons chiens' can be read as 'artist dogs' who 'present a picture of courage and honour wretchedly exploited' (313), part of a series of the theme of the artist defeated by life. He suggests that the prose poem invites association with Cervantes' picaresque tale of a dog's life *El Colloquio de los perros* and with E. T. A. Hoffmann's *reprise* of the Cervantes text in *Nachricht der neusten schicksalen des Hundes Berganza* (1814). 'Baudelaire would have appreciated Berganza's misogyny and his stand against Morality in art; but equally, the stress on the social pariahhood of the *Lumpenproletariat* in "Les Bons Chiens" makes Baudelaire's text as much a "criticism" of Hoffmann's themes as Hoffmann's exclusive insistence on Berganza's status as an artist is a limiting restatement of those of Cervantes.' On some further intertextual resonances linking the poem to the Cervantes text and to *The Golden Ass* of Apuleius, see my article 'Laurence Sterne and *Le Spleen de Paris*', *French Studies*, 42, 2 (1988), 172–5.

12 Fernande de George argues in her article 'The Structure of Baudelaire's *Petits Poèmes en prose*', *L'Esprit créateur*, 12, 2 (1973), 144–53, that the ordering in successive publications in 1865, 1866 and 1867 suggests that 'Les Bons Chiens' was placed at the end of the collection for a specific reason and not merely by chance.

13 *Oc* I, 365.

7 THE POET AS SAVAGE: REWRITING CLICHÉ

1 On the reactivating of cliché in literary texts, see Riffaterre's *Essais de stylistique structurale* (Paris, 1971), 162–79; also Laurent Jenny, 'Structures et fonctions du cliché', *Poétique*, 12 (1972), 495–517.
2 On Baudelaire's thought, viewed in the context of changing attitudes to nature in the eighteenth and nineteenth centuries, see Felix Leakey, *Baudelaire and Nature* (Manchester, 1969). For an analysis which draws on Lévi-Strauss, see René Galand, *Baudelaire, poétique et poésie* (Paris, 1969).

The association of poet-figure and 'sauvage' which is conspicuous in 'Le Crépuscule du soir' is consistent with Baudelaire's publication of some of the prose poems in 1866 as 'Petits Poèmes lycanthropes'. 'Lycanthropes', with its association of monstrosity and the *loup-garou*, prolongs the suggestion of *poèmes nocturnes*. Rousseau had associated the writer with *loup-garou*, suggesting wildness, unsociability and solitariness. Baudelaire describes himself in similar terms in a letter to Hugo of 23 September 1859 (*Correspondance* I, 598):

> Je me trouve forte à l'aise sous ma *flétrissure*, et je *sais* que désormais, dans quelque genre de littérature que je me répande, je resterai un monstre et un loup-garou.

3 *Oc* I, 703.
4 *Oc* II, 576.
5 See the poet's letter to Poulet-Malassis of 13 March 1860 (*Correspondance*, II, 9). The proposed subtitle 'idéal de la beauté noire' invites comparison with the 1862 subtitle to 'Un Hémisphère dans une chevelure' ('Poème exotique'). Barbara Johnson suggests that the latter contributes to the text's acknowledgement of its own literariness (*Défigurations*, 40). The variant of the other prose poem 'Dorothée, idéal de la beauté noire' allows a similar reading.
6 See Robert Kopp's edition, 239–41, and Barbara Johnson, *Défigurations*, 78. For a more detailed discussion of Baudelaire's refutation in 'Le Gâteau' of the notion that 'l'homme est né bon', see Melvin Zimmerman, 'Trois Etudes sur Baudelaire et Rousseau, 1. Autour du "Gâteau"', 31–51.
7 *Oc* II, 323.
8 These portraits of women bring to mind the comments made in *Mon Cœur mis à nu* ('La femme est le contraire du Dandy...La femme est *naturelle*, c'est-à-dire abominable' (1, 677)) and in *Le Peintre de la vie moderne* ('Elle représente bien la sauvagerie dans la

civilisation. Elle a sa beauté qui lui vient du Mal... Elle porte le regard à l'horizon, comme la bête de proie' (II, 720)).
9 Balzac, *Œuvres complètes* (Paris, 1953), VI, 254.
10 *Oc* I, 287.
11 *Oc* I, 281.
12 *Oc* I, 334.
13 *Oc* I, 312.
14 This view is clearly revealed in his comments on commerce in *Mon Cœur mis à nu*: 'Le commerce est *naturel, donc* il est *infâme*' (*Oc* I, 703).
15 *Oc* I, 690. Baudelaire viewed the process of civilisation as an indirect by-product of art rather than as an artistic end in itself (see for example his summary of Poe's argument against didactic poetry (*Oc* II, 333) repeated in his 1859 article on Gautier (*Oc* II, 113)). He despised Castagnary's utilitarian approach to art, and although he echoes Castagnary's phrase, he would no doubt have wanted to put a completely different interpretation on it. See *Oc* I, 1495, and note 6 above.
16 Georges Blin, 'Les Fleurs de l'impossible', *Revue des sciences humaines*, 127 (1967), 461–6.
17 See Robert Kopp's critical edition of the *Petits Poèmes en prose* (Paris, 1969), 253–5.

8 MUSICALITY

1 *Oc* II, 1452.
2 Jocelynne Loncke (*Baudelaire et la Musique* (Paris, 1975)) argues that Baudelaire's understanding of musical technique is quite advanced. She concurs with André Ferran, 'Baudelaire et la Musique', in *Mélanges Huguet* (Paris, 1940), 387.

See also Serge Meitinger, 'Baudelaire et Mallarmé devant R. Wagner', *Romantisme*, 33 (1981), 75–90. Meitinger notes that Baudelaire recognised the importance of the *leitmotif* and he relates this to the fact that Baudelaire had long been an exponent of 'une poésie critique'. He rightly emphasises that Baudelaire's vision of Wagner, unlike Mallarmé's, 'met l'accent sur... la maîtrise concertée de tous les éléments en vue d'une globalisation de l'effet' (90).
3 Baudelaire suggests that the modern artist's achievements are realised in spite of the society in which he lives (*Oc* II, 634). In his essay on William Shakespeare Hugo had condemned the Horatian maxim 'Odi profanum vulgus' and had praised Shakespeare for speaking the language of the people. When Baudelaire, in his

article on Delacroix (1863), enthusiastically adopts the same Horatian phrase rejected by Hugo (*Oc* II, 761) he is referring not to the common people and their language, as Hugo had done, but to the bourgeois public whose materialistic, utilitarian values dominated the society of his day (in his 1865 letter to Jules Janin he defines 'la canaille' as 'ceux qui ne se connaissent pas en poésie', (*Oc* II, 233)). The same 'aristocratic' bias can be found in the contemporary *Projet de préface aux fleurs du mal*. Here Baudelaire comments that were he to give an explanation of how and why he wrote *Les Fleurs du mal* he would print only ten or so copies, and again he despairs of the intellectual capacity of the crowd (*Oc* I, 85). In his article on Leconte de Lisle (1861) he writes of the 'sentiment d'aristocratie intellectuelle' which characterises De Lisle's poetry and comments that 'l'impopularité, en France, s'attache à tout ce qui tend vers n'importe quel genre de perfection' (*Oc* II, 177). The descent into the 'carrefour' associated with writing prose poetry under the aegis of 'la muse familière' ('Les Bons Chiens') does not mean a capitulation to 'la canaille' (in the sense in which Baudelaire uses the word in the letter to Jules Janin), although the poem 'Laquelle est la vrai?' offers a humorous exposition of the tensions involved. The concluding lines of the 'Epilogue' poem make it plain that the choices of urban muse and a discourse characterised by recondite indirection need not be mutually exclusive:

> Je t'aime, ô capitale infâme, courtisane
> Et bandits, tels souvent vous offrez des plaisirs
> Que ne comprennent pas les vulgaires profanes.

4 Bruce Morrissette suggests that certain leitmotifs in music may be equated with *mises en abyme* in literature. See 'Un Héritage d'André Gide: La duplication intérieure', *Comparative Literary Studies*, 7, 2 (1971), 125–42.
5 Lucien Dallenbach, *Le Récit spéculaire: Essai sur la mise en abyme* (Paris, 1977), 123.
6 The references to music in other poems contribute to the association between music and poetry. For example, in 'Un Hémisphère dans une chevelure', 'L'Invitation au voyage' and 'Le Thyrse' music is associated with 'vagabondage', a theme which is, in turn, associated with lunacy, intoxication, digression and (self-reflexively) with the processes of association and analogy which form the fabric of the poetic structure itself. In 'Le Tir et le cimetière' discordant rifle shots, mimicked by the '*soubresaut*' effect of the poem itself, are compared to 'l'explosion des bouchons de

champagne dans le bourdonnement *d'une symphonie en sourdine*' (my italics).

Travelling clouds figure in 'L'Etranger', 'Les Bienfaits de la lune', 'Les Vocations' and 'La Soupe et les nuages', where they appeal to lunatic, outcast or imaginative individuals, presented as analogues of the poet.

In other poems reflecting surfaces are associated with ironic *dédoublement*, a quality which Baudelaire described in his *1859 Salon* as being fundamental to literature ('l'imagination...contient l'esprit critique', *Oc* II, 623). For example, the description in 'L'Invitation au voyage' where the 'pays de Cocagne' is said to be 'riche, propre, et luisant comme une belle conscience' is also recalled in 'Portraits de maîtresses', where the fourth narrator comments:

L'histoire de mon amour ressemble à un interminable voyage sur une surface pure et polie comme un miroir, vertigineusement monotone, qui aurait réfléchi tous mes sentiments et mes gestes avec l'exactitude ironique de ma propre conscience. (*Oc* I, 348)

The same terms (reflecting surface of sea or mirror, journeying, and the limpidity of a specular consciousness) occur in both the above poems, whilst a third, 'Le Miroir', provides an even more succinct *jeu de mots* on the equation of mirror and self-scrutinising consciousness:

je possède le droit de me mirer; avec plaisir ou déplaisir, cela ne regarde que ma conscience. (*Oc* I, 344)

Even the briefest of allusions can contribute to this play of specularity which dominates the collection of prose poems both referentially and on the level of the literal organisation of the collection itself. For example 'La Belle Dorothée', a poem which at first might appear to offer an escapist route, rapidly returns the reader to the 'étincelante fournaise intérieure', for when Dorothée smiles her white smile as in some cliché of the 'good savage', of the exotic and the natural (i.e. that which is not art), it is 'comme si elle apercevait au loin dans l'espace un miroir reflétant sa démarche et sa beauté'.

7 Lucien Dallenbach, 'Reflexivity and Reading', *New Literary History*, 11, 3 (1980), 440.
8 *Ibid.*, 441.
9 The expression is from a passage by Philippe Hamon, quoted by Dallenbach, 'Reflexivity and Reading', 439.

10 *Ibid.*, 441.
11 Gisèle Brelet, *Le Temps musical: Essai d'une esthétique nouvelle de la musique* (Paris, 1949); Leonard Meyer, *Emotion and Meaning in Music* (Chicago, 1959); Umberto Eco, *L'Œuvre ouverte* (Paris, 1965), especially 99–114.
12 For two contrasting approaches to the problem of oxymoron see Léon Cellier, 'D'une rhétorique profonde: Baudelaire et l'oxymoron', *Cahiers Internationaux du Symbolisme*, 8 (1965), 3–14, and Maurice-Jean Lefebve, *Structure du discours de la poésie et du récit* (Neuchâtel, 1971), 76. Cellier writes that Baudelaire's lyricism was characterised by antithesis and by oxymoron, both of which conformed to a philosophical necessity, but oxymoron differs from antithesis in that although it brings together two terms which should logically exclude one another it tends to unite these two terms. Basing his argument on H. Morier's definition of oxymoron, Cellier argues that its function is the opposite of antithesis in that it tends to reunite contraries. He argues that the irrational juxtaposition of contraries in language is a way of expressing the ecstasy produced by man's experience of the sacred.

Lefebve, on the other hand, sees the oxymoron not as a means of expressing the sacred, but as a means of drawing attention to the material of the language itself, and argues that it is poetic, or can be, not because it resolves the contradictions between its elements, 'mais au contraire parce qu'elle nous force à imaginer malgré tout une réalité dotée d'un pouvoir de présence d'autant plus grande qu'elle est contestée par son ambiguité' (76).
13 See Stephen Heath, *Vertige du déplacement* (Paris, 1974), 191–3 for a discussion of two types of irony, one of which is associated with 'fixation' or lack of hesitation (as in parody) whilst the other is 'plurivocal' and equivocal.
14 *Oc* I, 276 and II, 692.
15 For example, in 'Un Mangeur d'opium' Baudelaire's analysis of the memory process leads him to imply that there is a contradiction between harmony and dissonance (*Oc* I, 506). Or again, the notion of harmony to which Baudelaire refers in his description of Delacroix's circular ceiling in the Luxembourg library is inconsistent with the more sophisticated understanding of the term which he displays elsewhere. The implicit equation between harmony and consonance in this passage seems to reflect the difference between the views of nature expressed in the earlier and later works. A similar equation between harmony and consonance, or 'eurythmie', is to be found in 'Le Poème du hachisch', *Oc* I, 432. See Jocelynne Loncke's survey of Baudelaire's statements

about symphony, harmony and melody (*Baudelaire et la Musique*, 97–117).
16 *Poème en prose*, 131.
17 See David Kelley, *Charles Baudelaire's Salon of 1846* (unpublished Ph.D. Thesis, University of Cambridge, 1968), 304.
18 *Oc* II, 159–60.
19 *Oc* II, 43.
20 *Oc* II, 274.
21 'The Rationale of Verse', *The Complete Works of Edgar Allan Poe* (New York, 1965), XIV, 220 and 225–6.
22 Tzvetan Todorov, *Les Genres du discours* (Paris, 1978), 120, 122.
23 J.-M. Bailbé *Le Roman et la musique en France sous la monarchie de juillet* (Paris, 1969), 253–4.
24 Victor Hugo, *Théâtre complet* (Paris, 1963), I, 425.
25 *Ibid.*, I, 427.
26 Margaret Gilman draws attention to this omission in *Baudelaire the Critic* (New York, 1971), 96.

9 STRAIGHT LINES AND ARABESQUES

1 *Le Neveu de Rameau*, 105.
2 Laurence Sterne, *Tristram Shandy*, 64 and 313.
3 *Oc* II, 802.
4 The italics are by Baudelaire. *Oc* II, 80.
5 On 'Le Thyrse', see the article by Melvin Zimmerman, 'La Genèse du symbole du thyrse chez Baudelaire', *Bulletin Baudelairien*, 2, 1 (1966), 8–11, and the study by Marc Eigeldinger, '*Le Thyrse*, lecture thématique', *Etudes Baudelariennes*, 8 (1969), 172–83.
6 'Un Mangeur d'opium', *Oc* II, 444 and 515.
7 *Le Neveu de Rameau*, 105–6.
8 See Yoichi Sumi, *Le Neveu de Rameau: Caprices et logiques du jeu*.
9 *Ibid.*, 20.
10 In *Intertextuality: Theories and Practices*, edited by Michael Worton and Judith Still (Manchester, 1990), 11–12.
11 *Le Neveu de Rameau: Caprices et logiques du jeu*, 23–34.
12 *Oc* I, 703.
13 *Oc* I, 360.
14 See the account by Michael Worton and Judith Still of this aspect of Montaigne's writings in *Intertextuality: Theories and Practices*, 32–3.
15 *Tristram Shandy*, 92–3. See also my article 'Laurence Sterne and *Le Spleen de Paris*'.

16 The expression is Sterne's: *Tristram Shandy*, 428.
17 *Ibid.*, 575–6.

>She cannot, quoth my uncle Toby, halting, when they had marched up to within twenty paces of Mrs Wadman's door – she cannot, corporal, take it amiss. –
>
>– She will take it, an' please your honour, said the corporal, just as the Jew's widow at Lisbon took it of my brother Tom. –
>
>– And how was that? quoth my uncle Toby, facing quite about to the corporal.
>
>Your honour, replied the corporal, knows of Tom's misfortunes; but this affair has nothing to do with them any further than this, that if Tom had not married the widow – or had it pleased God after their marriage, that they had but put pork into their sausages, the honest soul had never been taken out of his warm bed, and dragged to the inquisition – 'Tis a cursed place – added the corporal, shaking his head, – when once a poor creature is in, he is in, an' please your honour, for ever.
>
>'Tis very true; said my uncle Toby, looking gravely at Mrs Wadman's house, as he spoke.
>
>Nothing, continued the corporal, can be so sad as confinement for life – or so sweet, an' please your honour, as liberty.
>
>Nothing, Trim – said my uncle Toby, musing – Whilst a man is free, – cried the corporal, giving a flourish with his stick thus –

[flourish]

>A thousand of my father's most subtle syllogisms could not have said more for celibacy.
>
>My uncle Toby looked earnestly towards his cottage and his bowling-green.

The corporal had unwarily conjured up the Spirit of calculation with his wand; and he had nothing to do, but to conjure him down again with his story, and in this form of Exorcism, most un-ecclesiastically did the corporal do it.

18 See Michael Riffaterre's study 'Compulsory Reader Response: The Intertextual Drive', in *Intertextuality: Theories and Practices*, 58.
19 *Oc* II, 636.

CONCLUSION

1 Quoted by M.-J. Durry, 'Autour de poème en prose', *Mercure de France*, 273 (1937), 505.
2 *Ibid.*, 495–503.
3 Barbara Johnson, *Défigurations*, 10.
4 These studies in literary history include the article by M.-J. Durry cited in note 1 above; Pierre Moreau, 'La Tradition française du poème en prose avant Baudelaire'. *Archives des lettres modernes*, 3, 19–20 (1959) (this brief but dense monograph contains comments on the affinity between the works of Aloysius Bertrand and Baudelaire (31–6) and on the musical conception behind *Le Spleen de Paris* (42–7); Marcel A. Ruff, 'Baudelaire et le poème en prose', *Zeitschrift für Französische Sprache und Literatur*, 77, 2 (1967), 116–30 (in this article the *Petits Poèmes en prose* are discussed in relation to the prose poetry of Alphonse Rabbe, Maurice de Guérin, Lefèvre-Daumier, and especially Aloysius Bertrand). In addition, Henri Ghéon, 'Les Poèmes', *Nouvelle Revue française* (1912), 345–54, saw a precedent for the prose poems in La Bruyère's *Caractères*, but makes no mention of the allusion to *Les Caractères* in 'La Solitude'; Suzanne Bernard, *Le Poème en prose de Baudelaire à nos jours* (Paris, 1959), contains an historical survey of prose poetry in the years preceding the publication of *Le Spleen de Paris* (21–93); Maurice Chapelan, in the introduction to his *Anthologie du poème en prose* (Paris, 1946), emphasises the dearth of good verse in the period 1690 to 1819 and stresses the importance in that period of prose writings such as those by Buffon, Rousseau and Chateaubriand, outstanding for their stylistic quality.
5 Maurice Chapelan, in his *Anthologie du poème en prose*, stresses the criterion of the absence of rational argument or narrative as a primary objective, suggesting that one may categorise as poetry 'tout texte qui ne se propose pas d'abord de raconter ou de démontrer, qui ne veut pas être d'abord raisonnement ou récit, mais accumulateur de cette énergie qui se manifeste par musique et visages...' (xv). Suzanne Bernard, in *Le Poème en prose*, sees the distinguishing characteristics of the modern prose poem as lying in

its organic unity, its gratuity, its 'intemporalité' and its brevity (14–15). This perception of the 'organic unity' of individual prose poems in my view encourages a misreading of *Le Spleen de Paris* and a failure to take account of the statement in the Dedication to Houssaye to the effect that 'tout y est à la fois tête et queue'. Bernard's arguments on the relationship of prose poetry to time owe much to Blin's *Introduction aux Petits Poèmes en prose* and *Le Sadisme de Baudelaire* (Paris, 1948). Both critics relate poetry's effect on the reader's time-consciousness to the question of harmony, and identify two types of poetry which exploit different methods of creating an impression of temporal evasion, or epiphany. The first category involves the 'harmonious' organisation of time, for example by conventional means of rhythm and rhyme; the second, by contrast, involves a rejection of rigid patterning, a dramatic unfettering of language which makes possible what Blin terms 'un certain état de grâce' (151) and Bernard describes as 'un *poème illumination*' (453). Both critics situate the *Petits Poèmes* in the second category, but Blin differs from Bernard in suggesting that the first category logically excludes all prose poetry, since in his view the choice of prose should involve abandoning the traditional devices of verse, such as repetition and rhythm. This view is shared by Jean Cohen, who argues that the prose poem might be rechristened 'poème sémantique' since 'il ne joue en effet que sur cette face du langage et laisse la face phonique poétiquement inexploité' (*Structure du langage poétique* (Paris, 1966), 9–10). However, the notion of a 'poème sémantique', however conceptually useful (like, say, Barthes's 'degré zéro de l'écriture'), does not reflect an empirically proven reality so much as a theoretical 'pole'. Thus, for example, Georges Blin himself notes the presence in the *Petits Poèmes en prose* of phonic patterns similar to those exploited in verse poetry, but he argues that these effects are unimportant (*op. cit.*, 159). Other critics of the prose poems have taken the opposite view: for example, Gilbert Guisan, drawing on the arguments of Henri Bremond (*Les Deux Musiques de la prose* (Paris, 1924), has stressed the importance of repetition and symmetry in prose poetry as a whole, and particularly in the *Spleen de Paris*, and has recalled the Abbé Batteux's assertion that 'la prose bien faite est nécessairement remplie de nombres poétiques, de manière qu'il en résulte une sorte de vers qui flatte en même temps l'oreille et l'esprit' (quoted in 'Prose et poésie d'après les *Petits poèmes en prose*', *Etudes de lettres*, 21, 3 (1948), 87–107); Jocelynne Loncke stresses the importance of rhythmic effects in the *Petits Poèmes en prose* in *Baudelaire et la Musique*, 205–11; Bernard analyses the 'procédé de reprises' within individual poems in the *Spleen de Paris* and suggests that these create 'à la fois une incantation et un rythme' (*Le Poème en prose*, 132–4). But her analysis of rhythmic and stylistic procedures in the prose poems differs from that of Guisan in that she believes that rhythmic symmetries are rare, and that Guisan accords an excessive importance to those symmetries of noun, adjective, verb and preposition which do occur (*ibid.*, 136–9).

6 For example, Y. G. Le Dantec, 'Sur le poème en prose', *Revue des deux mondes*, 5 (1948), 760–6. Suzanne Bernard suggests that some of the prose poems are virtual short stories (*Le Poème en prose*, 109). Regrettably, concern for accurate classification has sometimes been accompanied by reductive evaluation, as opposed to interpretation, of the *Petits Poèmes en prose*. Barbara Johnson gives a chastening account of examples of this sort of criticism (*Défigurations*, 20–1).

7 Early critics such as H. Dérieux concluded that the prose poems were anterior to their verse counterparts; see *Baudelaire* (Bâle, 1917), 39. More recently, the opposite view has prevailed. For example, Robert Kopp and Claude Pichois in their editions both suggest that the verse 'L'Invitation au voyage' was anterior to its prose counterpart, whilst J. Crépet and G. Blin, in their edition of *Les Fleurs du mal* of 1942, make a close comparison of 'La Chevelure' and 'Un Hémisphère dans une chevelure' which leads them to conclude that the verse poem was anterior to the prose. M. Ruff has drawn attention to evidence from *La Fanfarlo* which seems to suggest the anteriority of the verse poems ('Baudelaire et le poème en prose', *Zeitschrift für Französische Sprache und Literatur*, 77, 2 (1967), 116–23). The prose poem 'Un Hémisphère dans une chevelure' was published on 24 August 1857, the verse poem 'Chevelure' on May 1859, but the order of composition of the poems remains unknown. However, it should be remembered that Baudelaire himself was concerned that the relationship of the prose poetry to verse should not be misunderstood. Referring to the prose poems in a letter to Houssaye, he made it clear that above all he did not want to give the impression that he was putting forward 'le plan d'une chose à mettre en vers' (*Correspondance* II, 207).

8 See especially the analysis made by J. Crépet and G. Blin (see note 7 above), and the comparison of 'La Chevelure' and 'Un Hemisphère dans une chevelure' by Barbara Johnson (*Défigurations*, 31–55). See also Suzanne Bernard, *Le Poème en prose*, 141–2; J.-P. Ratermanis, *Etude sur le style de Baudelaire d'après 'Les Fleurs de mal' et les 'Petits Poèmes en prose'* (Bade, 1949), 417–64.

9 See for example J.-H. Bornecque, 'Les Poèmes en prose de Baudelaire', 178-9.
10 These include, notably, Jocelynne Loncke, *Baudelaire et la Musique*; André Ferran, 'Baudelaire et la Musique', Suzanne Bernard, *Le Poème en prose: De Baudelaire jusqu'à nos jours*.
11 See above, p. 178.
12 See above, p. 129-38.
13 *Oc* II, 644: 'car la fantaisie est d'autant plus dangereuse qu'elle est plus facile et plus ouverte; dangereuse comme la poésie en prose, comme le roman... dangereuse comme toute liberté absolue'.
14 Yoichi Sumi, *Le Neveu de Rameau: Caprices et logiques de jeu*.
15 Ross Chambers, 'The Artist as Performing Dog', 312-24.
16 See Jean Pommier, *Dans les chemins de Baudelaire* (Paris, 1945), 146, 149, 173, 175, 187, 193-5, 316-17; Melvin Zimmermann, 'La Genèse du symbole du thyrse chez Baudelaire', 8-11; also, by the same critic, 'Trois études sur Baudelaire et Rousseau'; *Petits Poèmes en prose*, ed. Robert Kopp; Jean Thomas, 'Diderot et Baudelaire', *Hippocrate* (1958), 328-42; Walter Benjamin, *Charles Baudelaire: A Lyric Poet in the Era of High Capitalism*, 48-9 and 129-30; Rosemary Lloyd, *Baudelaire et Hoffmann: affinités et influences* (Cambridge, 1979), especially 217-19, and her article, 'Sur Hoffmann, Poe et Baudelaire', *Bulletin Baudelairien*, 11, 2 (1976), 11-12; Barbara Johnson, *Défigurations*, 78-9; Graham Chesters, 'Sur "Les Bons Chiens" de Baudelaire', *Revue d'histoire littéraire de la France*, 3 (1980), 416-21.
17 Marie Maclean, *Narrative as Performance: The Baudelairean Experiment* (London and New York, 1988). This lively study emerges from an initial focus on narrative theory rather than Baudelairean studies. See also Nathaniel Wing, *The Limits of Narrative: Essays on Baudelaire, Flaubert, Rimbaud and Mallarmé* (Cambridge University Press, 1986), and his article 'Poets, Mimes and Counterfeit Coins: On Power and Discourse in Baudelaire's Prose Poetry', *Paragraph*, 13, 1 (1990), 1-18.
18 Charles Mauron, *Le Dernier Baudelaire* (Paris, 1966).
19 Leo Bersani, *Baudelaire and Freud*.
20 *Le Spleen de Paris*, edited by Max Milner (Paris, 1979).
21 Lucien Dallenbach, *Le Récit spéculaire*, 123.
22 *Tristram Shandy*, 509 and 510-11.
23 *Ibid.*, 215.
24 On contemporary metafiction and the problem of 'framing', see Patricia Waugh, *Metafiction: The Theory and Practice of Self-Conscious Fiction* (London, 1984), 28-31.
25 See Chapter 3 above.

26 *Oc* I, 505–7.
27 Inger Christensen, *The Meaning of Metafiction* (Bergen and Oslo, 1981), 155.
28 *Oc* II, 788.
29 Banville, *Petit Traité de poésie française* (Paris, 1872), 6.

Select bibliography

WORKS BY BAUDELAIRE

Œuvres complètes, ed. Claude Pichois (Paris: Bibliothèque de la Pléiade, 1976), 2 vols.
Petits Poèmes en prose, Le Jeune Enchanteur, ed. Jacques Crépet (Paris: Conard, 1926)
Petits Poèmes en prose, ed. H. Daniel-Rops (Paris: Les Belles-Lettres, 1934; reprinted in 1952)
Petits Poèmes en prose, ed. Melvin Zimmermann (Manchester: Manchester University Press, 1968)
Petits Poèmes en prose, ed. Robert Kopp (Paris: Corti, 1969)
Le Spleen de Paris, ed. Max Milner (Paris: Imprimerie Nationale, 1979)
Les Fleurs du mal, ed. Jacques Crépet and Georges Blin (Paris: Corti, 1942; reprinted 1950; new edition in 2 vols. by Georges Blin et Claude Pichois, 1968)
Journaux intimes. Fusées. Mon Coeur mis à nu, ed. Jacques Crépet et Georges Blin (Paris: Corti, 1949)
Salon de 1846, ed. David Kelley (Oxford: Clarendon Press, 1975)

OTHER WORKS

Alain, Olivier, *L'Harmonie*, 2nd edition (Paris: Presses Universitaires de France, 1969)
Alter, Robert, *Partial Magic: The Novel as a Self-Conscious Genre* (London and Berkeley, 1975)
Antoine, Gérald, 'La Nuit chez Baudelaire', *Revue d'histoire littéraire de la France* (1967), 375–401
Apuleius, Lucius, *The Golden Ass*, translated by Robert Graves (Harmondsworth: Penguin, 1972; first published 1950)
Aretino, Pietro, *Œuvres Choisies*, translated with notes by P.-L. Jacob (Paris: Charles Gosselin, Libraire, 1845)
Bailbé, Joseph-Marc, *Le Roman et la musique en France sous la monarchie de juillet*, with a preface by Pierre Moreau (Paris: Minard, 1969)

Bal, Mieke, 'Mise en abyme et iconicité: *Le récit spéculaire, essai sur la mise en abyme*, par Lucien Dallenbach', *Littérature*, 29 (1978), 116–28.
Balzac, Honoré de, *Œuvres complètes*, text revised and annotated by Marcel Bouteron and Henri Lognon (Paris: Louis Conard, 1953), 40 vols.
Illusions perdues, ed. Michel Déon (Paris: Gallimard et Librairie Générale Française, 1962)
La Rabouilleuse, with an introduction and commentary by Roger Pierrot (Paris: Librairie Générale Française, 1972)
Barbey D'Aurevilly, Jules, *Goethe et Diderot*, reprint of the 1913 Paris edition (Geneva: Slatkine Reprints, 1968)
Barthes, Roland, *Le Degré zéro de l'écriture* (Paris: Seuil, 1953)
'De l'œuvre au texte', in *Revue d'esthétique*, 3 (1971), 17–24
Beguin, Albert, *L'Ame romantique et le rêve: Essai sur le romantisme allemand et la poésie française* (Marseille: Editions des Cahiers du Sud, 1937; 1946 reprint)
Benedetto, L. F., 'L'Architecture des *Fleurs du mal*', *Zeitschrift für französische Sprache und Litteratur*, 39 (1912), 18–70
Benjamin, Walter, *Charles Baudelaire: A Lyric Poet in the Era of High Capitalism*, translated from the German by Harry Zohn (London: NLB, 1973)
Bennington, Geoffrey, *Sententiousness and the Novel: Laying Down the Law in Eighteenth-Century French Fiction* (Cambridge: Cambridge University Press, 1985)
Benveniste, Emile, *Problèmes de linguistique générale* (Paris: Gallimard, 1966)
Bernard, Suzanne, *Le Poème en prose: De Baudelaire jusqu'à nos jours* (Paris: Nizet, 1959)
Bersani, Leo, *Baudelaire and Freud* (London: University of California Press, 1977)
Bertrand, Aloysius, *Gaspard de la nuit: Fantaisies à la manière de Rembrandt et de Callot*, with a Preface by Sainte-Beuve (Paris: Labitte, 1842 original edition)
Gaspard de la Nuit: Fantaisies à la manière de Rembrandt et de Callot, ed. Max Milner (Paris: Gallimard, 1980)
Blin, Georges, *Le Sadisme de Baudelaire*, with *Introduction aux Petits Poèmes en prose* (Nogent la Rotrou et Paris: Corti, 1948)
'Les Fleurs de l'impossible', *Revue des sciences humaines*, 27 (1967), 461–6
Bonnet, Henri, *Roman et poésie: Essai sur l'esthétique des genres* (Paris: Nizet, 1951)
Bony, Alain, 'Terminologie chez Sterne', *Poétique*, 29 (1977), 28–49

Bornecque, Jacques-Henry, 'Les Poèmes en prose de Baudelaire', *L'Information littéraire*, 5 (1953), 177-82
Brelet, Gisèle, *Le Temps musical: Essai d'une esthétique nouvelle de la musique* (Paris: Presses Universitaires de France, 1949), 2 vols.
Brémond, Henri, *Les Deux Musiques de la prose* (Paris: Le Divan, 1924)
La Poésie pure (Paris: Grasset, 1926)
Brombert, Victor, 'Petrus Borel et les Prisons Noires', *Saggi e ricerche di letteratura francese*, 14 (1975), 349-65
'Hugo: L'édifice du livre', *Romantisme*, 44 (1984), 52-3
Victor Hugo and the Visionary Novel (Cambridge, MA: Harvard University Press, 1984)
Brooks, Peter, *Reading for the Plot: Design and Intention in Narrative* (Oxford: Clarendon Press, 1984)
Bruns, Gerald, *Modern Poetry and the Idea of Language: A Critical and Historical Study* (New Haven and London: Yale University Press, 1974)
Butor, Michel, *Histoire extraordinaire: Essai sur un rêve de Baudelaire* (Paris: Gallimard, 1961)
Caplan, Jay, *Framed Narratives: Diderot's Genealogy of the Beholder* (Manchester: Manchester University Press, 1986)
Castex, Pierre Georges, 'Balzac et Baudelaire', *Revue des sciences humaines*, 89 (1958), 139-51
Caws, Mary Ann and Riffaterre, H. (eds.), *The Prose Poem in France: Theory and Practice* (New York: Columbia University Press, 1983)
Cellier, Léon, 'D'une rhétorique profonde: Baudelaire et l'oxymoron', *Cahiers Internationaux du Symbolisme*, 8 (1965), 3-14
'Baudelaire et l'enfance', in *Baudelaire: Actes du Colloque de Nice, mai 1967* (Nice: Minard, 1968)
Baudelaire et Hugo (Paris, Corti, 1970)
Cervantes, Miguel de, *Nouvelles choisies de Cervantes* (*Le Mariage frauduleux, Dialogue des deux chiens, Léocardie ou la Force du sang*), new translation by Bouchon Dubournial (Paris: C.-L.-F. Panckoucke, 1825)
Chambers, Ross, 'L'Art sublime du comédien ou le regardant et le regardé', *Saggi e ricerche di letteratura francese*, 11 (1971), 189-260
'The Artist as Performing Dog', *Comparative Literature*, 23, 4 (1971) 312-24
'Change and Exchange? Story Structure and Paradigmatic Narrative', *Australian Journal of French Studies*, 12 (1975), 326-42
Chapelan, Maurice, *Anthologie du poème en prose* (Paris: Julliard, 1946)
Charles, Michel, *Rhétorique de la lecture* (Paris: Seuil, 1977)
'Digression, régression (Arabesques)', *Poétique*, 40 (1979), 395-407
Charlton, D. G., Gaudon, J., Pugh, Anthony R. (eds.,) *Balzac and the Nineteenth Century* (Leicester: Leicester University Press, 1972)

Chateaubriaud, François-René de, *Atala, René*, ed. Phyllis Crump (Manchester: Manchester University Press, 1966 reprint: first published 1826)
Chesters, Graham, 'Baudelaire and the Limits of Poetry', *French Studies*, 32, 4 (1978), 420–31
'Sur "Les Bons Chiens" de Baudelaire', *Revue d'histoire littéraire de la France*, 3 (1980), 416–421
Christensen, Inger, *The Meaning of Metafiction: A Critical Study of Selected Novels by Sterne, Nabokov, Barth and Beckett* (Bergen and Oslo: Universitetsforlaget, 1981).
Citron, Pierre, *La Poésie de Paris dans la littérature française de Rousseau à Baudelaire* (Paris: Editions de Minuit, 1961), 2 vols.
Cohen, Jean, *Structure du langage poétique* (Paris: Flammarion, 1966)
'Poésie et redondance', *Poétique*, 28 (1976) 413–22
Culler, John, *Structuralist Poetics* (London: Routledge and Kegan Paul, 1975)
Dallenbach, Lucien, *Le Récit spéculaire: Essai sur la mise en abyme* (Paris: Seuil, 1977)
'Du fragment au cosmos', *Poétique*, 40 (1979), 420–31
'Le tout en morceaux', *Poétique*, 42 (1980), 156–69
'Reflexivity and Reading', *New Literary History*, 11, 3 (1980), 435–49
De George, Fernande, 'The Structure of Baudelaire's *Petits Poèmes en prose*', *L'Esprit créateur*, 12, 2 (1973), 144–53
De Man, Paul, *The Rhetoric of Romanticism* (New York: Columbia University Press), 1984, 243–62
Delcroix, Maurice, 'Un Poème en prose de Charles Baudelaire: "Les Yeux des pauvres"', *Cahiers d'analyse textuelle*, 19 (1977), 47–66
Delesalle, Jean-François, 'Baudelaire rival de Jules Janin', *Etudes Baudelairiennes*, 3 (1973), 41–53
'Miettes baudelairiennes', *Bulletin Baudelairien*, 8 (1973), 19–22
Derrida, Jacques, *De la grammatologie* (Paris: Editions de Minuit, 1967)
Diderot, Denis, *Le Neveu de Rameau*, ed. Jean Fabre (Geneva: Droz, Lille: Giard, 1950)
Le Neveu de Rameau et autres dialogues philosophiques, ed. Jean Varloot, with notes by Nicoles Evrard (Paris: Gallimard, 1972)
Jacques le fataliste et son maître, ed. Simone Lecointre and Jean le Galliot (Paris and Geneva: Droz, 1976)
Oeuvres esthétiques, ed. P. Vernières (Paris: Garnier, 1959)
Dublin, P. G., *La Vie de l'Arétin* (Paris: Fernand Sorlot, 1937)
Eco, Umberto, *L'Oeuvre ouverte*, translated by C. Roux de Bézieux with the help of A. Bouceurechliev (Paris: Seuil, 1965)
Eigeldinger, Marc, *Poésie et métamorphoses* (Neuchâtel: Editions de la Baconnière, 1973)

"'Le Thyrse'', lecture thématique', *Etudes Baudelairiennes*, 8, 2 (1976), 172–83
'Trois études sur Baudelaire et Rousseau', *Etudes Baudelairiennes*, 9 (1981), 9–78
Evans, Margery A., 'Laurence Sterne and *Le Spleen de Paris*', *French Studies*, 42 (1988), 165–76
Fairlie, Alison, 'Observations sur les *Petits Poèmes en prose*', *Revue des sciences humaines*, 127 (1967), 449–60
'Quelques Remarques sur les *Petits Poèmes en prose*', in *Baudelaire: Actes du Colloque de Nice, mai 1967* (Monaco: Minard, 1968)
Felman, Shoshana, *Writing and Madness* (New York: Cornell University Press, 1985)
Ferran, André, *L'Esthétique de Baudelaire* (Toulouse and Paris: Hachette, 1933)
'Baudelaire et la musique', in *Mélanges de philologie et d'histoire littéraire offerts à E. Huguet* (Paris: Publications de M. E. Huguet, 1940)
Feuillerat, Albert, 'L'Architecture des *Fleurs du mal*', in *Studies by Members of the French Department of Yale University*, decennial volume (New Haven: Yale University Press, London: Oxford University Press, 1941), 221–329
Fokkema, Douwe W., *Literary History, Modernism, and Postmodernism* (Amsterdam and Philadelphia: J. Benjamins, 1984)
Foucault, Michel, *Folie et déraison à l'âge classique* (Paris: Gallimard, 1972)
Galand, René, *Baudelaire, poétiques et poésie* (Paris: Nizet, 1969)
'Baudelaire's Psychology of Play', *The French Review*, 44 (1971), 12–19
Genette, Gérard, *Figures II* (Paris: Seuil, 1969)
Ghéon, Henri, 'Les Poèmes', *Nouvelle revue française*, 8 (1912), 345–54
Gilman, Margaret, *Baudelaire the Critic* (New York: Columbia University Press, 1943; reprinted 1971)
'Baudelaire and Emerson', *The Romantic Review*, 9 (1943)
The Idea of Poetry in France: From Houdar de la Motte to Baudelaire (Cambridge, MA: Harvard University Press, 1958)
Glendinning, Nigel, *Goya and his Critics* (New Haven and London: Yale University Press, 1977)
Grava, Arnold, *L'Aspect métaphysique du mal dans l'oeuvre littéraire de Charles Baudelaire et d'Edgar Allan Poe* (Geneva and Paris: Slatkine Reprints, Honoré Champion, 1976, reprint of the Lincoln edition, 1951)
Guichard, Léon, *La Musique et les lettres en France au temps du Wagnérisme* (Paris: Presses Universitaires de France, 1963)

Guiette, Robert, 'Des *Paradis Artificiels* aux *Petits Poèmes en prose*', *Etudes Baudelairiennes*, 3 (1973), 178–84

Guinard, Paul, 'Baudelaire, le Musée espagnol et Goya', *Revue d'histoire littéraire de la France*, 2 (1967), 310–28

Guisan, Gilbert, 'Prose et poésie d'après les *Petits Poèmes en prose*', *Etudes de lettres*, 21, 3 (1948), 87–107

Hall, Joan Joffe, 'The Hobbyhorsical World of Tristram Shandy', *Modern Language Quarterly*, 24 (1963), 131–43

Hamon, Philippe, 'Texte et architecture', *Poétique*, 73 (1988), 3–26

Hiddleston, James A., *Baudelaire and Le Spleen de Paris* (Oxford: Clarendon Press, 1987)

Hoffmann, E.T.A., *Œuvres complètes*, vols. II–XII, 'Contes fantastiques', translated by M. Loève-Weimars with a historical preface by Walter Scott (Paris: E. Rendvel, 1830-2), 20 vols.

Contes fantastiques, new translation with a preface by Henri Egmont (Paris: Camuzeaux, 1836), 4 vols.

Horatius, Flaccus (Quintus), *Satires*, translated by Jules Janin, with a preface by Sainte-Beuve (Paris, reprint 1931)

Hughes, Randolph, 'Baudelaire et Balzac', *Mercure de France*, 1, 40 (1934), 476–518

Hugo, Victor, *Œuvres romanesques, dramatiques et poétiques* (Paris: Pauvert, 1963), 38 vols.

Œuvres complètes, ed. Jean Massim (Paris: Le Club Français du Livre, 1969)

Hunt, Leigh, *An Answer to the Question 'What is Poetry?' Including Remarks on Versification*, ed. Albert S. Cook (Boston: Ginn and Co., 1893)

Jakobson, Roman, *Fundamentals of Language* (The Hague: Mouton, 1956)

Selected Writings (The Hague: Mouton, 1962–71), 4 vols.

Janin, Jules, *Le Gâteau des rois*, facsimile of the 1847 edition; illustrated edition with an introduction and notes by Joseph-Marc Bailbé (Paris: Minard, 1972)

Jankelevitch, Vladimir, *L'Ironie* (Paris: Flammarion, 1964)

Jenny, Laurent, 'Structure et fonctions du cliché', *Poétique*, 12 (1972), 495–517

'Le Poètique et le narratif', *Poétique*, 28 (1976), 440–9

Johnson, Barbara, *Défigurations du langage poétique* (Paris: Flammarion, 1979)

Kelley, David, *Charles Baudelaire's Salon of 1846* (unpublished Ph.D. thesis, University of Cambridge, 1968)

'Delacroix, Ingres et Poe: Valeurs picturales et valeurs littéraires dans l'œuvre critique de Baudelaire', *Revue d'histoire littéraire de la France*, 4 (1971), 606–14

'*Modernité* in Baudelaire's Art Criticism', in *The Artist and the Writer in France*, ed. Francis Haskell, A. Levi, R. Shackleton (Oxford: Clarendon Press, 1974)

King, Russell, S., 'Dialogue in Baudelaire's Poetic Universe', *L'Esprit créateur*, 13 (1973), 114–23

Klein, Richard, 'Straight Lines and Arabesques: Metaphors of Metaphor', *Yale French Studies*, 45 (1970), 64–86

'"Bénédiction"/"Perte d'Auréole": Paraboles of Interpretation', *Modern Language Notes*, 85 (1970), 515–28

Kremen, Barbara, 'Baudelaire's Spiritual Arabesque', *Romance Notes*, 9 (1967), 57–65

Kristeva, Julia, *Recherches pour une sémanalyse* (Paris: Seuil, 1969)

Laclos, Choderlos de, *Les Liaisons dangereuses*, with a preface by André Malraux (Paris: Livre de Poche, 1958)

Leakey, F. W., 'Baudelaire: The Poet as Moralist', in *Studies in Modern French Literature, Collected Essays for P. Mansell Jones* (Manchester: Manchester University Press, 1961), 196–219

'A Festschrift of 1855: Baudelaire and the *Hommage à C. F. Denecourt*', in *Studies in French Literature presented to H. W. Lawton*, ed. J. C. Ireson, I. D. McFarlane and Garnet Rees (Manchester: Manchester University Press, 1968), 175–202

Baudelaire and Nature (Manchester: Manchester University Press, 1969)

Lebois, André, 'Prestiges et actualités du *Spleen de Paris*', *Archives des lettres modernes* (1958), 1–32

Le Dantec, Yves-Gérard, 'Sur le poème en prose', *La Revue* (15 October 1948), 760–6

Lefebve, Maurice-Jean, *Structure du discours de la poésie et du récit* (Neuchâtel: Editions de la Baconnière, 1971)

Lehan, Richard, 'Urban Signs and Urban Literature: Literary Form and Historical Process', *New Literary History*, 18, 1 (1986), 99–113

Levi, Eliphas, *Transcendental Magic and its Doctrine and Ritual*, translated, annotated and introduced by Arthur Edward Waite (London: Rider and Co., 1958; first published 1896)

Lévi-Strauss, Claude, *La Pensée sauvage* (Paris: Plon, 1962)

Levoinnois, Louis, 'De la dédicataire des *Paradis Artificiels*', *Bulletin Baudelairien*, 12, 2 (1977), 3–18

Lloyd, Rosemary, *Baudelaire et Hoffmann: affinités et influences* (Cambridge: Cambridge University Press, 1979)

Baudelaire's Literary Criticism (Cambridge: Cambridge University Press, 1981)

Lodge, David, *The Modes of Modern Writing* (London: Edward Arnold, 1977; reprinted 1979)
Loncke, Jocelynne, *Baudelaire et la Musique* (Paris: Nizet, 1975)
Lucan, *The Civil War (Pharsalia)*, with an English translation by J. D. Duff (Cambridge and London: Loeb Classical Library, 1969)
Maclean, Marie, *Narrative as Performance: The Baudelairean Experiment* (London and New York: Routledge, 1988)
Mallarmé, Stéphane, *Œuvres complètes* (Paris: Pléiade, 1945)
Mansell Jones, P., 'Poe, Baudelaire and Mallarmé: A Problem of Literary Judgement', *Modern Language Review*, 39 (1944), 236–46
Maurin, Mario, 'Le Saltimbanque héroique; de Baudelaire à Henri de Régnier', *Revue d'histoire littéraire de la France*, 74 (1974), 1010–14
Mauron, Charles, *Des Métaphores obsédantes au mythe personnel. Intro à la Psychocritique* (Paris: Corti, 1963)
Le Dernier Baudelaire (Paris: Corti, 1966)
Menard, Maurice, 'L'Arabesque et la Ménipée', *Revue des sciences humaines*, 48 (1979), 11–31
Meyer, Leonard, *Emotion and Meaning in Music* (Chicago: University of Chicago Press, 1959)
Michaud, Régis, 'Baudelaire, Balzac et les correspondances', *The Romantic Review*, 29 (1938), 253–61
Milner, Max, *Le Diable dans la littérature française: de Cazotte à Baudelaire 1772–1861* (Paris: Corti, 1960), 2 vols.
Baudelaire: Enfer ou ciel qu'importe? (Paris: Plon, 1967)
Moreau, Pierre, 'En Marge du *Spleen de Paris*', *Revue d'histoire littéraire de la France*, 59 (1959), 539–43
'La Tradition française du poème en prose avant Baudelaire'; followed by 'Anti-roman et poème en prose', *Archives des lettres modernes*, 3, 19–20 (1959)
Morrissette, Bruce, 'Un Héritage d'André Gide: La duplication intérieure', *Comparative Literature Studies*, 7, 2 (1971), 125–42
Nojgaard, Morten, *Elévation et expansion. Les deux dimensions de Baudelaire. Trois essais sur la technique poétique des Fleurs du mal* (Odense: Odense University Press, 1973)
Pachet, Pierre, 'Baudelaire et le sacrifice', *Poètique*, 20 (1974), 437–51
Le Premier Venu: Essai sur la politique baudelairienne (Paris: Denoël, 1976)
Peyre, Henri (ed.) *Baudelaire*, 'Twentieth Century Views' series (Englewood Cliffs, NJ; Prentice-Hall, 1962)
Pichois, Claude, *Baudelaire à Paris* (Paris: Hachette, 1967)
Pichois, Claude, and Jean Ziegler, *Baudelaire* (Paris: Juillard, 1987)

Pizzorusso, Arnoldo, '"Le Mauvais Vitrier" ou l'impulsion inconnue', *Etudes Baudelairiennes*, 8 (1976), 147–71
Poe, Edgar Allan, *The Complete Works*, ed. James A. Harrison (New York: AMS Press, 1965), 17 vols.
   Œuvres en Prose, translated by Charles Baudelaire; ed. Y.-G. Le Dantec (Paris: Gallimard, 1969, new edition)
Pommier, Jean, *La Mystique de Baudelaire* (Paris: Publications de la Faculté des Lettres de Strasbourg, 1932)
   Dans les chemins de Baudelaire (Paris: Corti, 1945)
Poulet, Georges, *Les Métamorphoses du cercle* (Paris: Plon, 1961)
   La Poésie éclatée: Baudelaire/Rimbaud (Paris: Presses Universitaires de France, 1980)
Prendergast, Christopher, *Balzac: Fiction and Melodrama* (London: Edward Arnold, 1978)
Prévost, Jean, *Baudelaire* (Paris: Mercure de France, 1964, second edition; first edition 1953)
Ratermanis, J. B., *Etude sur le style de Baudelaire* (Bade: Editions Art et Science Bade, 1949)
Rees, Garnet, 'Baudelaire et Balzac', in *Balzac and the Nineteenth Century*, ed. D. G. Charlton, J. Gaudon and A. Pugh (Leicester: Leicester University Press, 1972)
Régnier, Mathurin, *Œuvres complètes*, new edition with a commentary by Brossette (Paris: Lequiem Libraire, 1822)
Ricardou, Jean, *Pour une théorie du nouveau roman* (Paris: Seuil, 1971)
   Nouveaux problèmes du roman (Paris: Seuil, 1978)
Richard, Jean-Pierre, *Poésie et profondeur* (Paris: Seuil, 1955)
Riffaterre, Michael, *Essais de stylistique structurale* (Paris: Flammarion, 1971)
   Semiotics of Poetry (Bloomington and London: Indiana University Press, 1978)
   'Compulsory Reader Response: The Intertextual Drive', in *Intertextuality: Theories and Practices*, ed. Michael Worton and Judith Still (Manchester: Manchester University Press, 1990)
Rousset, Jean, *Forme et signification* (Paris: Corti, 1962)
Ruff, Marcel A., *Baudelaire, l'homme et l'œuvre* (Paris: Hatier-Boivin, 1955)
   'Baudelaire et le poème en prose', *Zeitschrift für Französische Sprächе und Literatur*, 77, 2 (1967), 116–30
   L'Esprit du mal et l'esthétique Baudelairienne (Geneva: Slatkine Reprints, 1972; reprint of the Paris edition, 1955)
Ruthven, K. K., *Critical Assumptions* (Cambridge: Cambridge University Press, 1979)
Sainte-Beuve, Charles Augustin, *Vie, Poésie et Pensées de Joseph Delorme*, ed. Gérald Antoine (Paris: Nouvelles Editions Latines, 1956)

Slott, Kathryn, 'Le Texte e(s)t son double. *Gaspard de la nuit*: Intertextualité, parodie, auto-parodie', *French Forum*, 1 (1981), 28–35

Souriau, Etienne, *La Correspondance des arts* (Paris: Flammarion, 1947; new edition 1969)

Starmand, Barton Levi, 'A Superior Abstraction: Todorov on the Fantastic', *Novel*, 1 (1975), 260–7

Starobinski, Jean, 'Sur quelques répondants allégoriques du poète', *Revue d'histoire littéraire de la France*, 77, 2 (1967), 402–12

Portrait de l'artiste en saltimbanque (Geneva and Paris: Albert Skiral, 1970)

Stauble-Lipman Wulf, Michèle (ed.), *Charles Baudelaire, un mangeur d'opium*, with the parallel texts *Confessions of an English Opium-Eater* and *Suspira de profundis* by Thomas de Quincey, *Etudes Baudelairiennes*, 6–7 (Neuchâtel: Editions La Baconnière, 1976)

Still, Judith, and Michael Worton (eds.), *Intertextuality: Theories and Practices* (Manchester: Manchester University Press, 1990)

Sumi, Yoichi, *Le Neveu de Rameau: Caprices et logiques du jeu* (Tokyo: Librairie-Editions France Tosho, 1975)

Thomas, Jean, 'Diderot et Baudelaire', *Hippocrate*, 6 (1958), 328–42

Todorov, Tzvetan, *Introduction à la littérature fantastique* (Paris: Seuil, 1970)

Poétique de la prose (Paris: Seuil, 1971)

'Théories de la poésie', *Poétique*, 28 (1976), 385–9

Théories du symbole (Paris: Seuil, 1977)

Symbolisme et interprétation (Paris: Seuil, 1978)

Les Genres du discours (Paris: Seuil, 1978)

Towers, A. R., 'Sterne's Cock and Bull Story', *ELH*, 24 (1957), 12–29

Trahard, Pierre, *Essai critique sur Baudelaire poète* (Paris: Nizet, 1973)

Ullmann, Stephen, *Language and Style* (Oxford: Blackwell, 1966)

Uspensky, Boris, *A Poetics of Composition*, translated by Valentina Zavarin and Susan Wittig (Berkeley, Los Angeles and London: University of California Press, 1973)

Valéry, Paul, *Variété* III (Paris: Gallimard, 1936)

van Slyke, Gretchen, 'Dans l'intertexte de Baudelaire et de Proudhon: Pourquoi faut-il assommer les pauvres?', *Romantisme*, 45 (1984), 57–77

Vouga, Daniel, *Baudelaire et Joseph de Maistre* (Paris: Corti, 1957)

Waugh, Patricia, *Metafiction: The Theory and Practice of Self-Conscious Fiction* (London: Methuen, 1984)

Wing, Nathaniel, *The Limits of Narrative: Essays on Baudelaire, Flaubert, Rimbaud and Mallarmé* (Cambridge: Cambridge University Press, 1986)

'Poets, Mimes and Counterfeit Coins: On Power and Discourse in Baudelaire's Prose Poetry', *Paragraph*, 13, 1 (1990), 1–18
Wright, Barbara, and David Scott, *Baudelaire: La Fanfarlo and Le Spleen de Paris* (London, Grant and Cutler, 1984)
Zilberberg, Claude, *Une Lecture des Fleurs du mal* (Tours: Maison Mame, 1972)
Zimmerman, Melvin, 'La Genèse du symbole du thyrse chez Baudelaire', *Bulletin Baudelairien*, 2, 1 (1966), 8–11
 'Baudelaire et Montaigne: Les thèmes Carpe Diem et Vita Brevis', *Romance Notes*, 8, 2 (1967), 197–9
 'Trois études sur Baudelaire et Rousseau', *Etudes Baudelairiennes*, 9 (1981), 31–71

Index of names

Apuleius, Lucius *The Golden Ass* 97

Bailbé, Jean-Marc 136
Balzac, Honoré de xi, 5, 10, 47, 56–8, 108, 156
  Le Faiseur 26
  Ferragus 15
  La Muse du département 57
  La Peau de chagrin 42, 44
  Le Père Goriot 14, 117
Banville, Théodore de 2, 137
Barthes, Roland
  'Pouvoir nous brûle' 26
  Le degré zéro xii–xiii
Benjamin, Walter 33
Bennington, Geoffrey 59
Bernard, Suzanne 97, 133
Bersani, Leo 47, 153
Bertrand, Aloysius xi
  Gaspard de la nuit xi, xiii, 27, 81–3, 150
Blin, Georges 120
Brelet, Gisèle 129
Brombert, Victor 14, 16
Butor, Michel xii

Cervantes, Miguel de 10, 97, 152
Chambers, Ross 37, 152
Cohen, J. 75

Dallenbach, Lucien 128, 129, 154
Defoe, Daniel 10
  Robinson Crusoe 76–7
De Quincy, Thomas
  Suspiria 141
Diderot, Denis
  Le Neveu de Rameau xi, 14–15, 17, 43, 44, 61, 64, 65, 73, 81, 88–93, 142–7, 155

Eco, Umberto 130

Felman, Shoshana 73, 75
Foucault, Michel
  Histoire de la folie 75
Frank, Joseph
  Spatial Form in Modern Literature 7

Gautier, Théophile
  Spirite
Genette, Gérard 42
Goya y Lucientes, Francisco de
  Los Caprichos 75, 79–80, 81

Hamon, Philippe 19
Hoffmann, Ernst Theodore Amadeus 13, 152.
Horace 10, 60, 81, 147
Hugo, Victor 126, 134
  Les Contemplations 159
  Légende des siècles 5
  Notre-Dame de Paris xi, 12–14, 64–5
  Preface de Cromwell 136–7
  William Shakespeare 10, 19, 110

Janin, Jules
  Le Gâteau des rois 125
Johnson, Barbara
  Défigurations du langage poétique xii, 73, 94, 97, 104

Kopp, Robert 120

La Bruyère, Jean de 77
Laclos, Choderlos de
  Les Liaisons dangereuses 49, 62, 72
La Fontaine, Jean de 10, 60
Liszt, Franz 123, 124, 139–40

Index of names

Lucan 10
  Pharsalia 83–4

Maclean, Marie 152–3
Mallarmé, Stéphane 9, 10, 11, 121
Mauron, Charles 153
Meyer, Leonard 130, 131
Milner, Max 82, 153
Montaigne, Michel Eyquem de 13
  Des Cannibales 115
Moreau, Hégésippe 134

Nerval, Gérard de 10
  Sylvie 54–5

Pascal, Blaise 60, 61, 76, 77
Pichois, Claude xi, 38, 40
Poe, Edgar Allan 72, 114, 126, 134, 138
  Marginalia 73
  Philosophy of Furniture 101
  The Poetic Principle 3
  The Rationale of Verse 134–5
  Tale of the Ragged Mountains 15
Prévost, Jean 79
Proust, Marcel 19–20

Rabelais, François 10, 64–5
Régnier, Mathurin 10, 60, 61, 95
Riffaterre, Michael 6

Rousseau, Jean-Jacques 10, 60, 61, 113–14
  La Nouvelle Héloïse 62

Sainte-Beuve, Charles Augustin 10
Slott, Kathryn 83
Stendhal (Henri Beyle)
  La Chartreuse de Parme 42
  Le Rouge et le noir 34, 62
Sterne, Laurence
  Tristram Shandy xii, 10, 15–16, 17, 27, 43, 44, 56, 66, 69, 73, 81–2, 92, 95, 105, 108, 139, 147–8, 154–8
Still, Judith 143
Sumi, Yoichi 91, 142–3, 152
Swedenborg, Emanuel 115
Swift, Jonathan 147

Theocritus 10
Todorov, Tzvetan 135

Valéry, Paul 21
Vauvenargues, Luc de Clapiers, Marquis de 10, 60–1, 77
  Réflexions sur divers sujets 60
Virgil 10
Voltaire 150

Wing, Nathaniel 153
Worton, Michael 143

46 'Perte d'auréole' 17, 29, 38, 98
47 'Mademoiselle Bistouri' 33-4, 45, 47-50, 54, 56-7, 71, 80, 86, 93-4, 131
48 'Anywhere out of the world' 72-4, 76, 85
49 'Assommons les pauvres!' 17, 52, 61, 65, 67-8, 85, 88-93, 97, 98, 99, 136, 144
50 'Les Bons Chiens' xii, 5, 15-16, 25, 26, 35-7, 43, 44, 46, 56, 77, 80, 105-9, 115, 117, 147-8

Index of prose poems

The prose poems in this index are listed in the order in which they appear in the 1869 edition.

'A Arsène Houssaye' xi, xii, 1, 8–9, 14, 59, 82, 106, 121, 124, 128, 132, 140
1 'L'Etranger' 23–4, 31, 66, 99
2 'Le Désespoir de la vieille' 101, 115
3 'Le Confitéor de l'artiste' 31, 44–6, 49, 50, 54, 58, 76
4 'Un Plaisant' 21, 76, 80, 117
5 'La Chambre double' 34, 51, 97, 118
6 'Chacun sa chimère' 78–81, 85
7 'Le Fou et la Vénus' 17, 50, 136
8 'Le Chien et la flacon' 26, 60, 97, 99, 107, 136
9 'Le Mauvais Vitrier' 17, 60–1, 71–2, 76, 85, 92–3
10 'A une heure du matin' 29–30, 85, 117
11 'La Femme sauvage et la petite-maîtresse' 62, 70, 86, 87, 101, 102, 103, 110, 116, 118, 144
12 'Les Foules' 15, 57–8, 60–1, 77, 84, 86
13 'Les Veuves' 14, 50, 57, 60, 71, 77, 101–2, 107, 115, 127, 131
14 'Le Vieux Saltimbanque' 18, 34, 52, 61, 85, 106, 112–13
15 'Le Gâteau' 77, 97, 101, 104, 113, 136
16 'L'Horloge' 33–4, 41, 50, 51
17 'Un Hémisphère dans une chevelure' 51, 85, 103, 104
18 'L'Invitation au voyage' 30–1, 85, 96, 97, 103, 120, 126, 127, 131
19 'Le Joujou du pauvre' 52, 85, 99, 115, 131
20 'Les Dons des fées' 37
21 'Les Tentations' 46–7, 97, 100, 101
22 'Le Crépuscule du soir' 18, 76, 77, 84, 85, 86, 87–8, 95–7, 99, 102, 110–11, 112, 117, 118
23 'La Solitude' 61, 76, 77, 85
24 'Les Projets' 85, 113
25 'La Belle Dorothée' 32, 103–4, 113–14, 116–17, 119
26 'Les Yeux des pauvres' 18, 24–5, 50, 52–3, 56, 100, 101
27 'Une Mort héroïque' 37, 38, 44, 47, 50, 56, 71, 86, 131
28 'La Fausse Monnaie' 25–8, 32, 83, 107
29 'Le Joueur généreux' 83, 84, 85, 91–2
30 'La Corde' 37–8, 118–19
31 'Les Vocations' 31, 32, 34, 66, 85, 99, 118, 119–20
32 'Le Thyrse' 17, 31, 34, 65–7, 84, 85, 139–48
34 'Déjà' 31, 86
35 'Les Fenêtres' 18, 49, 50, 56, 131
36 'Le Désir de peindre' 41, 45, 54, 58, 83–4, 87, 115, 119
37 'Les Bienfaits de la lune' 17, 51, 76, 81–2, 85, 87
38 'Laquelle est la vraie?' 28–9, 85, 118
39 'Un Cheval de race' 116–17, 119
40 'Le Miroir' 50, 60
41 'Le Port' 31, 127
42 'Portraits de maîtresses' 50, 51, 53, 69–70, 102–3, 144
43 'Le Galant Tireur' 54–5
44 'La Soupe et les nuages' 31, 85, 97, 99, 104, 106
45 'Le Tir et le cimetière' 27, 54–5

Cambridge Studies in French

GENERAL EDITOR
Malcolm Bowie

Also in the series (* denotes titles now out of print)

1. J. M. COCKING
   Proust: Collected Essays on the Writer and his Art

2. LEO BERSANI
   The Death of Stéphane Mallarmé

*3. MARIAN HOBSON
   The Object of Art: The Theory of Illusion in Eighteenth-Century France

4. LEO SPITZER
   Essays on Seventeenth-Century French Literature, translated and edited by David Bellos

5. NORMAN BRYSON
   Tradition and Desire: From David to Delacroix

6. ANN MOSS
   Poetry and Fable: Studies in Mythological Narrative in Sixteenth-Century France

7. RHIANNON GOLDTHORPE
   Sartre: Literature and Theory

8. DIANA KNIGHT
   Flaubert's Characters: The Language of Illusion

9. ANDREW MARTIN
   The Knowledge of Ignorance: From Genesis to Jules Verne

10. GEOFFREY BENNINGTON
    Sententiousness and the Novel: Laying Down the Law in Eighteenth-Century French Fiction

11. PENNY FLORENCE
    Mallarmé, Manet and Redon: Visual and Aural Signs and the Generation of Meaning

12. CHRISTOPHER PRENDERGAST
    The Order of Mimesis: Balzac, Stendhal, Nerval, and Flaubert

13 NAOMI SEGAL
The Unintended Reader: Feminism and Manon Lescaut

14 CLIVE SCOTT
A Question of Syllables: Essays in Nineteenth-Century French Verse

15 STIRLING HAIG
Flaubert and the Gift of Speech: Dialogue and Discourse in Four 'Modern' Novels

*16 NATHANIEL WING
The Limits of Narrative: Essays on Baudelaire, Flaubert, Rimbaud and Mallarmé

17 MITCHELL GREENBERG
Corneille, Classicism, and the Ruses of Symmetry

*18 HOWARD DAVIES
Sartre and 'Les Temps Modernes'

19 ROBERT GREER COHN
Mallarmé's Prose Poems: A Critical Study

20 CELIA BRITTON
Claude Simon: Writing the Visible

21 DAVID SCOTT
Pictorialist Poetics: Poetry and the Visual Arts in Nineteenth-Century France

22 ANN JEFFERSON
Reading Realism in Stendhal

23 DALIA JUDOVITZ
Subjectivity and Representation in Descartes: The Origins of Modernity

24 RICHARD D. E. BURTON
Baudelaire in 1859: A Study in the Sources of Poetic Creativity

25 MICHAEL MORIARTY
Taste and Ideology in Seventeenth-Century France

26 JOHN FORRESTER
The Seductions of Psychoanalysis: Freud, Lacan and Derrida

27 JEROME SCHWARTZ
Irony and Ideology in Rabelais: Structure of Subversion

28 DAVID BAGULEY
Naturalist Fiction: The Entropic Vision

29 LESLIE HILL
Beckett's Fiction: In Different Words

30 F. W. LEAKEY
   Baudelaire: Collected Essays, 1953–1988

31 SARAH KAY
   Subjectivity in Troubadour Poetry

32 GILLIAN JONDORF
   French Renaissance Tragedy: The Dramatic Word

33 LAWRENCE D. KRITZMAN
   The Rhetoric of Sexuality and the Literature of the French Renaissance

34 JERRY C. NASH
   The Love Aesthetics of Maurice Scève: Poetry and Struggle

35 PETER FRANCE
   Politeness and its Discontents: Problems in French Classical Culture

36 MITCHELL GREENBERG
   Subjectivity and Subjugation in Seventeenth-Century Drama and Prose: The Family Romance of French Classicism

37 TOM CONLEY
   The Graphic Unconscious: The Letter of Early Modern French Writing